CAMUS
AND
SARTRE

CAMUS AND SARTRE

Crisis and Commitment

Germaine Brée

A DELTA BOOK

A Delta Book
Published by
DELL PUBLISHING CO., INC.
1 Dag Hammarskjold Plaza
New York, N.Y. 10017
Delta ® TM 755118, Dell Publishing Co., Inc.
Reprinted by arrangement with Delacorte Press
Library of Congress Catalog Card Number: 71-185418
Manufactured in the United States of America
Third Printing

Designed by Ann Spinelli

Contents

Foreword

We have reason to think that, in the seventies, we are fast moving away from the dramatic issues, the moral tensions and the sensibility of the mid-century. Significant in France, for instance, is the unwillingness of a new generation to accept unconditionally the mystique born of the Occupation years, summarized in the word "Resistance." Many young writers, more particularly, have not been disposed to adopt the literary ostracisms suffered by writers accused thirty years ago rightly or wrongly of "collaborating" with the enemy. In the Europe of the Common Market, the ferocity of the political passions of the past that led to the "purging" of the literary establishment is, no doubt, distasteful and puzzling. A reevaluation of that past is taking place. And, of necessity, it entails a reexamination of the positions taken by the writers who emerged at that time, Camus and Sartre. It was quite early in the fifties that writers questioned Sartre's 1945 call for a literature of commitment. But they did not in general openly question Sartre's proclamation of the total sociopolitical responsibility of the writer.

Today this is no longer true. French political scientists, like Raymond Aron,[1] are questioning the validity of the fundamental concepts of socio-political theory upon which Sartre based his doctrine of commitment, subsequently assimilating it to a mandatory involvement in revolutionary leftist activities. The severest indictment is couched as follows:[2] Like the activities of their predecessors, the Romantics, who developed an acute case of social concern after the Napoleonic wars were over and the bourgeois society was securely established, the present-day activism among intellectuals came after 1945, when the crucial conflict was over. Again, as was the case with the Romantics, the revolutionary rhetoric adopted referred to social structures of the past. Political "commitment" then in practice was tantamount to a complete evasion of real responsibility, to "political stagnation" in small segregated cells. "They see nothing and dream of a world that has passed. They want to act at all costs, but act with no reference to anything real." They are self-sequestered. Sartre's great battles in this context are absurd, for they have no bearing on the new patterns of social organization now emerging. Hence they are purely chimerical.

This in large part is true. But one is puzzled by the conclusion, couched in unmistakably Sartrean terms. Artists and intellectuals have failed, consequently, in their task, which is to keep the culture rooted in the developing

society. "One of the functions of the artist and the intellectual in a given society, is a critical function . . . A culture is designed to manifest the freedom of man who concurrently expresses, questions, contests and stimulates the
society in which he lives." The failure of the committed
artists and intellectuals is then connected with their failure
to detect the patterns of an emerging technological society, with its computerized and abstract modes of opera-
tion. In other words the task assigned them is, in present
confusions, to detect what clearly appears to an observer,
and a specialized one, a third of a century later. What
about later perspectives still? How far-reaching must the
visionary power of the artist or intellectual be into the
future potentialities of trends hidden to his contemporaries? Here we may fail to be convinced. For the implications are clear: artist and intellectual quite arbitrarily are
given a responsibility that may very well not be theirs,
certainly not theirs alone. Furthermore, one may question
the assimilation of "artist" to "intellectual" and inquire as
to the exact meaning of the second term. The confusion
has been constant and unhelpful; and Sartre to his detriment has been instrumental in keeping it alive.

Historical perspectives change. But whatever the argument, certain facts remain. It is more interesting to find
out why, at certain moments in history, writers and artists
are more deeply concerned about the social significance of
their activity than at other times; and when, as has been so
clearly the case in this century, they have voiced the concerns of a wide public, the accusation of "evasion" may
seem ill-founded. For only if we accept the premise that
the changes writers and artists may bring about in our
culture must be short-term and directly or immediately
reflected in contemporary social institutions, can we conclude for example that the Romantics "failed" as artists

in their own sphere. And there is as yet no evidence that the deep concern of men like Camus and Sartre did not contribute to rather than deter from the value of their work. Céline too was a deeply concerned writer, though in a different vein, whose present stature points up the paradoxes imbedded in Sartre's attempt at setting up the political frame which "judged" the writer.

In any case it is an old problem; and at present, in an aftermath of skepticism, it seems to be fast fading into the background of our still uneasy minds. Why then raise the question again? Why not write the whole thing off? And why speak of two men who belong to a past era? It is perhaps because we are still close enough to discern the compelling forces that moved the writers' conscience in those years and their uncertainties, and yet distant enough to see them more dispassionately than heretofore, that such an appraisal may have its present value. To no small extent, these two receding voices have also been ours, alternatively perhaps, or even simultaneously. Without in any sense presuming to pass judgment on the men and on their work, it is Camus's position that has seemed to me, though not the easiest, the most fruitful for the artist. This is a personal view and not a thesis, for the dilemma is real and not easily resolved. In answer to Ellul one can say that the question Sartre raised, although it becomes acute only in certain circumstances which involve a whole community—a dictatorial political regime, occupation by a foreign power, civil war—can only be discussed openly when a measure of political freedom exists. In the first case circumstances present an "all or nothing" pattern bearing on certain well-defined issues. On these, there are no shadings; and at the extreme are three possible attitudes: to conform; to be silent; to oppose and risk being silenced. It is only in the second case that the question of the writer's role and responsibility can appear in all ambiguity. Over a quarter of a century the French writer was placed in rapidly changing, sharply contrasted socio-political situations, in itself a definition of crisis as opposed to inclusion in a long-term "establishment." Thus the intensity of a discussion some phase of which, in different and often starker circumstances, is being lived out almost everywhere in the world.

Notes to Foreword

1. From a close study of *The Critique of Dialectical Reason* Aron draws the conclusion that one could read Sartre's treatise as a justification of Stalinism—that is of tyranny as an inescapable consequence of his Hobbesian-like vision of human relations as founded on implacable conflict. See *Contrepoint*, No. 5, Winter 1971.
2. J. Ellul, "Le néo-romantisme moderne," *Contrepoint*, No. 4, Summer 1971.

CAMUS
AND
SARTRE

1.

A Camus-Sartre Encounter

The voice of the intellect is a soft one, but it does not rest until it has gained a hearing. Ultimately after endlessly repeated rebuffs, it succeeds. This is one of the few points in which one may be optimistic about mankind.   SIGMUND FREUD

You say in big strident tones: I am a man. *That is enough . . . If it were possible you would like to go on saying* I am a man *ad lib in order to hide the more terrible stage whisper* I am an artist *and from there to the ultimate blinding conclusion* Iamgod!!
LAWRENCE DURRELL

In 1971, two books came out in France whose conjunction awakened echoes of the past. Camus's first novel, *La Mort heureuse* (A Happy Death), composed a third of a century earlier and abandoned by a then obscure young man in his early twenties, now dead; and Sartre's two-volume *Idiot of the Family*, the first part of a projected four-volume study of Flaubert. *La Mort heureuse* soon rose to the top of the best-seller list. It would be foolish to assume that Sartre's highly academic work of more than two thousand pages would join it there. But its publication created a characteristic flurry of interviews in a press where, since the war years, Sartre's activities have always attracted considerable attention.

It was his first major book since *The Words*, eight years earlier. In the meantime Sartre's political activities had continued to make news, often international; but of late, except for his participation in the Russell-inspired tribunal on American war crimes in Vietnam (1966–67), they had become more specifically militant within the French context. A biography of Sartre would in itself be a record of the political issues of our time, pinned down verbally and "judged" by him according to his own peculiar ethico-intellectual code; there hardly seems to be a situation great or small, national or international, on which he has not pronounced. Furthermore, all his personal decisions—his refusal of the Nobel prize and his refusal to deliver a promised series of lectures at Cornell, inevitably became a matter of public debate. In 1968 he had supported the student rebellion and adopted the students' language and slogans. In 1970 passers-by might encounter him and Simone de Beauvoir on street corners distributing the banned Maoist-student paper, *La Cause du peuple—J'accuse*; and skeptical Parisians derived passing and rather affectionate diversion from the image of a short, tubby, elderly man of considerable renown with a ravaged face, hoisted on a barrel, surrounded by a group of student "enragés"—extreme Maoist revolutionaries—at the exit of the large automobile works in the suburbs of Paris, exhorting the generally indifferent passing workmen to join the students who punctuated his appeal with the cry of "Revolution!"

Sartre's barrel was, for many, the symbol of a kind of existential protest rather than a relevant political act. And the affectionate respect his person generally elicits stems rather from a sense of his obdurate refusal to capitulate to common sense, his quixotic stance and unsparing labor. His intellectual authority is nonetheless a thing of the past.

And one can sustain the view that although his political positions have consistently been accompanied by elaborate discussions and demonstrations, they have not greatly influenced the actual evolution of French, European or world politics. Sartre, in other words, has become an exemplary though controversial figure rather than an actually effective one. He is now a figure of the past; and because the conclusion of his arguments has by now become entirely predictable whatever the situation, their force is blunted by their monotony. One would never ask, concerning Sartre, the question he put at Camus's death: What would he say now, in this particular instance? We know. He seems to have been completely stymied only once in his attribution of right and wrong—and that was in the Israeli-Arab conflict.

Meanwhile Sartre, the writer, is definitely being integrated into the traditional patterns of academic study; and, with his Flaubert, participating in them. An annotated and scholarly edition of his literary work too, in the respected Pléiade series of Gallimard, is in preparation. A retrospective light has been cast upon his vast achievement and activities by the publication of a thoroughly documented academic bio-bibliography entitled *Les Écrits de Sartre* (*The Writings of Sartre*).[1] It was a different kind of retrospection perhaps from that which *La Mort heureuse* might call for. But once again, in 1971, as in the forties and fifties, the names of Sartre and Camus had made literary news.

One is always aware, when considering literary events, that one runs the danger of overemphasizing their significance;[2] all the more so when wrestling with the often distorted ego-centered view rather comically apparent in some of the statements of Sartre himself.

Sartre has not lost the habit which he developed in the

postwar years—and which is consistent with his existential perspective—of placing himself at the hub of the world. Yet the chance conjunction of the two books in 1971, and the sense that a different intellectual climate is apparent here and in France invite a backward glance at the role they played and the questions they debated in the postwar years. Camus, needless to say, was, like Sartre, a representative figure, in a sense that the next generation of French writers, however ardently discussed in academic circles, never succeeded in being, wanted to be, nor were called upon to be.

No two books could possibly be more profoundly different than these: the latest to date of Sartre's works, written in his late sixties, and the first of Camus's, composed before he was twenty-five and finished but left unpublished in a tentative state.[3] One has the feeling that Sartre's Flaubert developed with Sartre's own life, in a kind of slow incubation. Sartre knew whole passages of *Madame Bovary* by heart by the time he was ten and even today, when he speaks of Flaubert, it is with a kind of fascination. Over the years he has entertained with Flaubert a kind of hate-love relationship: until his study produced an empathetic and compassionate understanding of the man. As for Camus's novel, its vivid freshness, passion, and revolt recall the young man untouched as yet by the experience of war. It is a book both obscure and brilliant—tender and harsh—still very close to an intellectual autobiography.

It is a purely personal and literary work, a first singularly remarkable fictionalizing of an inner experience, struggle, and resolution that engaged his whole sensibility. Camus's early published works still reflect, but only obliquely, this first unguarded young man, with his violent dismay at his own vulnerability—at the sterile frittering away of his time in the daily drudgery of petty employs; his wild aspiration to larger horizons, even at the price of burning himself out; his zest for life, his feeling for language and literature, his strong and subtle personality. This was the Camus who was overshadowed in the somber business of war, its violence and ruthlessness, but whose voice surfaced again, in 1951, calling an end to the dismal frittering away of time in the dreary political morass of postwar Paris.

> We are advancing together toward a prodigious alternative: a final apocalypse, or a world of values and realizations which may astonish those who still remember our fall. The first task of our public life is to preserve the fragile chance of peace, and to that end to serve none of the forces of war in any manner whatsoever. Without peace, I confess I see only agony. With peace, all is possible and the historical contradiction in which we live will be transcended . . . In the meantime, we must live, we must create in the storm. That is why, in accord with my vocation, I justified art; my book finished, I feel I have the right to say that we must now stop commenting on our time in order to give it form.[4]

The book in question was *The Rebel*. Camus, who had been doing battle because of that work on many fronts—more particularly against Sartre's *Les Temps modernes*—though still somewhat battered, was reformulating, in more simple terms, the position he had taken in his essay. *The Rebel*, in fact, had been Camus's way of sloughing off the obsessions and attitudes that the war had required; more particularly the heavy burden of involvement, responsibility, and anxiety that it had placed upon a small group of writers in France—himself among them. In a sense *The Rebel* was a reordering of priorities; the recognition that the heroic political and ethical stance of the

Resistance years was no longer called for in France, and that without abandoning his political responsibilities a man might now make room legitimately for other concerns. Camus's own bent was toward literature. For him literature was not just "writing," any form of writing. It was the practice of an artform. And notwithstanding outer circumstances as devastating for him as the Algerian war, and more private difficulties—his health and family situation—it was indeed his literary work after the publication of *The Rebel* that most deeply engaged him. Not that he intended to withdraw from political concerns. The passage just quoted is witness to that. But the postwar political vacuum in France, however shakily, was being filled; institutions, however faulty, were running. Camus sensed the time of the apocalypse was past. Rather ironically, possibly because of the peculiar form in which he cast his essay or because of the curiously circuitous path he took in reaching his conclusion, his essential reassessment of the situation was lost. And the Algerian war further contributed to obscure it.

Although the controversies that fused around *The Rebel* reveal much concerning the politico-literary tangles of the time, they missed the fact that Camus had intuitively glimpsed the French political situation returning to relative normalcy. The short-term tensions and dramas of the occupation and immediate post-occupation years, and the rhetoric they had engendered, had become obsolete and, sustained, would lead writers to sterile political isolation and literature into irrelevancy. Therefore, the concluding chapter of *The Rebel*, with its quasi-lyrical invocation to creativity. It was Camus's release from political bondage. He had begun making notes for his book even before the war had ended, and the focus had changed in the half-dozen years of its writing, a fact

Camus himself realized only confusedly in the ensuing turmoil. What went unnoticed or was jeered at was the anticipatory thrust of the book.[5] Camus had questioned the adequacy, in the modern situation, of the Marxist-Leninist view of the historical process on which left-wing intellectuals so obdurately based their interpretations of France's future. He saw it as a recoil from reality, a blindness to the present, its dangers and potentialities. A new situation was emerging which did not fit the catastrophist patterns of social change through a proletarian revolution. Thence, at the end of *The Rebel*, the call to a new outlook upon the world to come. He did not attempt to predict what kind of world. As political analysts have shown, this point of view was widely held among Communist Marxists in the sixties: there is no dearth of documentation on that score. Communist eschatology, which *The Rebel* attacked, was definitely a point of embarrassment to the later Marxist theoreticians. But this was not the case with Sartre and *Les Temps modernes* in the fifties. Sartre was convinced at the time that, in its doctrinaire Leninist formulation, Marxism, both as a total world view and as a revolutionary doctrine unifying theory and practice, was the only rational guide to the future, and to responsible action.

Camus, as his *Notebooks* show, tired of theoretical discussions and verbal duels, was anxious to disentangle literature from its subordination to immediate political "relevancy" and himself from the guilt-responsibility syndrome of the war years. He was seeking his freedom as writer from the issues that had dictated his activities and the directions of his thought in the wilderness of the war years; and, as he had done in *La Mort heureuse*, but now in the form of an essay, confronting the grim contradictions and ironies it had yielded with the will not to let his mind and sensibility be bounded by them. It still seemed to him a man's job to seek and to create happiness and, if possible, forms of beauty.

A decade later, in *The Words*, Sartre went the opposite way: the book he said, was his "good-by to literature." But though he had said good-by to literature he never ceased talking about it—and generally quite ambivalently. Lately, he has conceded he considered literature as a "mini-praxis," seemingly relegating it to a peripheral place in his concern; but he appeared to apply that reductive term only to the "commitment to turn out books," whereas he placed the real literary commitment on a quite different and awesome plane—familiar to his readers: "The real literary commitment, finally, is the fact of assuming the entire world—in its totality. To take the universe as a whole, with man inside it, and to give an account of it from the point of view of nothingness (*le néant*)—that is a deep commitment, it is not simply a literary engagement in the sense in which one 'is committed to write books.' "[6]

Furthermore, he was still fascinated by literary figures —major writers of the past: Flaubert and Mallarmé. He had just brought out *The Idiot of the Family*, the first two volumes of a monumental study on Flaubert; the first three were, he said, to lead to a fourth, an exhaustive analysis of Flaubert's novel, *Madame Bovary*, which would fuse into his own system the methods of textual analysis developed by the structural linguisticists, who, in France, sometimes share his Marxism but deny the validity of the linkages he establishes between text, author, and historical circumstances. His Flaubert was, Sartre commented, the only one of his present "tasks" that gave him pleasure, and it was a task which, in the next three years, he would finish.[7]

In a lengthy interview, he spoke of his biography paradoxically in terms of the novel, that is, of a fictional narrative: "It seems that when you wrote *The Family Idiot*,"
his interlocutors said, "you were pursuing two ambitions:
on the one hand, you wanted to write a novelistic-type
work which, in spite of its novelty, could be linked to the
nineteenth-century 'Bildungsroman'; on the other [you
wanted] to present a study which by its rigorous character would be a scientific model." Sartre asserted: "I
should like my study to be read as a novel, since it is in
fact the story of an apprenticeship which leads to the
failure of a whole life. At the same time I should like
those who read it to think that it is the truth, a *true* novel.
It is Flaubert as I imagine him: but since I had a method
which seemed to me rigorous, I think it is Flaubert as he
is and Flaubert as he was"; Sartre's Flaubert, in his confrontation with the world, is, in Sartre's terms, a creation
of Sartre's imagination, *and* the re-creation in words of
the real man, a "scientific" contribution to philosophical
anthropology.

Sartre's "novel" in his view is then also a demonstration
and a demonstration with philosophical and political implications. It proves, he argues, that to a man who pos-
sesses the right conceptual tools—in this instance a psy-
choanalytic-Marxist-existentialist-dialectical method of
analysis—and applies them to an exhaustive examination
of all the data available to him, another man can be made
entirely "transparent." "The underlying intent of the
Flaubert is to show that at bottom everything can be
communicated and that, without being god, any man who
has access to the appropriate data can succeed in understanding another man perfectly." His aim, he said, was "to
prove that any man is completely knowable, on condition
that one uses appropriate methods and has the necessary

documents." Both of these he felt he had. His work then would prove that there existed no "mystery" in the development of a human life, that all the structures of the "self" could be laid bare and its inner dynamism made clear. His own "imagination," Sartre said, had provided the interconnections between the various kinds of facts yielded by Flaubert's life—the outer pressures of family and society, the inner subjective options; and so had made it possible to uncover how Flaubert had realized his project, and made it his destiny not only to write but to write a particular book, *Madame Bovary*. This exhaustive re-creation, from within, of Flaubert's "total" personality from childhood on is the "true novel" of which Sartre spoke.

There is paradox in the entire affair, a chink in the armor. Until one confronts *Madame Bovary*, Sartre appears to suggest, the history of Flaubert's life and his modes of behavior could be entirely deciphered in sociological (Marxist) and existential-psychoanalytical terms. What Sartre had written in the first volumes was a case history which laid bare the fundamental structures and basic orientation of the bourgeois society of mid-nineteenth-century France that shaped the responses of the child and man. Flaubert's life is the account of his impotence—a failure; until he writes the book, a unique accomplishment, which is his victory. *Madame Bovary* then, it would seem, is another example of the paradox Sartre read into the development of the life of another writer, Jean Genet. "The secret failure of every triumph, is that the winner is changed by his victory and the loser by his defeat." Turning to literature as the only way out of a personal disaster, both men transformed their defeats on the social plane into a triumph over the society that had condemned them; and in so doing they changed it while they themselves became respected figures within it. However that may be, it seemed then that the literary process was once again at the center of Sartre's preoccupations, and that beyond Marx and Freud and the linguisticists he was weaving it doggedly back into what Stanley Burnshaw has called "the seamless web" of a man's concrete existence, an expression of "the unsurpassable singularity of the human adventure." One might, after all, call it mystery.

I do not propose in this study to do more than retrace briefly some of the issues concerning the literary endeavor that the experience of the war years raised. And I have centered my study on the Sartrean theory of commitment with all the questions and confusions it generated. If I have chosen to develop it in the form of a parallel it is because the cleavage ran deeper than the confrontation at the time of *The Rebel* revealed. I must state at the outset that I share Camus's skepticism in regard to what George Lichtheim has called Sartre's "grandiose synthesis" and his compulsion to build universal systems he regards as "real." I shall not attempt to deal with it. Others more competent have followed his ever more detailed patterning of his original scheme. It seems to me as though Sartre had designed in the first part of *Being and Nothingness* a rather simple kaleidoscope and kept slipping in more and more elements to vary its patternings. As a philosopher he clearly belongs to the group A. J. Ayer called the Pontiffs—men whose aim it is to give a complete and definitive account of reality. Camus was surely not one of these; in fact, his own mode of thought rested on the premise that this could not be done, at least in the present. I am more in sympathy with Sartre's personal attempt at playing God to his own life, forcing it into the molds he shaped, turning the successful bourgeois writer into the man on the barrel. The magnitude of his achievement is a guarantee of respect. As a human being, Camus was a figure more elusive and more secret—more vulnerable and deeply sensuous, silently observant and guarded; yet toughly realistic with a strange kind of humor, sometimes cynical. He was a man of few words, and strong commitments: "Politics," Lawrence Durrell once quipped, "is an art that deals in averages. Art is a man that deals in people." This, of course, is hardly exhaustive. But Camus, whether in art or politics, was a man who essentially dealt in people. Sartre, if I may venture the criticism, eventually dealt mainly in abstractions—which he confused with averages: and yet was deeply preoccupied with people.

For both men I think the war years were a detour; but not a futile one. When they met in 1943 both knew that "the search for truth on the level of thinking is but the reflection of the search for meaning on the level of living."[8] Both shared the same conviction that present social and political systems and institutions were alarmingly outdated or showed dangerous proclivities. Politically, both men were to become progressively more aware of the planetary implications of local political moves and, simultaneously, of the shift in power away from its former European center. And both, from a secular viewpoint, sought, in their daily actions, to go beyond the intellectual relativism which in practical politics generates opportunism and cynicism. They differed greatly, not so much at first in the positions they took as in the way they related to them; thence, the later parting of the ways. That there is a Camus-Sartre dialogue still alive among us, the evidence seems to show. That it is not merely a Camus-Sartre dialogue but a dialogue which in one form or another still permeates modern thought, the many books devoted to the questions raised bear witness. I owe a great deal to them, but hope that this book can throw some new light on the significance of that dialogue and encounter.

Notes to Chapter 1.

1. Contat and Rybalka, *Les Écrits de Sartre* (Paris: Gallimard, 1970).
2. The late sixties and early seventies did seem to show a surge of interest for the "older generation" of writers— Julian Green's *Journal*; Malraux's *Anti-Memoirs*, and the rising fame of Céline, are possibly straws in the wind. The abstruse experiments of the "new, new novel" in the sixties did not attract a reading public which seemed happy to turn to less self-conscious writers. The interest in Sartre and Camus is not necessarily peculiarly significant in itself.
3. *La Mort heureuse* was displaced by *The Stranger;* one feels, judiciously. It is a typically young book, a novel of initiation with considerable originality and brilliance, but without the mastery apparent in *The Stranger*. For a further discussion of the book see pp. 64–66.
4. *Essais*, 1715.
5. George Lichtheim's study, *Marxism in Modern France* (New York: Columbia University Press, 1966), clarifies the confusing intellectual debate in relation to which *The Rebel* takes on meaning: the awareness among Marxists that society was "undergoing a structural transformation" not foreseen by Marx, that made a transformation of Marxist theory, in particular its eschatology, necessary. For a brief but clear summary of Sartre's position in 1966 see in particular pp. 99–101.
6. "Un entretien avec Jean-Paul Sartre" in *Le Monde*, May 14, 1971, 19–22. The two interlocutors, Contat and Rybalka,

the authors of the bio-bibliography had clearly prepared their interview with intelligent care—eliminating the flow of long Sartrean digressions. All the following quotations concerning Flaubert refer to this interview.

7. Sartre seemed somewhat self-conscious about the unfinished state of some of his major enterprises; he mentioned the *Ethic* that was to complete *Being and Nothingness*, his *Tintoretto*, and the second volume of his *Critique of Dialetical Reason*. He had obviously given up the idea of finishing his novel *Roads to Freedom*, since it was scheduled for publication as it was, including the unfinished drafts of the fourth part. He was vaguely planning without enthusiasm a "political testament" and a play.

8. Robert E. Meagher, *Personalities and Powers* (New York: Herder and Herder, Inc., 1968).

2.

A Manifesto: The Writer and the Moral Imperative

I cannot see how to refute the arguments for the subjectivity of ethical values, but I find myself incapable of believing that all that is wrong with wanton cruelty is that I don't like it.

BERTRAND RUSSELL

It was immediately after World War II that, in an eloquent and brash manifesto, Sartre first outlined in concrete terms his concept[1] of "engagement"—commitment. He was placing it in a context of great importance to him at that time. Launching a new review, *Les Temps modernes*, in October, 1945, he urgently wished to demonstrate the value of his chosen activity—writing. In postliberation France, beset by desperate problems of all kinds, the publication of a new review could hardly be considered a notable event. Sartre, who was emerging during those years as one of the two intellectual leaders of the "new" France—Camus being the second—was still little more than a name to the majority of his country-men. Unquestionable, however, was his ranking among the young men and women who haunted the left-bank cafés of Saint-Germain des Prés. There, during the occupation years, Sartre, Simone de Beauvoir, and Camus, although Camus to a lesser degree because he was more deeply involved in clandestine activities, had helped many bewildered students through the moral and intellectual ordeal of growing up in a defeated and occupied country. As some of those students later recalled, for them, Sartre and Camus were then the very embodiment of integrity. It was with the problem of integrity as reflected in the writer's profession that Sartre's manifesto concerned itself.

There were some among Sartre's few readers who missed the point. Sartre, in part, was to blame. His "presentation" of *Les Temps modernes*, semipolemical, semi-didactic in tone, belonged to a peculiarly Sartrean type of pamphleteering which, in the following years, he was to cultivate. Dogmatic in its formulations, pugnacious and brilliantly barbed in style, yet pedantically overargued and overdocumented, it was directed at scoring points over an implied—or real—adversary rather than at establishing balanced perspectives or lining up solid facts.

To the Paris literati the procedure was so familiar that it obscured the intent. For over a century, each generation of writers in France, in order to establish a literary identity, had proclaimed its freedom from the constraints of tradition ritually, by issuing manifestoes. Like Sartre, they attacked literary canons with scant regard for fact and logic and with varying degrees of insolence and conviction. Barely a quarter of a century earlier the Surrealists had gone further. They had announced their rejection of the French Establishment *in toto*—political, social, ethical, and cultural—on the grounds that it, not they, had become radically alienated from the vital sources of existence. Now, with his peremptory assertion concerning the writer's social responsibility, Sartre in turn was entering the game.

Nothing was further from his intent. Sartre, a critic remarked when he later refused the Nobel Prize, never played according to the rules. He was not thinking in terms of a *literary* movement, although literature was then of great importance to him. In the thirties and forties writing, his autobiography, *The Words*, and Simone de Beauvoir's *Memoirs* make clear, had been the marrow of his life. His manifesto made no concessions on that score. Literature for the sake of literature was out of the question. The writer was no "flute player"; writer and writing were to be taken seriously. An activity like any other, writing, Sartre claimed, was not merely a personal venture, it was a social act. A book proposed a certain view of society which either concealed that society's shortcomings, thereby condoning them or, by revealing them, disturbed readers so deeply that they could not continue blindly to accept them. A social act, it had thereby political implications.

On the face of it this position was scarcely new. It had been debated among intellectuals in the West for close on a hundred years.[2] There had been many instances in the past in which French writers had effectively intervened in social issues or had raised the question of the writer's responsibility. Writers had certainly not waited on Sartre to commit themselves politically. Zola, Barrès, Maurras, Péguy, Romain Rolland, at the turn of the century, are well-known examples, to mention only French writers. Outside France, the greatest example of all was Tolstoy. The Russian Revolution, Fascism, the Spanish Civil War

had further politicized the literary establishment everywhere in the West. By 1945, André Malraux—only four
years older than Sartre—had, for some twenty years, been
engaged in political action, while Louis Aragon, not ten
years Sartre's senior, had been a militant Communist for
some fifteen years, viewing the world and the writer's
function in it from an orthodox Marxist standpoint. It
had been the adherence of Sartre's friend Paul Nizan to
the Communist Party that had brought about the semi-
estrangement of the two young men in the prewar years.

On the whole, in the thirties, the literary establishment
in France, dominated by the urbane, elusive figure of
André Gide, had been oriented toward left-wing positions
in the conflict of ideology generated by the Fascist-Com-
munist dichotomy. There were also those writers who had
supported other views—the antidemocratic nationalism
of Charles Maurras or a French brand of fascism. The
German occupation of France had, to some extent, sorted
the two groups out. During the brief four-year interim it
lasted it had created a bitter cleavage between "resistant"
and "collaborationist" writers, the latter—Céline, Brasil-
lach, Drieu la Rochelle—rather arbitrarily grouped together as "rightists." In 1945, those writers were being
held answerable in courts of law for the political opinions
they had proffered during the occupation, even when no
reprehensible acts could be held against them. The ferocity of the trials at a time when passions were running
high, and the confusion in their motivation—retaliatory,
political, judiciary—created bitter controversy.

Sartre's 1945 manifesto came at a particularly dramatic
moment. "Commitment" as such was not in fact the essential issue, but the question of "right" and "wrong" commitments and the degree to which a writer could justifiably
be impugned for the viewpoints explicitly or implic-

itly contained in his work. Sartre's answer was uncompromising. Writers were not "singing birds," nor did they exist somewhere in the stratosphere: they were people situated in a particular, circumscribed situation, and the specific over-all view that shaped their writing immediately concerned that situation. A writer, in other words, was to be considered responsible for the limitations of his *awareness*, answerable for his "Weltanschauung," for his words and his silences, in terms of the attitudes coiled in them like dormant electric charges. Sartre, using a different vocabulary, was advancing the idea that any piece of writing had cultural connotations and revealed a writer's relation to the entire fabric of society. That relation was open to moral judgment and determined the extent of the writer's social responsibility and, one could infer, ultimate relevancy. Though Sartre does not seem then to have had in mind Jdanov's definition of the ideal writer as an "engineer" of souls, conditioning his readers to the needs of a specific regime, he was viewing literature in Marxian terms as a cultural rather than an aesthetic phenomenon. This, in France, was somewhat overdue. But his manifesto aimed at something more. In fact, Sartre was intent on annexing the socio-historical domain, on absorbing it into the over-all view of human reality he had defined and systematized in *Being and Nothingness*.

Behind the apparent arbitrariness of his manifesto stretched a dozen years at least of philosophical disquisition and literary achievement. They had not been years conducive to frivolity. In the thirties, as Simone de Beauvoir describes him in her *Memoirs*, Sartre had been a fairly typical, though exceptionally gifted, French intellectual. His sharply critical mind easily ranged over most topics but he did not question certain key assumptions of the French literati, among them the relevancy of his enterprise: to become a writer. The six years that stretched between 1939 and 1945 radically altered his outlook. The war plunged Sartre, with many of his contemporaries, into what an American theologian has called a "crisis of integrity." To its resolution, he had stubbornly addressed his resilient and restless mind. The confident tone of his literary manifesto conveyed his sense of triumph. His bulky ontology, *Being and Nothingness*, published two years earlier, had staked out the theoretical ground and laid down the terms for a reappraisal and reorientation of his former understanding of life—his, and he assumed, his contemporaries'.

In the prewar years Sartre had already felt that some such radical reorientation was urgently needed. Like most young people turning thirty, although, Simone de Beauvoir notes, more belatedly and reluctantly, Sartre in the thirties had begun to sense a discrepancy between reality as it impinged on his life and the view of the world, the hierarchy of values he had begun to absorb as a child and which had been reiterated by his masters in school and the university. Unlike most people he could not tolerate the dichotomy. It had thrown him into a state of revolt and anxiety reflected in his first novel *Nausea* and in his short stories. Philosopher that he was, he had set himself the task methodically to examine the structures of his consciousness, in order to reach a true, or at least a dependable understanding of his actual relations with the world around him—in perception, imagination, emotion—an understanding so basic that it could apply to all men. He had proceeded along the lines of traditional philosophical criticism and speculation, adapting to his own ends the methods of the German phenomenology he had recently discovered—a highly specialized undertaking. He had not extended the re-examination to the political conditions or the historical situation that circumscribed his activity as thinker and writer.

Conventionally antibourgeois, his political sympathies had been on the side of socialism, and of the kind of international arbitration represented by the League of Nations, but he considered political action as no business of his. Literature and philosophy were, in his eyes, activities engaging the mind in an over-all view of human beings that transcended such accidental features as being born a Jew, for example, in Hitler's Germany, or a Frenchman in a petit-bourgeois family in twentieth-century France. All men, in his eyes, could be described in terms of a basic model, as Western philosophers had long since taken for granted. Sartre rejected both the Christian and the rationalistic models on which Western thought rested. In the thirties he was intent on recasting that model in an existential mold that could more aptly and genuinely describe his own sense of the human adventure.

When war struck France in 1939, and overwhelming defeat, it changed the frame of Sartre's life and of his thinking. War, he found, was the concrete reality that had awaited him, the particular war he must live as a Frenchman, a dimension of his existence that he had not perceived situated in a particular time. For this major deficiency in his mental outlook he bitterly reproached himself. It ironically qualified his former attitude and point of view, exposing the unexamined assumptions upon which they had rested. Concurrently, his concrete experience as a soldier in the French army, then as a prisoner of war, then as a professor of philosophy in occupied Paris, had had repercussions that deeply modified his understanding of what he called "human reality," hence of the writer's role and responsibility.

A prisoner of war, in 1940, he had been asked to write a Christmas play for his fellow prisoners, the ordinary rank and file of men regularly conscripted into the French army. His play *Bariona*[2a] used the Christmas theme to dramatize their common concerns as prisoners of war, and for the first time Sartre sensed the immediate presence of an audience and the power of words to create a community of feeling binding together a group of individuals. In Paris, in 1943, in another play, *The Flies*, Sartre likewise succeeded by the particular use he made of the Orestes myth, in voicing the common yearning for freedom mutely alive in an otherwise silenced public. By 1945, Sartre, in his role as writer and as mentor to the young, had in fact assumed a position of responsibility and moral leadership. His manifesto then was a necessary critique of his prewar attitude toward the writer's function, both as regards theory and practice. It was, characteristically, his own prewar assumption that he had submitted to scrutiny, and instantly generalized.

Armed with his new sense of the immediate social import of writing and with the understanding of human reality described in *Being and Nothingness*, he faced the task of gearing his activity as writer to the outer world so that he would prove both justified in his decisions and efficacious in his writing. The area of a writer's action Sartre defined as social. To write, Sartre argued, was implicitly or explicitly to take positions in the social issues of one's time, even if one didn't mention them. And, Sartre had already contended in the thirties in his early critical essays, whether he knew it or not, a writer was responsible to his reader for the total view of reality that his work implied. Sartre now pushed his point even further: he formulated criteria for distinguishing right and wrong options and took up a characteristic stance—the stance of

prosecutor. The great majority of French writers, he
claimed, had failed to convey an authentic view of the
actual circumstances in which they and their readers
were placed. They had failed in the most serious obligation of writers. In their role as "singing birds" they offered
their readers fake worlds and values, a fool's paradise.
Thence the limitations and decline of literature itself, its
fundamental irrelevancy to any of the real issues of the
hour and its share of responsibility in the French disaster.

In the next two years Sartre followed up his initial
manifesto with a series of four lengthy articles, grouped
under the title *What Is Literature?* In these he further
expanded, justified, and somewhat refined his thesis, liberating the poets from its strictures. "What is writing?,"
"Why write?," "For whom does one write?" Sartre had all
the answers. They led to a final blueprint, a guide for
immediate application: "Situation of the Writer in 1947."
And it was topical. The role of the "intellectual," more
especially of the writer, had been a major theme at the
opening of UNESCO in Paris, in November and December 1946. The first group of speakers who dealt with the
question of "culture" in a changing world, with the single
exception of the British philosopher A. J. Ayer, had all
been French, and all men of the Resistance: Emmanuel
Mounier, a "progressist" Christian philosopher, the director of the left-wing review *Esprit*; Pierre Bertaux, a high-
echelon administrator; André Malraux, who had now
thrown the full weight of his prestigious personality behind General de Gaulle; Louis Aragon, the most influen-
tial and brilliant of France's orthodox Marxist writers;
and Jean-Paul Sartre.[3]

All were concerned with the future, all deeply impressed still by the immediate past. But now the ideologies and divergences that had surfaced so quickly among

French intellectuals, destroying the unity imposed by the German occupation, were mirrored in their communications. That these were political in essence was unmistakably emphasized when Louis Aragon hit out specifically at André Malraux. Malraux had spoken of an "Atlantic culture"; Aragon, Russian-oriented, took violent exception to the idea. The cultural "cold war" had begun.

The broader and more peremptory formulations of Sartre's point of view in *What Is Literature?* owe, it would seem, more than a little to the UNESCO lectures —in particular to the stress they placed on culture in its broad sense. One particularly abrasive address seems to have had some impact upon him: Pierre Bertaux's "The Intellectual and Action."

Bertaux's thesis was simple and direct: society was moving rapidly into an era of collectivization; intellectuals in the new society in the making must prove to be of use, practically. If writing in itself is a private function, to publish is not. To publish "is to exercise that function publicly." Whereas the nineteenth-century writer in nineteenth-century Western European society could be the detached "seeker after truth," the twentieth-century writer in the future collectivized state would have to consider himself as a "technician"—a man who could show how those truths he came by could apply directly to the problems of society. He could no longer cast himself as the "spiritual" guide of humanity. He would have to be a participant, a man whose function it was to accompany the mass of men in their human adventure, and he must consent to "go with open eyes" where they were going. For a new world, a new type of intellectual must emerge "linked more closely to the world"; a man involved in action, "for whom action was a source of experience, a reason for being and, for others, a measure of his sincerity."[4]

Sartre's UNESCO paper—written with unusual care —was strictly academic in form. Within the metaphysical frame of his ontology, he duly defined the writer's responsibility as the consequence of the writer's ontological freedom. And he made a clear distinction between political and literary action: "A political man can have as his aim the realization of freedom, but he has no means to realize it other than through violence. Violence can be reduced to a minimum, but he cannot avoid it, for he will have to use it against those who attempt to attack the freedom he wishes to make available to the world . . . The writer in contrast refuses violence." Yet, Sartre continued, proceeding through contradiction to qualification, in a world permeated by violence, the writer cannot, in practice, exercise any influence if he condemns all violence unconditionally. He must therefore distinguish necessary from useless violence, combating the latter. The distinction calls for a unifying philosophical viewpoint—Sartre's own—that allows for a clear definition of the "relation of the means to the ends." Essentially, the writer's urgent responsibility, in the present historical circumstance, would be "always, unceasingly and without respite to meditate upon the question of the end and the means *and* upon the relation between the ethical and the political."[5] Sartre's position was the traditional position of the moral philosopher, which Bertaux had decried with considerable brio a couple of days earlier.

Significant throughout this debate was the paucity of reference to literature proper. "Writer" and "intellectual" seemed to be more or less interchangeable terms for the speakers with little regard to the immense variety of activities to which the words might refer. When, in 1947, Sartre further developed his theme, he related it more closely to the literary enterprise, but he was clearly more concerned than heretofore with a new image of the writer as a man of action, an active participant in the shaping of the collective human future; and when he defined the writer's function he was more self-consciously intent on relating it to the situation of French "culture" considered as an organic whole. It was then that Sartre spelled out a three-pronged task for the "new" writer: to discern behind the surface chaos of the times the interdependent processes that pattern human lives and orient humanity toward its future forms of collective existence; through conscious practice in his personal and political life and relentless self-criticism, to participate effectively in the shaping of that future; and, through his writing, to communicate to as broad a public as he could reach the nature of the patterns in the making, the issues they involved. The idea of a "new-style" intellectual called for by a new historical era still preoccupied Sartre in 1971. Of the three goals he had adumbrated, it was the last which at that date admittedly still eluded him. "According to me the new-style intellectual today must give everything to the people. I'm sure one can go far in this direction. As yet I don't know how. It's one of the things I'm searching for."[6] "To give to the people": Sartre still thought of the intellectual as "going to" the people, teaching the people, an elitist attitude which, in spite of himself, he had not shed.[7]

In 1947, Sartre's survey of the past situation of the French writer was arbitrary, the logic of the demonstration and the reliability of the facts were far from unimpeachable. But the whole had an inner cogency, a persuasiveness and plausibility that carried conviction. And he was laying down what amounted to a positive ethic for the writer in a new age. He couched it in terms of situation, choice, commitment, responsibility, and freedom. Beneath the "existentialist" vocabulary he had put to work, Sartre in those years had in fact been applying to French literature a Marxian type of analysis completely new in his writing. It emphasized rather schematically the relation between the mental perspective and ambience of French writing and the class structure of French society. The blueprint of activities Sartre outlines for *Les Temps modernes*—a massive program of systematic investigation of social and political problems—was the means whereby he and the highly distinguished team of intellectuals he had recruited planned to develop a more accurate view of that structure as a first step in ridding themselves of past "myths" and deficiencies. As for their own position within the structure—their "situation"—Sartre defined it too in broadly Marxian terms: they were "petit bourgeois" intellectuals in a society whose cultural future would be defined by the rising proletariat.

Sartre, in other words, was asking French intellectuals to see that certain of their attitudes were dated; and he was proposing a radical critique of the assumptions on which these attitudes rested; he was also proposing an ideological frame of reference, a set of basic positions. Since in his view the "middle-class" culture of the last two centuries was on the decline, and as the war had shown, doomed to disappear, only one choice was left open to the bourgeois writer: actively to assume the role of cultural critic, thus preparing his bourgeois readers to view themselves as realistically as the "hostile" proletariat viewed them. The first task of the writer then was to see beyond the onerous distortions of reality inherent in the outlook of a class that in the past had equated humanity with itself. Radically changing his outlook he must, according to Sartre, learn to appraise society and himself from the vantage point of society's least favored members —a generous proposition. It jibed with Sartre's prewar

definition of writing as an act of generosity, the only absolutely disinterested form of communication between
two minds. But whereas that generosity had first been
defined by Sartre as a free creative exchange between
writer and reader, it was now defined in concrete social
terms. Sartre was prescribing, dictating, and excluding: an
attitude that changed the context, hence the meaning of
his vocabulary. The writer was only conditionally free, in
the service of a qualified though generous ideal of human
freedom.

Sartre's basic existential vocabulary, though it pur-
ported to be descriptive, had always been charged with
ethical connotations. Now, his new awareness of the social aspects of literature took on a dogmatic cast and
turned what had been a conjectural theory into a mandatory doctrine, coercive in its formulation. No one was
likely to quarrel with the proposition, stressed a century
before Sartre by the French realists, that literary works of
scope can arise only out of the writer's sense of the social
reality in which he partakes, and that his sensibility
changes with that reality. But Sartre had now added further specifications. Writing was triply relevant: to a view
of history in the making, essentially Marxian, though defined in Sartrean terms as the upsurge of freedom inherent in the proletariat's struggle for emancipation; to the
deciphering, within that general perspective, of the immediate social issues at hand; and to the writer's actual
position toward those issues. The integrity or the inadequacies of a writer's vision could thus be gauged objectively at any time in terms of a total social configuration
unfolding in the course of history. To err was to be guilty
vis-à-vis the future. History was precisely what had caught
up with the collaborationists revealing the dose of self-
deception in their view of reality, and the real, hidden

meaning of their commitment thence of their guilt: in the name of patriotism and the future of France what they had supported, Sartre claimed, was the enslavement for themselves and all men inherent in the Nazi "Weltanschauung." This was clearly proven by the outcome and by the limitations of their creative work. One could not, Sartre argued, be an anti-Semite and a great writer. Anti-Semitism in itself was an attempt at establishing one man's right to destroy another, and it conflicted with the writer's basic project, as Sartre had defined it: to communicate, and liberate. Plausible on the surface, the argument has by now been thoroughly discredited. It established what amounts to literary guilt and ostracism on ideological grounds: a man's literary achievements were judged by another in terms of political disagreements. The stage was set for the postwar confusions: the banning of literary works, the ideological condemnations. The cases of Pound and Céline are sufficiently illustrative. And it ran counter to Sartre's previous position.

Between Sartre's prewar detachment and his postwar conviction lay a momentous historical experience and a world in ruins. Sartre had been deeply affected emotionally and intellectually, and as Simone de Beauvoir notes, had felt a measure of guilt for his selfish and unrealistic individualistic "anarchism." He attributed his blindness to the bourgeois culture he thoroughly detested, and which he held responsible for his initial bout with anxiety in the thirties. He was triply committed in those years: to ridding himself of all intellectual "bourgeois" preconceptions that limited his view of the present; to accurately situating himself within that present so that he could fruitfully, by his actions, take part in its shaping; to acting upon the course of events through his writing by awakening his readers to an awareness of the built-in inadequacies of their most cherished assumptions. A single verbal pattern, evolved in major part in *Being and Nothingness*, served as a schematic frame for all three commitments. It defined the spirit in which *Les Temps modernes* would play its role, reorienting the cultural ambience of France. Sartre was earnest about it all, sure of the rightness of his attitude and optimistic as to the effectiveness of his enterprise. The outcome of the war had rerooted him in a basic rationalism, no longer Cartesian but Hegelo-Marxian and holistic in its dialectic. Given a proper view of social reality founded on a clear analysis of the multiple forces at work in its shaping, Sartre was confident that men could direct the course of their history, manipulate it so that it would serve rational human purposes.

Applied in this case to writing, the word pattern he proposed could be extended to all spheres of individual activity. Men, Sartre had claimed in his ontology and proceeded to demonstrate in plays, novels, articles, and essays, direct their own affairs and must be held responsible for the course of their history, individual and collective. Whether or not they are intentionally responsible—responsibly responsible people one might say—was quite another question. Sartre wanted intentionally responsible men and intentionally responsible writers, on his own terms. But it was only by a curious twist in his own sensibility that, for him, the word "responsibility" implied moral guilt. To be responsible was to be guilty.

When, jumping geographic and linguistic barriers, Sartre's terminology began to crop up everywhere, it became evident that Sartre by his very vocabulary had singled out one of the areas of crucial perplexity for numbers of people not particularly drawn to philosophical argumentation. With or without reference to Sartre, it was increasingly in Sartrean terms of situation, commitment, choice, responsibility, guilt, and freedom that people did their soul-searching and discussed the issues that troubled them: Nazi guilt, religious dogma and practice, social injustice, racial discrimination, colonialism, the Algerian War, the Vietnam War, civil rights, revolution. A previous generation had spoken in terms of ideals, of abstract entities such as democracy, communism, and capitalism, or of principles: justice, peace, freedom, truth. Freedom was, perhaps, the one term the two generations still had in common, but they used it differently. Freedom in Sartre's initial terminology was a psycho-metaphysical component inherent in all human beings, not a social or political state. It was also the source of human guilt.

In its broadest connotations, Sartre's vocabulary referred to one of the more familiar and perennially unsolved dilemmas of Western philosophy: the rational justification of our moral options as reflected in our attitudes and acts.[8] The widespread interest in Sartre made clear how shaky current standards appeared to many. The crisis had been long in the making and has often been analyzed.[9] World War II dramatized it. In a culture undergoing great pressures, traditional responses no longer sufficed. Whole collectivities lived the violent contradictions between proclaimed standards and facts. Thence a prevalent uneasiness and sense of guilt, a vague sense of inadequacy. Given the right circumstances, might not the most apparently honorable of men be found to harbor a torturer and a brutal wholesale murderer? Or the society the most genuinely dedicated to humane principles reveal propensities as ugly and destructive as those so freely manifested in World War II? Where was the right and wrong of it? To what authority could one appeal when outer guideposts failed? Who or what was responsible for the violence exploding in human affairs? What future was in preparation for the human communities confronting each other on our planet? These were common questions and common anxieties and Sartre was tenaciously wrestling with them.

It was the time that Walter Kaufmann has called the "high tide" of Sartre's creativity. The short ten-year span between 1938 and 1949 saw the publication of a first great chunk of his work: novels, short stories, plays, literary criticism, political analyses and debate, a major philosophical treatise. It was during those years that for intellectuals he became a world figure, what the French call "un grand intellectuel." He was in fact the committed writer incarnate.

"For the last ten years or so," Jean-Paul Sartre wrote less than twenty years later as he approached his sixtieth year, "I've been a man who's been waking up, cured of a long bittersweet madness"[10]—a thirty-year neurosis he called it, a "lucid blindness." What did Jean-Paul Sartre mean? The gradual awakening which, according to him, began in the fifties had not impaired his fabulously active mind. In *The Words*, Sartre wryly alluded to his epic cast of mind. The dimensions of his enterprises were truly epic. A new massive edifice of work was under construction. Fragments of it were appearing: a first volume of a huge socio-philosophical work with a Kantian title—*Critique of Dialectical Reason*; the first installment of his autobiography, *The Words*. But the ambiance of his writing had changed.

By the sixties the first impact of Sartre's work was spent. It had been explicated, explored, appraised, placed in historical perspective. Philosophers, psychologists, sociologists, literary critics dealt with its many facets. With astonishing velocity Sartre was getting the treatment he most despised: analyzed, classified, he was being "frozen," "petrified," turned into an object by others. He was being absorbed into the "bourgeois" culture from which he had fled.

It is rather amusing to remember that, as late as 1944, Simone de Beauvoir could ask the philosopher Gabriel Marcel, in all good faith, a question with a future: What is existentialism? Today the question has been answered. We have learned what existentialism is. Around the cradle of the child Descartes, Kant, Hegel, Kierkegaard, Marx, Nietzsche, Bergson are now gathered. The Pre-Socratics, Plato, and Aristotle are its distant but recognizable relatives. Sartre's many debts to Hegel, Husserl, Heidegger, Marx, and later, Freud, along with his own idiosyncrasies, have all been pinpointed and assessed. What concerns us here is not to produce another appraisal of his work but rather to follow the itinerary of the man, through some of the twists and turns of his thought. What did the awakening in the fifties signify? Since his questions and answers reverberated so widely in our time, could it be that his "neurosis" was also in part ours? For we have been burdened, in the West, with a sense of our culpability. What was the "commitment" finally relinquished and, to use his own terms, what was the "fundamental project" uncovered in the relinquishment? Was Sartre merely recognizing in *The Words* that he had toiled for thirty years only to set up another "God that failed?"

Sartre's career has not been an easy one. It has been strewn with controversy. In the sixties he published two major essays that recall two periods of his intellectual life, in relation to two men who had been his close friends and from both of whom at one point, for intellectual reasons, he had become estranged: a preface to Paul Nizan's

Aden Arabie; an article in memory of the distinguished philosopher, Merleau-Ponty. Nizan, killed in 1939 at Dunkirk, had been the alter ego of Sartre's schoolboy and student days; Merleau-Ponty, his closest collaborator on *Les Temps modernes* from its inception as a project in 1943 until his withdrawal from it ten years later. The two essays are excellent examples of that perennial and peculiarly Sartrean exercise in criticism, a perspective opening upon a perspective, and are thereby doubly revealing. Both essays are rather bitter re-appraisals of the past, self-justifactory in essence, whose substance we shall discuss later. Revealing, too, is the narrow circle of Sartre's really significant friendships, very parochially limited to a small inner core of "normaliens," alumni of one of France's highly selective academic institutions, very similar to himself in their modes of thought. In the fifties, controversy separated him from a very different type of person, Albert Camus.

Camus seldom made use of the term "engagement" (commitment) except, ten years after it was launched, to voice his distrust of the word and of the connotations it had acquired. Yet he had used it before the war in a review of Ignazio Silone's novel, *Bread and Wine*. *Bread and Wine* he described as a novel "engaged in the problems of the hour." A year before he had discussed *La Conspiration* (*The Plot*), a novel by Sartre's Communist friend, Paul Nizan, from the point of view of political commitment:[11]

> Nizan requires a commitment in which a man relinquishes himself, and with himself his prejudices and choices . . . And that is how Nizan puts the great question for the intellectuals of our time; commitment. We cannot follow him on that terrain. For some years now, much has been written and debated concerning commitment. But all

things considered it is as futile a problem as the problem of immortality, something a man solves for himself and upon which one should not pass judgment. One adheres in the same way as one gets married. And when we deal with a writer, it is in his work that we can judge the effect of adhesion.

In contrast, the quality of Silone's novel in young Camus's eyes was that it had transcended militancy to reach back to the doubts and the faith in which Silone's revolutionary action was rooted, that is, love of the people and their ways, respect for a dignity he was resolved to defend. "A return to those gestures and that truth and, from an abstract philsophy of revolution, a return to the bread and wine of simplicity, is the path Ignazio Silone took and the message of the novel."

Camus then could hardly have been overly impressed by the tenor of Sartre's manifesto, even though in the meantime, he had been affected, like Sartre, by an experience he had not foreseen. He once ironically proposed an equivalent for the term "committed": "impressed," a literature "impressed" or conscripted into compulsory service. Discussing at a later date the writer's situation today, as he saw it, he gave a humorous twist to Sartre's mandate. Unlike Sartre, Camus was not adept at argumentation; it bored and irritated him. He often preferred to rely on illustrative, concrete, frequently semi-burlesque metaphors. In this case, he evoked History as a Roman amphitheater complete with its lions, and the writer as a recently designated and rather reluctant martyr. "History's amphitheater has always contained the martyr and the lion. The former relied on consolations in an eternal future and the latter on raw historical meat. But until now the artist was on the sidelines. He used to sing voluntarily, for his own sake, or at best to make the lion forget his appetite." Now, Camus continued, the artist is *inside* the ring, "of necessity, his voice is not quite the same."[12] But he agreed in substance that the era of what he called the armchair genius, the artist with a camellia in his buttonhole, was a thing of the past. Over and over again he came back to the subject: "We want to think and to live in our history. We believe the truth of this age can be found only by living through, to their limit, the conflicts it presents. . . . It seems to me that the writer must be fully aware of the conflicts of his time and that he must take sides every time he can or knows how to do so."[13] His was a tentative position, the position of the ordinary well-intentioned citizen. It made no claim to the kind of total responsibility Sartre had defined.

When he met Sartre in 1943 Camus, who was just turning thirty, was a reader for the famous Gallimard publishers and more deeply involved than Sartre in clandestine activities, actively engaged in the editing, printing, and distribution of the underground paper, *Combat*. With the publication of his first novel, *The Stranger*, and an essay, *The Myth of Sisyphus*, he had just made a brilliant entry into the world of letters that two plays in the next two years, *Caligula* and *The Misunderstanding*, would consolidate. Behind him lay ten years of what we would today call activism. In his early twenties in Algiers he had been a militant Communist Party member for a short while, then had withdrawn, infuriated by what he considered as the coldly calculated exploitation of Muslim misery by the party for purely political ends. As a young journalist on the staff of the liberal left-wing daily *Alger-Républicain* his reports on scandalous miscarriages of justice had in several instances proved effective and a series of articles, coldly factual, on the desperate economic plight of the Berber peasants of Kabylia had thoroughly displeased the colonial administration in Algiers. Younger than Sartre by eight years, he had behind him a far tougher experience of men and society. He had earned his living at various jobs while working toward a degree in philosophy at the University of Algiers; had directed and run an activist theater group; had married, divorced, remarried. Meanwhile he had had to fight the pulmonary tuberculosis that had plagued him since he was seventeen. He had been actively engaged in underground activities during the war. In 1943, both he and Sartre belonged to the clandestine National Council of Resistance writers, grouping men and women of all shades of political opinion who hoped that, out of the shared ordeal, a new consciousness would emerge in France demanding a thoroughgoing reform of the country's obsolete political institutions, inaugurating a viable democratic regime.

Because of historical circumstances, dramatic to the extreme; because they had ventured to stake their future in the conflict; because of their literary talent and personal vitality, both men found themselves, almost in spite of themselves, at the hub of the ideological and political controversies that shook France—and Europe—in the climactic and fast-moving years that followed: Hiroshima, Nuremberg, the Cold War, Korea; the disconcerting complexities of French decolonialization in Indo-China, Madagascar, and Africa. And both men continued to be deeply affected by the current sweep of events. They had a great deal in common: literature, philosophy, theater, journalism, their serious concern with social justice and freedom, and the sense that they lived in a time which required that the writer re-examine and redefine the nature of his activity and calling. And both men felt that it was incumbent upon men to live, not merely to speak, as they thought.

Yet, from the very beginning of their careers as writers, Sartre and Camus were in fact engaged, at first obliquely, then more and more directly, in a debate that revolved around the issue of commitment. A young and still obscure Camus had raised it when reviewing Sartre's first novel *Nausea* and his 1939 collection of short stories in which Camus detected a quasi-obsessional dream of destruction and ruin, an almost frightening power of negation. In the immediately postwar years Camus's second novel *The Plague* and his play, *The Just Assassins*, were counterbalanced by Sartre's two plays *Dirty Hands* and *The Devil and the Good Lord*, and the as yet unfinished novel, *The Roads to Freedom*. Camus, in *The Fall*, deliberately and sardonically alluded to Sartre's *Saint-Genet, Comedian and Martyr*, an exhaustive psychoanalysis of Jean Genet, thief, informer, sexual pervert, jailbird, and the writer of talent who has been widely hailed in the West. In the concluding pages of his book, Sartre had spoken of Genet as "a hero of our time." "A hero of our time," the words echo ironically in the epigraph that Camus chose to designate the fictional soliloquist of *The Fall*, Jean-Baptiste Clamence, comedian and self-appointed martyr. The confrontation of the fifties had long been in the offing.

Saul Bellow, in a partial and somewhat indiscriminate attack on university critics in general, accused them of trying to "form a new model of civilized intelligence for the twentieth century,"[14] of scrutinizing literary works only in terms of "postures, life-styles and positions." There are signs that this is changing; but perhaps the horizons of "civilized intelligence" have, in fact, changed so rapidly that it is they, not the academic critics, that are forcing writer and critic alike to think in terms of new perspectives, new attitudes, and new themes. France, in the mid-century years, was so situated that her writers could hardly evade the issue. It was a country in which literature, highly self-conscious both in its theory and its practice, was a matter of national import and cultural pride; in which the rationalist conception of man and society, inherited from the Enlightenment, was firmly rooted, despite an articulate minority of dissenters. It had been, in fact, as Sartre so clearly saw, a whole way of looking at life that, for the French, 1914 had shaken and 1940 had shattered. It had come to be, in twentieth-century circumstances, or so it seemed to many at the time, a dangerously illusory fiction if not a downright lie. Ethical values and intellectual perspectives were inextricably entangled in the process of reevaluation. In 1945, in Sartre's vocabulary of commitment, unquestioning allegiance to the traditionally accepted hierarchy of values was seen as a double evasion, intellectual and ethical, a diabolical caricature of morality. For Camus, as his first work makes clear, such an allegiance could only be, at worst, a hollow lie, an evasion, at best, a protective shell. For both men, it was a refusal to face reality, hence responsibility. Morality understood in this passive way made of men, to use Sartre's image, a species of crab, beings soft inside, shut into their small closed universe, scuttling through life in sideways gait. Or, as Camus saw it, blind participants in their own annihilation.

This "waste-land attitude"—as Saul Bellow has called it—toward social values was hardly new. In literature and philosophy, alienation, estrangement, rebellion against the mechanical workings of society, and on a grander scale, against the blind forces of nature, were century-old themes of debate and elaboration. One could hardly avoid them. In their early work Sartre and Camus had modulated them each in his own manner. Their experience in the forties reoriented their thinking toward the social dimensions of the individual. They were in many ways still heirs of the Romantics in their literary themes and sensitivity. Camus in the realm of the practical politics of the hour was ahead of Sartre, but the semi-artisan and rural economy of French Algeria insulated him from the major trends developing in an increasingly technological age. Sartre and Camus are thus, in different ways, men who lived with particular intensity the accelerated passage from one era to another that two wars had punctuated. They are to a certain degree representative, because articulate men. Today we can see their progress through the years as illustrative of a period rather than as a guide to the present. That his literary work outlasts immediately "relevant" political issues is quite obvious in Camus's case. And, his own attitude to the contrary, possibly in Sartre's. In a sense, for both men the notion of "commitment" had much in common with a term we have used, misused, and now thrown away: "relevancy." And it raised the same problems: Committed to whom? to what? that have troubled American "intellectuals" and many American writers in the last years.

In his book, *Cosmos and History*, Mircea Eliade speaks of modern man's effort to come to terms with the "terror of History," to make tolerable its increasingly powerful pressures. The "terror of History" weighed heavily in Western Europe on the men who, like Sartre and Camus, were reaching maturity in the forties. The "waste-land" outlook then became, for both men, the ghost to be laid. Had they been diametrically opposed in thought and action, their disagreement might have been more easy to understand and perhaps of lesser interest. In the mid-sixties one chapter of their history seemed closed. Camus had died and with the end of the war in Algeria the pressures of history, the responsibilities of decision-making had moved away from Western Europe. It was in America that, under different circumstances, a dialogue was taking place that involved many of the same elements of discussion: civil rights, segregation, war in Vietnam, the questioning of the power structures of society, became centers of a debate affecting the social and moral consciousness of a whole society. Then, dramatically, student unrest swept through the world, achieving a first paroxysm in the United States, then in the 1968 Paris demonstrations. Though the name of Camus was sometimes mentioned, though Sartre engaged in a "dialogue" with the Paris students whose actions he unreservedly—and somewhat nostalgically—approved,[15] it was not to Sartre and Camus that the activists referred. Ché Guevara, Régis Debray, Ho Chi Minh, Mao Tse-tung, Bakunin, Marcuse were now their mentors; but also in France, symptomatically, and perhaps more eloquently, were André Breton and the anarchistic Dadaist-Surrealist rebels of the twenties whose impact upon themselves both Sartre and Camus had been at some pains to exorcise. By 1971, the whole era to which they had responded seemed to be receding into the past.

Yet though more soberly weighted by the earnest effort Sartre and Camus had made to come to grips with an immediately grim experience, the questions they had raised and the solutions they had adopted were still, though more chaotically stated, those debated by the insurgent students. Camus would have recognized his inclination no doubt in the Civil Rights movement, in the peace movements and also—pushed to an extreme limit perhaps—in the concern of the "commune"-minded for other human beings, and in their aspiration toward the aesthetic—although not in the forms in which those aspirations now sought fulfillment. But perhaps he would have felt a certain nostalgia for the positive, concerted, popular, yet nondoctrinaire mode of action and life they chose. The student movement seems to have taken Sartre by surprise and brought to a head his latent quarrel with the placid French Communist party. In no sense did the students refer to him as a leader, but he made himself the spokesman and "sponsor" as it were of the more articulate —Cohn-Bendit for instance—of the more extreme Maoist faction, and in a hasty post-mortem, he denounced as bourgeois reformism the reticent policy of the French Communist party.[16] In April, 1970 he took over the editorship of *La Cause du peuple* (*The People's Cause*),[17] the newspaper of the Maoist faction of the revolutionary Left. One could sense the fascination the students' physical carnage and iconoclasm held for Sartre, even when he found it hard to agree with them on certain points. He would no doubt defend, if not condone, the recourse to violence of the Weathermen.

This immediate presence of Sartre, the impact of his personality and his association with a small group of articulate intimates—Simone de Beauvoir more especially—who participate in his indecisions and help to turn them into positive interventions make it difficult to consider him in relation to the absent figure of Camus. Sartre has now outlived Camus by more than a decade. And he always had been a far more articulate man. In a recent and admirable bibliography of Sartre's writings,[18] 511 published items were listed; of these, of course, some were collections or re-editions; and a number were interviews or translations. But there is a good deal more to come and Sartre's publishing record also includes a history of lost manuscripts—a *Mallarmé*, notebooks—or unfinished ones, laid aside. In the sheer bulk of his work, he has far outdistanced Camus; in immediacy, too, and explicitness. The interviews and lectures Sartre has given explaining his literary works, his political positions or his decisions—his refusal of the Nobel Prize for instance— and his participation in colloquies are innumerable. As a member of a team, in *Les Temps modernes*, he has signed his name to declarations of policy drawn up by others, his friend the philosopher Merleau-Ponty, for instance; Simone de Beauvoir has on several occasions, it is said, edited and cut his articles. Sartre, figuratively speaking, has increasingly been on the barricades; carrying on verbal battles on several fronts, intervening wherever there is a confrontation, large or small, national or international.

Camus's work is far more limited in its scope, more concentrated in a single endeavor, essentially literary. In his editorials as a journalist he dealt with current situations in direct terms, stating the facts he possessed and expressing his opinions plainly within the limited space allotted him. He only rarely indulged in polemics centering on his work—the polemic with *Les Temps modernes* concerning *The Rebel* being the notorious exception; his comments on his writing are short and far between. Where Camus is concerned, for over a decade now, of necessity, the buzz of comment that personal notoriety assures and which accompanies Sartre's presence wherever he goes, perhaps in spite of Sartre himself, perhaps because he wants it that way, has died down; with it, some of the immediacy of reaction to his work. Yet in 1970 when, in relation with the student unrest, polls were taken inquiring what author the students preferably read, it came as a surprise to most to find Camus, ten years after his death, still in the lead: twenty-six per cent of the students voiced their preference for Camus; Sartre was the choice of another twenty per cent; Marx running a poor third with thirteen per cent of the votes. And that same year, when Gallimard released the sales figures for its cheaper paperback "pocket book" editions, Camus again topped the list, with close to two million copies of *The Plague* and *The Stranger* sold in that series alone.

It is difficult to gauge the extent of Camus's present appeal to the American reading public, the students in particular, who all, at some point or other, read Camus in the course of their studies. It seems to have fluctuated, lately again showing an upsurge, perhaps in a troubled reaction to militant student activism with the consequent campus disruptions, and the students' awareness of the hostile citizen reaction outside. To use the words of Camus's Caligula, it has seemed to some that these tactics and rhetoric were "not of the right kind." The *Village Voice* brought a strangely moving testimony to Camus's influence. In a memorial article for Robert Kennedy,[19] his friend Jack Newfield wrote as follows:

"The most concrete expression of Kennedy's existential quality was his involvement with the writing of Albert Camus. He discovered Camus when he was thirty-eight, in the months of solitude and grief after his brother's death. By 1968 he had read, and re-read, all of Camus's essays, dramas and novels. But he more than just read Camus. He memorized him, meditated about him, quoted him and was changed by him." And Newfield quotes a paragraph from Camus's *Notebooks* that Kennedy had underlined: "Living with one's passions amounts to living with one's sufferings, which are the counterpoise, the corrective, the balance and the price. When a man has learned—and not on paper—how to remain alone with his suffering, how to overcome his longing to flee, [the illusions that others may share,] then he has little left to learn." This concern for specific human beings is indeed the expression of an inner sensibility that most clearly separates the two worlds of Sartre and Camus, sharply distinguishing Sartre's point of view from Camus's.

Notes to Chapter 2

1. Actually he would now prefer the term "notion," applying the word "concept" to scientific ideas.
2. See, for instance, Christopher Lasch, *The New Radicalism in America* (1889–1963) (New York: Vintage Books, 1967), Chapters 6–9.
2a. For a summary of the play see p. 192 note 7. Genet recalled that Sartre spoke to him with emotion of that experience.
3. Under the overall heading "Culture" the general discussion in which those men participated was followed by more specific lectures on Indian, Arabic, Spanish, and Greek cultures closing with a paper on the situation of the plastic arts by Sir Herbert Read. Other lecture series were grouped under the headings of "Science" and "Education." Julian Huxley gave the final address entitled "The Conditions of Progress" on December 9.
4. Les Conférences de l'UNESCO, Fontaine, Paris, 1947, p. 31.
5. *Ibid.*, "La responsabilité de l'écrivain" (57–73) p. 63; p. 72.
6. Interview in *Le Monde*, May 14, 1971, p. 21.
7. For a brief but illuminating discussion of this view of the intellectual's role among French leftist intellectuals see H. Stuart Hughes, *The Obstructed Path* (New York and Evanston: Harper & Row, 1966), p. 190–91.
8. For a recent thorough and lucid analysis of the problem, see William Warren Bartley, III, *The Retreat to Commitment* (New York: Alfred A. Knopf, 1962).
9. See for example Stanley Rosen, *Nihilism: A Philosophical Essay* (New Haven: Yale University Press, 1969); and

Karl Löwith's essay "The Historical Background of European Nihilism" in *Nature, History and Existentialism* (Chicago: Northwestern University Press, 1966).

10. *The Words*, p. 138.

11. "Le Pain et le vin" d'Ignazio Silone, Alger Républicain, May 23, 1939 and "La Conspiration" de Paul Nizan, Alger Républicain, November 11, 1938. Included in *Albert Camus Essais*, pp. 1394–1398.

12. "Create Dangerously," *Resistance, Rebellion and Death*, p. 250.

13. "The Wager of our Generation," *Resistance, Rebellion and Death*, p. 288.

14. "Cloister Culture," the *New York Times Book Review*, July 10, 1966, pp. 2 and 4.

15. See *Le Nouvel Observateur*, Special edition, May 20, 1968, "L'imagination au pouvoir," an interview between Sartre and the student leader Daniel Cohn-Bendit.

16. See *Les Communistes ont peur de la Révolution* (*The Communists Are Afraid of Revolution*) (Paris: Éditions John Didier, 1968).

17. See, among others, *Le Monde*, April 29; *The Paris Herald Tribune*, April 28 and *Le Nouvel Observateur*, May 18–24, 1970 (pp. 47–56). Entitled "Jean-Paul Sartre gives the trashers (les casseurs) a chance to speak," this last item is almost entirely a statement of the aims and tactics of the group made by one of them, with few interventions by Sartre, who, as is the case in his famous interview with the leader of the 1968 student insurrection, Cohn-Bendit (*Le Nouvel Observateur*, special supplement, May 20, 1968), deliberately stands back and gives the young revolutionaries a chance to speak, clearly aware that his name will assure them an audience. Like the American Weathermen, *La Cause du peuple* advocates a policy of terrorist action, as a tactic to disrupt the "blocked" social structure and so prepare the transfer of power to the people. Its two previous editors had been arrested for incitement to murder

when Sartre announced that he was taking over the editorship and openly challenged the government to take him to court, an action which French authorities have always carefully avoided. There is something rather comical yet courageous in the actions of Sartre and Simone de Beauvoir, both now well over sixty and famous, who sold the banned paper at a street corner in Paris, and were temporarily apprehended but not arrested. It was, Sartre said, rightly, the proof that there were two forms of justice in France. But then, it should be remembered, they had some years before both signed a petition to have the prison sentence of Jean Genet waived on the grounds of his literary talent. They can hardly protest when the same leniency is extended to them. *La Cause du peuple* has usefully, though with questionable rhetoric, concentrated on cases of police brutality and disregard for basic civil rights. But the paper turns the policeman into a mythical incarnation of Evil as portrayed in comic strips.

18. Michel Contat and Michel Rybalka, *Les Écrits de Sartre* (Paris: Gallimard, 1970).
19. *Robert Kennedy: A Memoir*, pp. 58–59 (New York: E. P. Dutton & Co., 1969).

3.
The Backdrop: Social Facts and Personal Myths

Every man has his natural place; its altitude is determined by neither pride nor values: childhood decides.

JEAN-PAUL SARTRE

The facts are well known. Jean-Paul Sartre was an only child, born into a middle-class family of intellectual bent and moderate means. His father died when he was one year old and he was brought up in the home of his grandfather, Charles Schweitzer, a teacher of German. The Schweitzers were Alsacians who had opted for France after the Franco-Prussian war. In Sartre's lifetime they produced another internationally known figure and Nobel Prize winner, Dr. Albert Schweitzer.

Given his environment and his intelligence, the boy's life developed along predictable lines. His school career was normal, although it started late, and he was eventually admitted to France's École Normale Supérieure, an institution that recruits, every year, in competitive examination, the more intellectually gifted of the young *lycée* graduates in the liberal arts. France, in turn, expects that from their ranks will come an articulate and brilliant intellectual elite. "Normaliens," on the whole, seldom question their own pre-eminence. On this score, Sartre would be no exception. It was probably in the course of his studies—more particularly at l'École Normale—that Sartre developed certain stylistic idiosyncrasies that on occasion prove rather annoying to his readers whom at times he castigates as though they were rather backward students.[1] The end-product of the French system of education has been somewhat simplistically described as "the ability . . . to make a coherent case subtly and plausibly, out of a paucity of fact"[2] and to present it in the "magisterial and rhetorical" style of nineteenth-century oratory. The "rhetorical" style and "magisterial" tone are apt to crop up everywhere in Sartre's work. Even in his novels and plays he will italicize key words, marshal arguments in rhetorical order, setting up theses and countertheses, on his own terms scoring rhetorical triumphs. He is adept at proving himself right.[3]

Sartre early quarreled with the linear, Cartesian mode of logical analysis imposed upon him by his masters. But he never lost the compulsion to put facts neatly to work within a conceptual framework theoretically devised. One of the attractions the Marxian dialectic held for him when he really began to assimilate it in the forties, was the premium it put upon "reading" facts aright, decoding them according to a given ideological pattern. Although Simone de Beauvoir stated that he does not read much, his work seems to show that, throughout his life, he cultivated the habit of monumental, if sometimes hasty readings in specialized fields, documenting his own articles tirelessly from notes with the apparent thoroughness of the researcher, although he did not always feel the researcher's need scrupulously to acknowledge those sources.

If one can judge from the innumerable catch phrases, word patterns, book titles, quotes woven into the fabric of Sartre's writing—often for ironic effect—Sartre's memory for verbal expression must be or has been phenomenal. Like Simone de Beauvoir, he avidly seizes upon technical modes of expression new to him, culled from specialized fields—Marxian, psychoanalytic, structuralist terminology for example—using them massively with a kind of passionate intensity. And, specialists have noted, Sartre with each new terminology tends rather uncritically to endorse theories that may no longer be operative. Furthermore, in Sartre's pattern of rhetoric, hypotheses are seldom distinguishable from statements of fact. The hypothetical "if . . . then," basic to hypothetical deduction, persistently slips into the "since this is so . . . then this follows," by which the conditional is replaced by the affirmative. Sartre thus quite frequently uses hypotheses as proven facts to clinch an argument.[4] He is amazingly expert at public debate, skillful in the use of his unwieldy dialectic, never losing sight of the main points he wishes to make. His ability as well as his need to push his theories to and beyond the limit of common sense are intensified and partially redeemed by his lucidity.

In due course, armed with a degree in philosophy, Sartre, at the age of twenty-five, served his apprenticeship as teacher in a couple of provincial *lycées* and began to write. In the thirties, the novel was the literary form that attracted him. World War II came, he was conscripted, taken prisoner on June 21, 1940, without having participated in combat, released in March, 1941, and assigned a teaching post in a Paris *lycée*. The next step would normally have been a bulky thesis and the appointment to a university chair. Sartre broke with the pattern. He did in fact produce the bulky treatise, *Being and Nothingness*, but it was not then destined for academic scrutiny. Soon thereafter, in 1944, he abandoned teaching and started out on an independent career as a writer. As *The Words* reveals, he had been writing since about the age of seven. From 1944 on he has lived the life of his choice, free from economic constraints and the responsibilities of job and family.

Albert Camus was born into a destitute and illiterate working-class family. He was the second son of immigrants: his father's family had emigrated from Alsace, like Sartre's, after the Franco-Prussian war; his mother's had come from Spain. He was, again like Sartre, a fatherless child. Camus's father, an agricultural laborer, was killed at the front in 1914. His mother and grandmother brought him up in the crowded slums of Algiers. His mother was a cleaning woman; among his relatives one uncle ran a small cooper's workshop, another, more prosperous, was a butcher. The working-class milieu he knew was still geared to an agricultural economy, close to the small artisan-type workshop he later described in one of his short stories—*The Silent Men*. Destitute though his people were, their poverty, in the Mediterranean setting and climate of Algiers, was not scarred by the grim ugliness of the industrial cities of Europe. This Camus noted later when his clandestine activities brought him into contact with the industrial cities to the west of Lyons. Camus compared them to a form of hell. To have been brought up in Algiers he considered a major privilege.

Breaking with working-class patterns—at the instigation of his grade-school teacher and in spite of some family opposition to so much waste of time—Camus went as a scholarship boy through the same educational formation as Sartre, likewise majoring in philosophy, though at the University of Algiers, not at the prestigious École Normale. Barred from a teaching career for reasons of health, he turned to journalism for a living, and to writing. He had started to write around his seventeenth year. But throughout his student years he led a precarious life financially, working in diverse odd jobs that ran the gamut from docker to white-collar employee. He knew and enjoyed at firsthand the motley and picturesque population that walked in the streets of Algiers and he had a realistic concept of its joys and sufferings, its limitations, its aspirations, its potentialities for violence and all manner of braggadocio and, above all, its fundamental dignity. It furnished the cast of characters that surround the small white-collar employee, Meursault, the protagonist of Camus's first published novel *The Stranger*, close relatives to those he had sketched in a brief first work, *L'Envers et l'Endroit*.[5] They indelibly impressed themselves upon his sensitivity as the basic stuff of humanity. It was during World War II that he finally settled in Paris, as a minor journalist first, in 1939, then eventually, under the Occupation, as one of the editors of the clandestine paper, *Combat*. He had no great love for that city and never felt entirely at home there. His discomfort in the closed circles of the literati clustered around the publishing firms was apparent, and included the tight little circle that gravitated around Sartre and Simone de Beauvoir. He was twice married, had two children, and, although with the mitigations born of literary success, worked for a living until his death.

The facts in themselves are significant. More significant

is the crucial role they played in the initial orientation of the two men, in their attitudes and, eventually, in their understanding of themselves and their work.

In 1954, as both he and Simone de Beauvoir have informed us, Sartre, then around his fiftieth year, opening doors into his past, began to jot down notes concerning a childhood to which previously he had made scant reference. Some of these jottings produced *The Words*, published ten years later, just as Sartre was turning sixty. A best-seller, *The Words* gives a carefully patterned account of Sartre's childhood, more especially in the period between the ages of seven and eleven, a total psychometaphysical portrait of himself. The rest, he suggested, might follow. Later, he seems to have changed his mind, announcing instead an autobiographical political testament. Although from the mid-fifties on he sometimes referred in interviews to later episodes in his youth, information about him was scant until the Sartre of the years 1928–29 emerged in Simone de Beauvoir's *Memoirs* and again in a preface to Nizan's *Aden-Arabie*. From then on we can follow him almost step by step as he moves out of private into public life to become France's "leading intellectual" and as such one of its more controversial figures.

Long before he described his own, childhood had fascinated Sartre. A self-appointed psychoanalyst, at first anti-Freudian, he gradually steeped himself in the analytical-interpretative method, though not in the clinical techniques of Freudian psychoanalysis.[6] He scrutinized the childhoods of Baudelaire, Flaubert, Jean Genet—and may still, in the future, explicate the early days of Mallarmé and Tintoretto. He laid down rather schematic but significant childhoods for many of his characters—for the "prefabricated" young fascist in "Childhood of a Leader," the last story in Sartre's 1939 collection of short stories;

for Hugo, the would-be Communist militant in the play *Dirty Hands*;[7] for Ivich, the adolescent girl-child in *The Age of Reason*; for Franz, the self-sequestered central character in *The Prisoners of Altona*; and also, in 1953, for the real and courageous young workman, Henri Martin, who while serving in the navy, had been condemned to five years' incarceration for distributing leaflets that denounced the French military action in Indo-China, a sentence which a group of intellectuals, Sartre and Camus among them, successfully contested.[8]

Childhood, for Sartre, although at first he denied the fact, holds the key, at least in part, to a person's psyche, to his relationship to himself, to others, and to the world, and for Sartre probing its intricacies could, he seems to think, open most of the locks to the understanding of any man.

He seems always to have been a passionate investigator of the workings of other people's minds. Simone de Beauvoir's *Memoirs* describes the small circle of their intimate friends endlessly elucidating patterns of behavior and ascribing motivations, intellectuals as claustrophically shut in on themselves as the tireless trio of *No Exit*. Violently as he might disagree, Sartre is, in this area, the compulsive heir to a long line of French analysts of the human psyche. The method differs, but the end is the same—interpretation and moral evaluation. In our post-Freudian era he has increasingly put the emphasis on childhood. If "childhood decides," childhood is responsible and Sartre in *The Words* pronounced the final judgment on the child, Jean-Paul, only to rescind it later. In 1971, the child Jean-Paul comes into his own as the "loved" child in contrast to the "unloved" child, Flaubert. But he is always at the center of his small world.

Sartre's approach to his own childhood, consequently, is not merely evocative, although *The Words* draws its moving and vividly persuasive force from its evocative power. The facts and episodes he describes are conductors of meaning and are carefully controlled by an adult. Sartre was rather dangerously intent on exposing "objectively" the inner mechanisms of his own psyche. His account of his childhood is edited. Its substance was carefully selected and the perspectives deliberately imposed by the quinquagenarian, the famous writer and philosopher, Jean-Paul Sartre. It is fairly easy, however, to disentangle memory from the interpretation that shaped it into an architectural whole, rather simply contrived in some respects. The ideological perspective will not concern us here immediately, except insofar as *The Words* is a trial with a foregone conclusion. The child who salts the jam, burns a carpet, kills a fly is held accountable for all his small deeds; yet only apparently so, for there is a straw man in the background, Charles Schweitzer, symbol of the "bourgeois." Sartre the little boy, Sartre the writer, are simultaneously protagonist, accused, accuser, witness for the defense and prosecution, jury, judge, and court of appeal. They exonerate each other and point to the real culprit, Sartre's perennial whipping-boy: the bourgeoisie.

Flaubert, Baudelaire, even Genet are, like Sartre's own fictional heroes, responsible to Sartre and of necessity found wanting. They are after all not Sartre, who has taken upon himself the duty to judge their innermost thoughts according to his own specifications and to pronounce the verdict. Brilliant as they are, and questionable, Sartre's excursions into the psyches of others were trial runs, *The Words* was for a number of years their final culmination. Is Sartre not, as he rhetorically claimed in the last sentence of his little book and in defiance of Rousseau, "composed of all men and as good as all of them and no better than any"?

Yet perhaps, one feels, subconsciously aware of judging

himself a good deal better than Baudelaire or Flaubert;
at least, until, in the course of writing Flaubert's biography, "empathy" replaced Sartre's former antipathy
toward the man. Better too than the grandfather who
brought him up? And why the defiance? Sartre's claim to
"universality," standard in Western and more particularly
French tradition, is directed, almost violently, against the
exceptional in human affairs. If Sartre, desperately, has
gone to great lengths to prove that there is nothing mysterious about being Baudelaire, Flaubert, or Jean-Paul
Sartre, and that writing is in fact often a form of neurosis,
not a sign of superiority, it is because he is hammering at
a concept firmly rooted in his own mind and which he
wants to eradicate, the romantic concept of the writer as
a man set apart and accountable only to his own genius,
just such a man in fact as he has been. Why, *The Words*
makes clear. As Sartre sees it this concept of the "genius"
is a myth he had absorbed as a child and applied to himself, a myth he considers peculiar to a social class and a
specific culture—a bourgeois myth—which has been the
source of his thirty-year "neurosis." But the paradox remains whereby the first sense of freedom in life, as in
writing, came to the child, so Sartre insists, through in-
fringements of a moral code: a vase deliberately broken,
the deserving victim in his childish fantasies blinded
by his choice instead of being rewarded. Freedom,
action, and guilt are closely linked to the fascinating lure
of evil and to the myth of the good but "fake" little boy and
his real but "clandestine" disturbing double. Thence the
extreme personal preoccupation with the self and with the
perils of "inauthenticity." For the self controlled the world.

The Words therefore throws upon Sartre and Sartre's
life a penetrating if equivocal light. The book presents us
with a genuinely mythical childhood. In 1963, it exemplified Sartre's most recent understanding of himself, which

eight years later the account of Flaubert's childhood was
obliquely to complete and in part deny.

Camus found it difficult to project himself directly into
his writing. This led him, on occasion, to hide deeply
personal reactions under a cloak of impersonal rhetoric.
Whereas in *The Myth of Sisyphus* an inner lyricism permeated the armature of logic, that armature in *The Rebel*
tended to stifle the emotional sources of the work and to
mislead the reader. Camus's childhood eluded him. Again
and again he grappled with it. Around his twentieth year
he seems to have thought of fictionalizing it in a novel, a
project he abandoned, but to the substance of which he
had returned at the time of his death. *La Mort heureuse* is
a novel of initiation into manhood.

He alluded to his childhood only occasionally in random notes and letters and in brief essays written twenty
years apart: a short terse sketch, one of the earliest pieces
he wrote, entitled "Between Yes and No," and included in
the first small volume he published; and the preface for
the re-edition of that first volume. "Every artist," he wrote,
"preserves deep within him, a single source from which,
throughout his lifetime, he draws what he is and what he
says. When the source dries up the work withers and
crumbles. As for me, I know that my source is . . . the
world of poverty and light in which I lived for many
years . . ."[9]—the world of his Algerian youth. He too, like
Sartre, felt that for him childhood had decided.

In contrast with Sartre's, Camus's work as we have it
contains few references to children. These always refer to
the vulnerability of children, and the particularly unbearable quality of the violence they suffer. In Camus's
play, *The Just Assassins*,[10] the scruples of a terrorist whose
bomb, he realizes as he is about to throw it, would kill not

only his designated victim but two children, point up Camus's deep revulsion to the "massacre of the innocents" so implacably a part of our indiscriminately violent age. In *The Plague*, the men inured to suffering, who fight the epidemic, face its irreparable horror at the deathbed of a small boy dying in desperate pain; and it is the illness of the boss's child which, in "The Silent Men," a short story, changes the emotional mood of a group of workmen. There is no myth of childhood in Camus's work; there is an almost desperate sense of a child's vulnerability.

Camus was not, in Sartrean fashion, fascinated by the intricate workings of the human psyche; he was wedded to a stark and austere human setting in which explanations were few and words mostly factual. Whereas *words* were the forces that gave Sartre's childhood its shape, *silence* permeated Camus's.

Sartre's "whole" life as an intellectual and most particularly his "neurosis," he defined as bound up in his relation to words.

> I began my life, and I shall no doubt end it amidst books . . . I was born of writing. Before that, there was only a play of mirrors. With my first novel,[11] I knew that a child had got into the hall of mirrors. By writing, I was existing, I was escaping from grown-ups, but I existed only in order to write, and if I said "I" that meant "I who write" . . . I was prepared at an early age to regard teaching as a priesthood and literature as a passion.[12]

Grownups pressed around him: mother, grandmother, and grandfather, coddling and praising the docile golden-haired child—"little angel," "miraculous child," "infant prodigy." He had no playmates and he was the image they held out to him: their image of him which he tried to incarnate. He was the beloved grandson of a towering, godlike figure, Charles Schweitzer, he was a gift from heaven, his grandfather's anointed lamb. He had his appointed place in the "ceremonial" rites and relationships of the family circle. He learned the appropriate gestures and the appropriate words. The grandfather-grandson rites dominated his life, established so as to send out to the world a flattering image of the old man himself. A "fake," an "imaginary" Jean-Paul was the necessary adjunct to that image. The real Jean-Paul vegetated in a state of quasi-desperate boredom: "A spoiled child isn't sad; he's bored like a king, like a dog." The "fake" child gestured in a "fake" world while, sharpening his power of observation, the real little boy became confusedly aware that he was leading a double life. In his own scrupulous and inarticulate way, he was aware that he was turning "traitor," that he was an "impostor," quite unlike the "public" child.

One need not have recourse to Sartre's own explications to sense the burden of responsibility that a doting family had unwittingly placed on the shoulders of an only child anxiously straining to be the "expected" little boy, vaguely uncomfortable and guilty, in his own eyes, of failing to comply. The connection between guilt and responsibility is clear: the child could not live up to the image of himself daily reflected back to him. Furthermore, Sartre's quasi-irrational fear of being "statufied," "institutionalized," turned into an abstraction, a "Nobel-Prize winner," appears in a very sympathetic light: up to the age of eleven Sartre was, or at least feels he was in grown-up eyes, a "child of genius," an abstraction personified. The memory, as late as 1963, still drove him wild. All the more so because this is how, in the light of his accomplishment, one could describe him.

Central in his grandfather's world, hence in the child's, were books, gathered in the library, a sanctuary. Himself a maker of books—textbooks—Charles Schweitzer partook of their mystery. At an early age his grandson was given the freedom of the sanctuary. "I never tilled the soil or hunted for nests. I did not gather herbs or throw stones at birds. But books were my birds and my nest, my household pets, my barn and my countryside."[13] Books were, too, the child's only road to freedom. It was through the Larousse Encyclopedia that he became acquainted with a vast world, his possession. It was made of words: "It talks in my head" he would say to his mother. Presumably it has never stopped. A single persistent voice unrolls its tireless soliloquy through pages and pages of Sartre's nonstop writing, frequently left unfinished like the serials he loved. Sartre thus early discovered the writer's domain, the world of words.

Through words the child escaped from the "fake" world imposed on him into an "imaginary" world in which he could at least choose his role. And choose he did, with passionate singleness of mind. In his grandfather's library the infant prodigy officially read the classics for the edification of adult eyes. But a clandestine little boy avidly fed on the romanesque epics of popular adventure serials and the early silent films. A hero emerged, a young Saint George, the savior of helpless victims and the slayer of evil monsters. "Superfluous" in the static world where nothing was asked of him except to reflect a mirror image, the child was the indispensable champion of good in a simple, imaginary, Manichean universe. There came a unique moment when, as he sat writing one more variation of the stories he endlessly copied, Jean-Paul realized that, with a stroke of his pen, he could modify the pattern: he was the demiurge of his world, the distributor of both the evil and the good in it. It was his first conscious sense of himself as free agent: "I who write," the equivalent of "I who create the evil I redress and make exist a reality that without me would not exist."

No other writer, perhaps, has given so convincing, so genuinely moving an account of the impact of books on a child—as objects in themselves, as compendia of the universe; nor so clearly described the revelation attendant upon the acts of reading and writing. This is no doubt because young Sartre did not at first go to school. With a little help, he taught himself: books were his conquests and his playthings. In their company he had found a universe which he carried in his own head.

He had also absorbed a myth, carefully implanted by his grandfather—the myth of the writer as a man set apart, the spiritual guide of humanity along the road of progress—a banal and, more particularly, French concept. After Hugo, among the "beacons" would come Jean-Paul Sartre. Humble and effaced, he would accomplish his appointed task, and metamorphosed into a row of volumes on a library shelf, he would continue a posthumous life, a man "indispensable" to all men. One day, when he was in his teens, Sartre relates, referring to his atheism, God tumbled out of the sky. In God's place, abetted by his grandfather, he had, long before, placed the "spirit of mankind," doubly incarnate in his future self: as future writer, and as the teacher his prudent grandfather persuaded him to become—the legislator of the literary domain. Before he was seven, if we are to believe him, Sartre was a child with a mandate, "committed." What transpires in Sartre's account of his childhood is the preoccupation with the problem of a role to be assumed. It is the leitmotiv of the book. And, in relation of self to the world, it is the self that looms the largest, the consciousness of self, not the involvement with others or any great curiosity about the world.

Camus's most precious memories were enveloped in silence and enhanced by no solemn ceremonial or consecrations.

> On summer nights, workmen sit out on their balconies. In his house there was only a very small window. So they brought the chairs down in front of the house to savor the evening . . . A train might go by. A drunkard would sing to himself on a street corner, without managing to break the silence. The child's mother sat in silence. Occasionally someone would ask: "What are you thinking about?" "Nothing," she answered. . . . Sometimes . . . returning from an exhausting day . . . she found the house empty . . . She sank onto a chair and, eyes vague, became lost in the pursuit of a crack on the floor. Night thickened around her and her muteness was immediately desolate. If the child came in at that moment, he would distinguish the thin silhouette with the bony shoulders, and stop: he was afraid. He was hardly as yet conscious of his own existence. But he suffered to the verge of tears when confronted by that animal silence."[14]

> He discovered the substance of his sensibility the day he realized that his mother *saw him* and that she almost *never thought*.[15]

> I grew up in dusty streets, on dirty beaches. We swam out a short distance and reached the clear water. Life was hard at home and I was deeply happy most of the time.[16]

There were no mirrors and no books in Albert Camus's home, and no grandfather. There was an older brother, a domineering grandmother who made free use of blows and died of cancer, an infirm uncle and the mother who so seldom spoke: " 'Well Mother . . .' 'Well . . .' 'Do I bore you, I don't say much?' 'Oh! you never did talk very much.' True, he had never spoken to her." Yet it seemed to the young man who reports the conversation that "between those two there existed a feeling deep as death. Not the apparatus of tenderness, emotion and memory that one mistakes for love, but what in fact gives love its significance. A bond so powerful that no silence could damage it."[17]

From the outset, then, Camus was aware of a realm of human experience that lay beyond the reach of words, outside all conscious elaboration. The bond from which as a child he obscurely drew emotional sustenance was as fundamental as it was mute. Beyond the crude realities of working-class life—the coarse language, the paucity of thought, the early, unadorned initiation to sex, the crude gestures and elementary emotions—he perceived another reality, incarnated in his mother, beyond class or nationality, timeless. It was the way of life of tenacious men and women, anonymous and stoical, working in poverty for their bare subsistence. Cruelty and suffering for them were things to be endured. Camus himself, at seventeen, would endure, alone and in silence, the physical reality of the tuberculosis gnawing at his lungs. These people did not pontificate, judge, justify, or recriminate. Their existence was an evidence too solid to inspire merely pity and protest, though Camus was never to forget the indignities attendant upon deprivation: brutality, illness, insensitivity, lack of horizon. His mother's mute self-acceptance demanded something beyond pity—respect. "Nothing prevents me . . . from imagining," he later wrote in the preface to L'Envers et l'Endroit, "that I shall at long last succeed in placing at the core of [my] work the admirable silence of a mother and a man's effort to rediscover a justice or a love that could compensate that silence."[18]

Camus's characters, with notable exceptions, are men

and women of few words, and the garrulous among them
—the soliloquists of *The Fall* and the priest of *The Renegade*—are hardly exemplary. The most moving of them
all perhaps is the figure of Dr. Rieux's mother in *The
Plague*, a presence almost inarticulate and yet a luminous
source of dignity and strength. And he himself in general
preferred terse understatement and simple language in
contrast to Sartre's runaway rhetoric and often abstruse
vocabulary.

There was in Camus's early life a verbal void and no
mandate. He could have no sense of holding a privileged
place in the universe; but rather of sharing the same general fate. To live, as his people understood it, was to
become a man, to work and die. He was particularly sensitive to the physical realities of life, both to the impermanency and vulnerability of the human body and to its
immense potentialities for joy. As his two first brief collections of essays show, *L'Envers et l'Endroit* and *Noces*
(*Nuptials*), he early shared with the emperor Caligula—
one of the first characters he conceived—an initial insight: "Men die and they are not happy." The undertow
of poignancy is evident, and the reaching out to each
individual as a singular human being, not as a type. The
sentence holds the key to Camus's deepest preoccupation,
for no amount of thinking or action can change the initial
statement "men die"; but the second part of the statement
might, to some extent, be modified. There are forms of
man-made imprisonments that could at least be allevi-
ated: poverty, illness, oppression. And Camus as a young
journalist was to fight some of these. But the kind of
responsibility he assumed was free of guilt.

Nothing that Camus later wrote is more revealing in
this connection than *La Mort heureuse*. Its opening pages
enact a violent fantasy with an allegorical significance:

Mersault, a young man imprisoned in the mediocrity of a workaday life, confronts Zagreus, a paralyzed older man, his friend, deliberately shoots him, and takes the money uselessly stacked away in an envelope. Life is in fact given him with the money, the possibility of a passionate quest for a happiness such that, when death is exacted in the end, it does not seem too high a price to pay for the exalted consciousness of life to which he has acceded. The deliberate act of violence, at the start of the adventure, is in one of its dimensions a measure of young Camus's revolt against the numbing effect of poverty. Because Camus early confronted the knowledge that life is given each individual only once; because his own was so early threatened, and no doubt because his was the artist's exigency, the freedom he claimed, for himself and for all, was first the freedom to become a fully conscious human being, capable of reaching a full measure of joy as well as pain. At twenty, what he most feared, it is clear, was the stifling of his life, of any life. Mersault's quest is the quest for an experience so intense that it outweighs the sense of the futility of life inherent in the certainty of death, so that when he dies he may die "happy."

But the path is not easy that leads Mersault to that reconciliation. His murder of Zagreus is, on one level, the symbolic destruction of all the outer barriers to his enterprise, barriers social in kind: the possession of the money stolen is the condition of Mersault's freedom to live a fully conscious life. Mersault's quest and fulfillment throw a good deal of light on Caligula's plaint "Men die and they are not happy"; and on Camus's social commitments. His primary revolt was directed against what imprisons men, barring them from a full experience of the world in its sensory and emotional richness. His sense of injustice was closely tied to his passionate concern that no human being be wantonly cheated of his fragile chance to experience happiness as well as pain, and thereby be excluded from the full knowledge of the glory of life itself.

Mersault's own escape out of the humdrum everyday world, the shot and theft that free him from it, his quest and final accession to a revelation concerning the world and his own fate in it, are clearly connected with young Camus's sense of his needs as artist. At one point he had envisaged making of Mersault a would-be writer. Mersault's quest is a quest for unity—unity within the self, unity with the world—experienced and expressed by Camus in the oblique, analogical language of fiction. Communication here is an imaginary reenactment and reordering of experience. However inadequately, young Camus strove to give this first narrative not only unity of form, but aesthetic coherence. If his was the artist's need, his too was the artist's exigency: awkward though it be in some respects, *La Mort heureuse* is the work of a young man for whom words have an aesthetic value. Through the myth of Mersault he was attempting to confront the reality he feared—his death—and to transcend it by integrating it into a symbolic whole. The introducing of the figure of Zagreus is the clear indicator that the myth Camus has in mind is the Dionysian myth of the artist.

Young Camus drew from his early experience a consciousness of the relativity of human power and intelligence in human affairs, a sense of human solidarity and of the great diversity of human needs. He could not accept a view of the world in which individual human beings were considered expendable, whatever the end. In the thirties it was because he saw the Stalin-directed policy toward the Algerian Muslims, a policy in which he was involved, developing as a political game of checkers, that he broke with the Party. And one of the things most deeply alien to him in Christian thought was its glorification of the gratuitous suffering inflicted on a human being by other human beings, exemplified in the tortured figure of a man hanging on a cross.

Immersed in the light, the sea, the wind, he could merge with the natural world, escaping from the limitations of his life, exulting in a sense of power and wholeness, an experience that he knew was as real as it was temporary. It neither negated his sense of the impermanency of life nor was canceled out by it. It was a dimension of experience that enriched his awareness of the value of being alive, physically alive in and to the world.

The child's human experience was sparse and elemental, often brutal, but its genuineness was not open to question. His experience of nature was sensuous and rapturous. Silence was a dimension of existence: the silence of his mother, the silence of the earth, those things to which obscurely he acquiesced. It protected an intimate and precious domain of pure untainted emotion that sustained the child's life. There were at first no matching words.

He was seventeen when a novel read by chance opened up this dimension of his experience to expression: "My stubborn silences, my vague and sovereign suffering, the singular world around me, the nobility of my folk, their misery, my secrets in brief, all could be said. Deliverance was there, an order of truth where poverty, for instance, showed its real face—which I had vaguely distinguished and dimly revered."[19] Writing, for Camus, would then first be an act of reverence, the difficult communication of an inner, guarded domain, brought forth out of the silence that had kept it intact. His early novel is, in one of its aspects, a cry of revolt against the limitations placed by poverty on a young man's access to that guarded domain. What preoccupied him was not a role to be assumed, but a world to be revealed.

In a short essay on André Gide, another of his initiations to literature, he spoke of his discovery of "le monde de la création," the realm of literary creation, as a "secret domain"; and of Gide "the guardian, a king's son, who watched over the doors of a garden in which [he, Camus] wanted to live."[20] The image is rich in connotations. The need and attraction; the secret dedication, hardly as yet conscious; the sense of peace, order, and beauty conveyed by the "royal garden"; and the respect for and gratitude toward the guardian and initiator. It was hardly surprising then, that in later years Camus could not easily share Sartre's sentimentalized and schematic view of the "working class" and reacted rather sardonically to Sartre's somewhat patronizing suggestion that the writer's task was to "unveil" to the bourgeoisie the inarticulate proletariat's situation. Sartre who, much as he desired it, did not easily establish contacts with "le peuple," associated the masses with the excitement that participation in mass demonstrations aroused in him. He idealized the working class first as non-bourgeois victims of bourgeois injustice; later, in Marxian perspective, as the proletariat, "the only class capable of effecting a radical change in society." Hence his sustained concern with the political party that alone could claim to represent the French proletariat, the Communist Party. But he did not see them as his equals: he inevitably, and even to this day, adopts the role of he who knows, of the "enlightener." His attitude is Promethean.

With his early knowledge of the conditions of life in what is now called the urban "ghetto," Camus saw working men as persons rather than a "class." He had no sense of them or of himself as a brand of human beings set apart. "In the periodicals and books written by specialists of progress, the proletariat is described as though it were a tribe with strange customs and in such a way that it would give the proletariat nausea if they had time to read the specialists to find out how well progress is moving forward . . ."[21] If anything, it was the Paris intellectuals whose artificial mode of life, parochial views, and petty rivalries disconcerted him. He knew the brutality, but also the dignity, the appetites, but also the instinctive code of ethics and the independence of working men. It was not in Marx, he once noted, that he had learned about freedom but from his own people. He was not inclined to politicize culture nor the basic emotions of life. Access to that culture had brought him out of the silence that so irrevocably walled in his mother. It had changed his relation to his world, giving it depth and meaning. When Prometheus, he noted, decided to liberate men from the tyranny of Zeus he brought them not only fire but the arts. And for this liberation he was personally grateful, as his lifelong friendship for the two men who had made it possible shows. He seems to have been less drawn to the mind-ridden Sartre, than Sartre, for a time, was drawn to him.[22] In part, as Simone de Beauvoir's memoirs obliquely show, it was Camus's refusal to be cast in the role of "proletarian writer," as they envisaged it, that explains the harshness with which they dealt with him at the time of *The Rebel*.

It is tempting to emphasize the contrasts; they are sharp and obvious to the extreme. If "childhood decides," no two childhoods could have been more different. But what concerns us here is the nature of the experience, the initial commitment it determined. All the essential components of Camus's work are contained in his childhood, whose immediate horizons, narrow in some respects, were the horizons of a real world. To that childhood, harsh in many eyes, the man turned with gratitude. He repeatedly stressed that it was a happy childhood, from which he drew his greatest strengths. Sartre, in contrast, admits his dislike of those early years, his sense that the small adult he was had had no real childhood. And yet he also spoke of it as "paradise." The only issue open to him—whether hell or paradise—had been to create his own childish reality, and the only problems he had had to cope with had been the problems in his own head, linked with the enigma of his own identity and the concern with his "role."

For Camus, the essential givens were the concrete givens of experience, for Sartre the creations of his mind. Camus would reach out of silence toward the difficult communication of a real experience, Sartre reached out for words to create a world that was lacking. Camus, closely bound emotionally with the realities he had early experienced, found it hard to achieve detachment, to establish in his writing and in his life the distance from himself that would allow the play of perspective that is inherent in the irony, wit, and intellectual vigor of Sartre, more consonant perhaps with the critical moods of the recent past. But neither would he have Sartre's form of deadly earnestness, his obsessive logic-chopping, his will singlehandedly to dominate and "save" the world through words. For although Sartre claims, in *The Words*, justifiably, that he is no leader, the accompanying statement that he was "not consumed by the canker of power,"[23] is open to some question.

It was a form of power that the child discovered with the first intimation of his own identity "I, who write": the power to mold a world, to blind his heroine or stay his pen and so save her from that disaster; the power to distribute right and wrong at will, a prerogative he has never relinquished. Although in *The Words* he rather ruefully mocks his self-imposed role as righter of wrongs, Sartre's polemical writings are sprinkled with rhetorically final judgments of the "you no longer have the right to teach" type which he addressed to Raymond Aron, guilty of holding adverse opinions on the 1968 student insurgency. Pronounced in the heat of passion, such ostracisms usually turn out to be temporary. But the accusatory stance is natural to Sartre, witness the role played in his articles by the pronoun *on* . . . designating the faceless "they" who so often bear the responsibility for the evils he has denounced. The *on* may sometimes—often—turn into a "you"; and the "you" may emerge from a "we." Out of that "we," if it is denunciatory, Sartre usually extricates himself, incarnating the wrongdoers in a type, which he defines and explicates and then illogically, indignantly castigates in terms of the specific mental perspective he has just attributed to the type: the anti-Semite, the collaborationist, American capitalists, the recalcitrant Communist Party, or "we" white men; all these turn out to be, in some sense, avatars of a single hated figure, incarnate in Charles Schweitzer: the bourgeois.

Sartre's hatred of bourgeois life is too notorious to stress. But the host of things he has characterized with this epithet over the years is rather confusing and reveals the streak of irrationality that underlies many of his judgments and that, honorably, he contends with. In *The Words*, Sartre suggests that underlying his whole personality, guiding its development, is his deep, childish revulsion against the sham façade of noble rectitude behind which his bourgeois family hid from itself, and from him, its real dereliction. In the discovery of that dereliction, he would meet Camus on a common ground, though

in a different emotional climate. For Camus, dereliction
was not a matter of class or type nor a matter for condemnation. The movement of his imagination is inverse:
the "mask" falls, in the end, from the face of *The Stranger*
or *Caligula*, even of the disturbing Clamence of *The Fall*,
revealing the fellow creature it concealed.

Both men were concerned with examining anew in
terms of their total experience what it meant to be a
human being, in a twentieth-century world, with a twentieth-century awareness. In the thirties, neither had put
the question that erupted with obsessional violence in
Sartre's postwar writing: to what today are we, unknown
to us, committing the future? In what light will tomorrow's history place us? Sartre's obsession with history,
born of the war, directed his thought away from the men
of today to what he called "the masked men of the future." Camus was far more concerned with the present.

For most readers, as the literate population goes,
though less perhaps now than heretofore, Sartre's "ceremonial" middle-class family may seem more familiar than
Camus's, and his revolt against its tight little universe
thoroughly sympathetic. Between Camus's silent mother
and Sartre's grandfather there is indeed a world. Yet only
the brilliancy of Sartre's writing, helped by his acute
perspicacity, can mask the fact that, callously, Sartre
made of the old man a type, a foil for the sole purpose of
his demonstration. Charles Schweitzer is an idea he
wanted to communicate—an enemy he is unmasking, the
"petit bourgeois" in person, not a human being whose
quality he is attempting to communicate with due regard
for truth. Reaching back in his own memory Camus deciphered what was most difficult and best in his past,
those things that had been of value to him, which hence
perhaps might also be of value to others as destitute orig-

inally as himself. His austerely concrete experience thereby, in a curious reversal of perspectives, is stylized in expression, and conveys a sense of intense idealism. In contrast, Sartre's fundamentally abstract universe, enriched by a dazzling interplay of perspectives, has the multifaceted semblance of reality. Camus's practical activity would always stretch beyond the bounds he reserved to literature. Sartre would find it imperative to bring every facet of reality within a circumscribed but total and ordered universe of words, seen from a relative point, momentarily absolutized.

Sartre has always been preoccupied with the question of judgment, intellectual and moral. His main drive, he has said, was fully to understand "man." That is, to achieve a total objective view of all the elements that enter into the making of what he eventually designated as "the singular universal," an individual imaginatively reconstituted in his organic whole as a person. He uses the expression "singular universal"—a Hegelian term—because he conceives of all human behavior in terms of a single basic drive—"the urge to become completely self-sufficient, autonomous, independent of anything external . . ."[24] and believes that a complex enough application of general laws of human psychology and Marxian analysis to an individual's behavior will reveal its singularity and at the same time its "universality," its human patterning. This he believes he will achieve in his *Flaubert*.

Sartre for a time considered his personal experience with assurance as exemplary: "Through my own history," he said of his autobiography, "it is the history of my time that I want to transcribe."[25] The "I" "I" "I" of Sartre that has indisposed some critics, is thus always dichotomized: there is the "I" detached, objectified, universalized, and the "I" that tells its story. Stage by stage Sartre washes his hands of each one of his avatars. He who remains is the "I" who retraces the steps of the "other," at whatever level the game is being played, an "I" who is continually forced out of any position achieved. He it is who discerns all the "blocks," the restraints, the structures that must be done away with in the next forward movement.

Sartre's works always tell the story of the successive phases in his understanding of what the future requires of him, and concomitantly, in his terms, of all his contemporaries. Literature then was always an adjunct to his main purpose, even when he accepted it unquestioningly as an absolute. "A culture," he told students in a 1964 interview,[26] "is the critical mirror of total man and makes sense if man finds it possible to recognize himself in it and to contest himself in it." There are many reasons to think that Sartre's constant purpose has been to provide this mirror, the initial schema of *Being and Nothingness* furnishing a frame for what became an increasingly complex sense of that mirror our culture holds out to us. But having "man" in mind Sartre quite naturally spoke for "all men," in his commitments as well as in his condemnations. He often equates "the other" with that other he is rejecting in himself. His is always the role of mentor to humanity.

On occasion he has discussed his own ideological evolution in Marxist terms; Marxism today, he declared at the time, "is in itself culture, since it alone allows us to understand men, works and events."[27] One might of course see things in a different light. In her book, *Natural Symbols* (Pantheon, 1970), the British anthropologist Mary Douglas describes the social experience, which in groups ranging from the primitive to the most contemporary, creates the same "millennial" tendencies and destructive attitudes with regard to existing categories of

any kind that underlie Sartre's own career, from his tussle
with the image of his grandfather to his identification
with the small sect of "casseurs."[28] She does not, of
course, use the Marxist frame. Whatever the case may be
in this respect it merely underscores the mythical dimensions of Sartre's understanding of himself, and the circle
of conviction, assumption, and explanation through
which he moves. The patterns of dialectical argument he
adopted may override but do not necessarily dissolve the
contradiction inherent in his argument, based on an a
priori pattern of explication and an arbitrary selection of
facts sometimes wildly disparate in nature. Consequently,
for Sartre the main problem was the transition in actual
life from theory to practice, from verbal pattern to action.

Camus accepted from the outset that a secular view of
the world implied all the limitations of variety, relativity,
and uncertainty. "The writer," he wrote, "tries to draw
the materials of his art out of the complex world in which
he is involved, and which he understands only partly,
accepting the flux, pain and joy, fully yet without submission." The word "partly" is what irrevocably would separate him from Sartre. What most deeply engaged his attention even as a very young man—and his very first sketches
show it—was the zone of personal feeling within which
words are born and die and through which people reach
out or fail to reach out to others' needs, the manner in
which people deal with one another. He could not, he admitted in his Nobel Prize acceptance speech, personally
live without his art. And he felt that art, authentic art,
could not but be "in the service of truth and freedom."
Truth he saw as "mysterious, elusive, always to be con-
quered"; and freedom as "dangerous, as hard to live as it is
exalting." He was, and he admitted he was, a man of
strong passions, quick to react to provocation, unimpressed

by authority, stirred by injustice, and restive under constraint. Writing was first for him a form of self-discipline: through his writing, he said, he built the inner "dikes" he needed to contain the surging inner forces whose destructive potentialities seemed at times to have frightened the young man. Caligula, the first figure to come fully alive in his imagination, has more in common with the young Camus than may at first appear. Art for Camus was the very opposite of judgment, at least judgment of the negative kind; he envisaged it rather as the measure of his desire to be recognized for what he was, by a "living community of men": "If I need my art . . . it is because it cuts itself away from no one and allows me to live, as I am, at the level of all."

Part of what he had to express was his sense of the beauty in life, a beauty which also as an artist "he could not do without." Literary creation then was for him a way of life as well as a privileged means of communication.[29] It seems to have been through his writing that he forged for himself what he called an art of living in times of catastrophe, without foundering in self-contempt. He was interested in theories only secondarily to the extent that they helped in the formulation of that art. Political systems he judged, like ideological systems, according to the manner in which they dealt with human persons, not in terms of the rhetoric they deployed. And he was willing, if need be, to put his life on the line. But he disliked public explanations and justifications which turned the spotlight on actions he thought should be taken for granted in a man's life.[30] For him, the language of literature was a language that could encompass conflicts and contradictions and so throw light on "the obscurity of the heart." The search for that language was a primary enterprise, and an intimate one. He could hardly accept, either for himself or for his fellow writers, any mandatory commitment for literature as such. Had it not been for the inner need to write, he could quite easily have lived, in his own way, among other men, in conflict or friendship, with no sense that he was called upon to be their mentor, or otherwise assume a public role.

What most deeply marked the two men coming from such different horizons was an experience they shared because, beyond all that separated them, both were citizens of France. And it was the fate of France that, as thinking men, brought them, like most of their contemporaries, sharply up against a reality they had not foreseen, but which by 1938 had become obviously inevitable. Revolution they had foreseen as a possibility. It had almost occurred between 1934 and 1936. But defeat and occupation, no. This was for both of them a disaster that reached beyond issues and ideologies to a stable image of a spiritual "France," fashioned by its long history in the past. Governments could go wrong, and frequently did; and French individuals could be and were frequently reprehensible. But "France" in some way remained intact. The defeat of France, the Occupation, the Liberation and its aftermath were indeed a "fall." And these events were crowded into half a dozen brief years that seemed longer to those who lived them. There was a before and an after. This was true for other countries in Europe but no two confronted the same situation. As we look back over the thirties and early forties, the broad conflicts seem to us simple: Politically, democracy versus fascism and communism; the League of Nations versus war; war versus peace; collaboration versus resistance. None of these were specifically French issues; all Europeans confronted them. The postwar problems were clearly different; they were more confused and, because of the French defeat, took on a more particularly French color. Some concerned France more specifically: questions of reconstruction, of the nature of the political, economic, or social structures. Others concerned the place of France in Europe. Others widened out to include the world: decolonialization, nuclear armament, the relation of France to the large major powers, the United States, Russia, China; and to the United Nations. The communist-fascist polarization ended with World War II in the defeat of fascism. The new polarizations were more complex in kind. Between 1930 and 1970, three sharply defined situations split the country virtually in two, posing the question of choice in dramatic terms for intellectuals who customarily attempt to define issues and justify their options. These occurred each time the currently recognized alternatives no longer applied: The Spanish war in 1936; the German Occupation, 1940–44; the Algerian war, 1954–1961. None of these turned out to be merely ideological issues, though the "committed" intelligentsia too easily argued as if they were. But they all three sharply posed for the French the problem of the disjuncture between French government policies and the convictions of active and articulate minorities of French citizens. This disjuncture reached its climax in the Pétain-de Gaulle dichotomy.

From one point of view or another all Frenchmen were traitors in the Occupation years. This was merely an extension of the political situation in the preceding years: fascists and communists, tolerated by and suspect to successive French governments, considered each other and were considered by current opinion as potential traitors to French traditions and to French ideals. The conflict surfaced again during the Algerian war: there the question of dissent and treachery was sharply etched:

Frenchmen took sides against their country at war, and not in words only. Dissent then, contestation, confrontation, violence on political issues, had become a way of life. Through it all ran conflicting dialogues of the French with France, of the French with each other, with the rest of the world. Sartre and Camus were not the only men caught in the turmoil. But they were, outstandingly, the men whose hours of decision most exactly coincided with the moments of the nation's greatest inner dismay. They were talented enough and forceful enough to make themselves heard; and they were disciplined enough as writers to attempt to establish some form of consonance in the confusion of their experiences. Both resolutely accepted the necessity of political action and that it should be grounded on genuine thought.

Besides coming from different horizons, they were also separated by age and by the perspectives conditioned by the geographic as well as the social location from within which one looks out on the world. Sartre was twenty, in Paris, in 1925. He was at the hub of the French intellectual and artistic world at a time of great turmoil and excitement in the world of the arts. Surrealism had succeeded Dadaism in the revolt against the values of the Western world. Paris was still a center where the writers and artists from all over the world congregated, and where, in the wild postwar explosion of talents, major works had come out in great abundance. Paris had turned its back on the "last" of all wars; the Russian Revolution, the first signs of fascism were all present, but only somewhere on the periphery; Paris was enthralled by jazz, the silent movie, the grand turmoil in the culture itself. And Sartre was enthralled too, well into the late thirties, eager to enter "modern times." He would always remain a man of the city of Paris in spite of his world-wide travels.

Camus was twenty in 1933, in a more sober time and in

a sparser cultural setting, Algiers. The eight years that
separate him from Sartre put them on the two different
slopes of that dividing line, 1929–1930. Even though it
was a large and vigorous seaport with a good university,
Algiers was intellectually very far indeed from Paris.
Camus and his small group of friends attempted to fill the
vacuum. But their view of the world was both simpler
and broader than Sartre's and less oriented toward the
arts and literature. The European-Arab dichotomy existed but was less pronounced in the poor sections of Algiers than in the more prosperous sections of the city or
elsewhere in rural Algeria. Camus was in daily contact
with Algerian Muslims. It is quite true that at the level of
everyday life, the "Mediterranean" way of life in southern
Europe—the "diffuse and turbulent" life of Genoa, or the
"deserted squares at midday" in Spain, the habit everywhere of the midday siesta—was still in the early thirties
as Camus observed closer to Islam than to what we call
the "Western" rhythms of living. At that level he then
thought "North Africa is one of the only lands where
Orient and Occident cohabit" (*Essais*, 1325). He was
early aware of the difference between his Algerian sensitivity and the Parisian. He was in his twenties when he
spoke in terms of a "Mediterranean" sensitivity, a term
which later was to be ridiculed by some of his critics. We
are being strongly reminded today that our physical and
intellectual life is indeed shaped by the space around us;
by the sky, water, sun, and air that envelop us. The sun
and sea and atmosphere of a region as distinctive as the
Mediterranean may well affect the perceptions of its in-
habitants in certain fundamental ways. When the young
Camus spoke of a "Mediterranean" culture, he was no
doubt using the word "culture" in a rather vague way.
But to say, like some commentators, that his own culture

was entirely European and French is to omit all the aspects of culture anthropologists have obliged us to take into account. Camus's *literary* culture was European; his sensibility and his general approach to human beings were specifically marked by his Algerian upbringing; and away from Algeria he felt, as he often said, "a little in exile."

Characteristically, when he first used the term "Mediterranean," in 1937, he was trying to define the particular cultural climate of North Africa, on the frontier of European civilization but also on the frontier of Asia.[31] This was a sweeping view but it did show an awareness not bounded by the French horizon. The French frame of reference is far less prominent in his work than in Sartre's. And his Algerian and working-class origins opened his eyes, much earlier than were Sartre's, to the inequities of the colonial regime in Algeria.

They met in Paris in the dark hours of the War. Each shared the other's sympathies in regard to the Occupation and ideas in regard to the future of France. They fraternized, discussed, went to some of the same hectic parties which Simone de Beauvoir describes and which helped them to cast off the tensions of their daily life. But Camus, more deeply and secretly involved in the underground, never belonged to Sartre's "set." For a few years their courses were almost parallel. Yet neither seems to have deeply influenced the other. By 1938, when Camus read *Nausea*, his own first works were already being published or well along in the planning. *The Myth of Sisyphus* and *Being and Nothingness* came out almost simultaneously, *The Myth of Sisyphus* slightly earlier, in December, 1942, and before they had met—these were not books that had been written overnight. But in fact, and this Simone de Beauvoir's *Memoirs* make acidly

clear, there was a temperamental opposition between the
Sartrean group and Camus, a fundamental difference in
orientation that made them unmixable and in many ways
antithetical. What is particularly interesting in their case
is that they did not rally opposing camps on the major
confrontations of the era. They were both anti-fascist,
against the Franco forces in the Spanish civil war; and
after Camus's short adherence to the Communist Party,
non-communist left-wing men. They were on the side of
the Resistance against the policies of Vichy and both, in
the decolonialization period, were opposed to the repressive policies of the French government with regard to the
national liberation forces in its former territories. When
Camus was directly involved, he usually became more
actively involved than Sartre who has accepted no specific
concrete responsibilities in the political sphere. His support
of the Spanish Republicans and his friendship with the
Spanish exiles lasted as long as his life; during the war he
was far more deeply engaged in specific underground activities than Sartre who, on the whole, stayed on the sidelines. In the Algerian war both in a sense, which should
not be exaggerated, risked their lives: Camus in his personal intervention in Algiers in 1955, an intervention
which had been preceded by others less spectacular but
nonetheless of vital importance to the men he defended.
Sartre began to participate actively in the growing opposition to the Algerian war in 1956. From then until the war
ended, he took position with increasing vehemence and
indignation, until in 1960 he signed the famous manifesto
of the 121, declaring the legitimacy for French citizens of
armed resistance to French policy.[32] But from 1948 on
there was no mistaking the rift that was rapidly separating
them. Sartre's eloquent testimony to Camus at the time of
Camus's death came too late to bridge it. Both men fol-

lowed a complex itinerary, hedged by uncertainties; but they did in fact take different ways. These we shall attempt to explore.

Notes to Chapter 3

1. This is the tone he adopted in his argument with Camus and in his quite unjustifiable answer to Professor Grossvogel of Cornell who courteously reproached him for his decision to cancel an engagement to speak at Cornell. One of the reasons for the decision, he alleged, was that no dialogue was possible with Americans because of the Vietnam situation, and that his presence in the United States would be a disappointment to his Cuban friends. Sartre often explains his decisions by a variety of reasons, which leaves them wide open to interpretation.

2. Richard Mayne, "Why French Students Rebel," *Encounter*, July 1968, 39–44.

3. Simone de Beauvoir recalls rather amusing examples of this streak as, for instance, Sartre's stubborn proof by argument—seriously intended—that only those things exist that are immediately perceptible to us, concluding therefrom that such things as bacteria do not exist. The position in this case was of course temporary, but characteristic. Sartre is an inveterate and not overly cautious builder of theories.

4. Sartre relies on the ambiguity, in French, of the "si" (if). A burlesque example of this ambiguity for example would run as follows: "if (si) it rains, it is because (c'est que) the earth is parched"; in contrast with the conjectural "if it rained, the grass would grow." The "si . . . c'est que" is often at work in Sartre's arguments.

5. The title refers to the warp and woof of a piece of cloth, and refers to the two interwoven facets of life Camus

wished to depict, the harsh loneliness, the physical plunge into old age, illness, death; and the sensuous physical joy of life.

6. Sartre's debt to Freud, in spite of his characteristic initial hostility, was already evident in his *Baudelaire*. Although he still rejects the idea of the "subconscious" he now makes massive use of Freudian terminology and analyses of neuroses. To describe the full range of the conscious-unconscious realms of the mind he now uses the term "the lived" (le vécu). See *Le Monde*, May 14, 1971, p. 21 for his understanding of that term.

7. Translated under the title: *Red Gloves*.

8. *L'Affaire Henri Martin*, Commentaire de Jean-Paul Sartre (Paris: Gallimard, 1953). In Sartre's depiction, however worthy its intent, Henri Martin's youth is sentimentalized and schematized, and the young man himself is turned into a kind of soap-opera figure.

9. *Essais*, p. 5.

10. Translated under the title *The Just Assassins*.

11. Written, it would seem, at approximately the age of eight.

12. *The Words*, pp. 95, 25, 26.

13. *The Words*, p. 31.

14. *Essais*, pp. 24–25.

15. From an early draft, published posthumously in *Essais*, p. 1213.

16. Letter to the poet René Char in *Essais*, p. 1180.

17. *Essais*, p. 29.

18. *Essais*, p. 13.

19. *Essais*, p. 12.

20. *Essais*, pp. 1118-1120. Gobineau had used the connotations of the image, a "king's son," to designate a "royal race" of superior human beings. For Camus, it is his function as guardian of and initiator to art that gives the artist his royal status.

21. *Essais*, p. 1111. Nelson Algren's reactions to the Paris intellectuals he met, more entertainingly expressed, have much in common with Camus's.

22. This may explain the brittle tone and "ad hominem" arguments both Sartre and Simone de Beauvoir adopted at the time of their disagreement. Sartre asserted rather pompously that Camus had "entered into History and by the same token into solid union with all those who bear the scars of historical injustice" only at the time of German occupation. He overlooked Camus's early and sustained advocacy of the cause of the Algerian Muslims to which Sartre in those years paid scant attention. Simone de Beauvoir, freely impugning his motives, cast Camus in the role of "resolute champion of bourgeois values" (*The Force of Circumstance*, p. 259), a rather silly and typically erroneous judgment.

23. *The Words*, p. 13.

24. Ivan Soll, *An Introduction to Hegel's Metaphysics* (Chicago: The University of Chicago Press, 1969).

25. *Libération*, November 4, 1953.

26. "L'Étudiant de France," No. 5, February 1964.

27. "Le Réformisme et les fétiches," *Les Temps modernes*, February 1956.

28. Mary Douglas classifies that social experience in terms of a group-focused social unit and what she calls a "grid" or ego-focused experience. She gives Sartre's description of his childhood as an example of the first, with its rituals and its hierarchical symbolization in the powerful grandfather figure. She gives as a contemporary example of the grid-type experience, among others, the unstructured ego-centered student world, the world of Sartre in the thirties, and well beyond. In this type of social experience, when the social structures fail to work, "a person feels that his personal relations . . . are in the grip of a sinister social system. . . . The destruction of categories of any kind is a symbolic act which replicates social life overstructured by grid, the experience which has always driven people to value unstructured personal experiences and to place their faith in a catastrophic event which will sweep away all existing structures." (xvi.) The ego-focused grid leaves

an individual with a weakened sense of his relation to his society, hence his urge to identify with sects who erect "a high wall between themselves and the rest of the world" and live "in continual schism," proclaiming the goodness of one part of the world and the badness of the other, a schism reflected in dualistic metaphysics. Sartre's childhood experience then would reflect a personal social experience, analogous to others throughout time in all societies and would be only secondarily connected to Marxist class theories.

29. Camus's basic orientation could to some extent be related to the model described by Mary Douglas; it appears in an unstructured social situation where both the group and the "ego-focused" grid structures are weak, where "a man is expected to build his own career by transacting with all and sundry as widely as possible to the best of his ability" and individuals are considered, on the whole, as fairly reliable. "Men are not set on either side of a line dividing sheep from goats. They are seen to be unequally endowed with talents, but the inequality is random, unpredictable and unconnected with moral judgment." (p. 1250.) Camus seems to have started out from just such a perspective, which he found inadequate. It fits his case far better than the attempt to fit him into the Marxian mold and unconvincingly taint him with the sin of "bourgeois-ism."

30. This refusal to justify his positions or publicize his actions was evident at the time of the Algerian war. The extent of Camus's personal involvement only became known in 1969, when the Le Figaro littéraire published extracts from Yves Courteline's book, Histoire d'Algérie. Le temps des Léopards (Paris: Fayard, 1969), under the title "Albert Camus devant la guerre d'Algérie" (June 2–7 and 9–15, 1964), ("Albert Camus Confronts the Algerian War").

31. There is a political context to the lecture delivered in 1937. Camus was speaking at the "Maison de la culture," the Communist-initiated cultural center which he had set up.

There were, it seems, conflicts between the policies of the Communist Party and the point of view of its Algerian-Arab members; they concerned questions of religion and tradition. Camus wished to define a form of "collectivism," "different from the Russian collectivism"; and he asserted that the orthodox party doctrine must be changed and adapted to "realities stronger than ourselves," that is, to the complex cultural situation of North Africa. A characteristic attitude. Camus was not, even as a party member, a doctrinaire. In a 1945 interview, the interviewer noted that one of Camus's essential preoccupations was the "Arab problem" and that he was one of the rare men in France who had attempted to define a really creative Franco-Arab policy (*Essais*, 1429).

32. During the worst years of France's involvement in the Algerian war, Sartre often stayed outside France, as Madame de Beauvoir's *Memoirs* tell us. They were disgusted with French policies, with French opinion, and with the attitude of the French Communist Party, and spent much of their time in Italy. They were in Brazil when a first bomb was set off in Sartre's apartment. When a second bomb exploded there in January, 1962, he had recently moved. The four years, 1958–1962, were years of intense harassment and, for Sartre, of an intellectual activity comparable to his activity during the Occupation and to the surge of activity in 1968. He is clearly, as we have noted, what the French call "un oppositionnel": a man whose energies are galvanized by his indignation, a "contestant" or "protester," who is fired by a moral cause.

4.

Self and Commitment: Ideological Patterns and the Logic of Myth

Here I sit, forming mankind
In my own image
A race resembling me.

GOETHE, Prometheus

"I wanted to write novels and plays long before I knew what philosophy was. I still want to. I have wanted to all my life."[1] When he said this, in a 1959 interview, Sartre had been pouring the better part of his vast intellectual energy for over a decade into political polemics and social theory. Plays he had continued to write, but at an increasingly slower tempo. Two of his more significant plays frame the decade: *The Devil and the Good Lord* and *The Prisoners of Altona*, antithetical in mood. But Sartre's novel-writing days were well behind him; it was twenty years since he had planned and written in large part the unfinished *Roads to Freedom*, his last attempt at narrative fiction. Sartre's deliberate blueprint for a literature "committed" to social action had, paradoxically, deflected his career as novelist. It was a curious result, given the fact that *What Is Literature?* was more particularly addressed to the writer as novelist. It is plausible to think that Sartre's postwar decision to subordinate his philosophical and literary activity to the dictates of his social conscience gave the philosopher the preeminence over the novelist that Sartre later seems at times to have regretted; and transformed the author of *Being and Nothingness*, whose intent it was to release individuals from their bondage to various forms of conformism, into the social theorist of the unfinished *Critique of Dialectic Reason*, which theoretically reabsorbed them, as social beings, into social life. Concurrently, it turned the left-wing supporter of parliamentary democracy into an earnest prophet of social revolution who for some years now has stubbornly rejected the Western world and all its ways.

Sartre is not a simple man, nor a naive thinker. It is not easy to find a way through the immense bulk of his writing and to interpret it adequately without resorting to vast oversimplifications. The complexity of the work itself is paralleled by the bulk of commentary it has inspired. Furthermore, both he and Simone de Beauvoir have amply explained and documented their forty-year progress. In the fifties and sixties the documents fell thick and fast. There were, besides the *Memoirs*, Sartre's preface to a 1960 re-edition of *Aden Arabie*, a novel of the early thirties by his alter ego of the period, Paul Nizan; and a hundred-page meditation in 1961, at the time of the death of the philosopher Merleau-Ponty, a later alter ego, in which Sartre gave an account of their joint direction of *Les Temps modernes*, and retraced their respective intellectual development from the days of the German occupation to the mid-fifties. Finally came *The Words* (1963), the drastically reductive account of Sartre's childhood and the many interviews that punctuate that decade. In the light of these still fragmentary but fairly abundant documents, Sartre's entire work can be seen as a single vast story, a stage by stage account of his development in his attempt to lead a fully responsible life, an experiment carried out with earnest self-consciousness. In this perspective, Sartre's purpose when he wrote *The Words* is not really different from his purpose, thirty years earlier, at the time of *Nausea*.

In the sixties he was not primarily interested in his childhood, but rather in defining the cultural conditioning the family had imposed on him—at least as he now saw it—when he was a child. But this itself he undertook, he makes clear, in order to disclose, to himself and others, those assumptions which, interiorized in childhood, had preconditioned an attitude which for many years he valued as the assertion of his freedom. These assumptions exemplified the errors of a past epoch—the bourgeois-dominated nineteenth century—that, perpetuated in French culture, had blocked French comprehension of the deficiencies of that culture. The theoretic frame that underlies Sartre's account of his childhood may prove irritating to the less casual of Sartre's readers; and the sleight of hand whereby Sartre draws the child-with-a-mandate-to-become-a-great-writer out of the bourgeois hat may, on reflection, seem rather unconvincing, more so indeed than the adventure of Sartre's fictional hero, Roquentin, as recorded in *Nausea*. We easily accept that an experience can be transposed into fiction, but we balk when under the guise of childhood memories we are obliquely given a mandatory sociological interpretation along with the facts.

It is only fair to say, however, that Sartre had fully stated his presuppositions and explained his method elsewhere, at great length; and that it is the ideological frame which saves Sartre's writing from what might otherwise appear as an almost monstrous egocentrism, the ideological frame giving it a more universal cast. At the time of *Nausea*, although his readers may not immediately have been aware of it, he had not proceeded otherwise. Few of us today would overlook the methodically controlled development of the book and its philosophical intent. Roquentin's adventure is not told as an end in itself; it is ordered to a certain extent so as to illustrate a theoretical point of view concerning the nature of human existence. Yet the substance of the experience and its concrete unfolding are uniquely subjective. Sartre's language vehicles a powerful, obsessive and imaginative discourse that goes beyond its intellectual structure. The order imposed on the development of the story is intellectual. But it only obliquely controls the evocation of an overwhelming cosmic disorder, hostile to all mental constructs.

Sartre has always worked on the assumption that men can and ideally should become transparently understandable to themselves; and that if this were achieved they would control their actions, realize their potentialities and lead free and responsible lives. His reconstruction of Flaubert in *The Idiot of the Family* purports to prove that a man can be coherently and entirely understood objectively.

In the *Prime of Life*, the second volume of her *Memoirs*, Simone de Beauvoir describes the small circle of young teachers who, in the early thirties when she and Sartre first started to teach philosophy in provincial high schools, talked and argued endlessly in provincial cafés. To the puzzled question of an outsider who wondered how they could keep this up, one of them rather grandly answered that they were re-inventing man. Nietzsche, Rimbaud, the Surrealists among others, had said the same thing. Sartre's own reliance on human freedom as a given, beyond all social or physical restraints, owes a good deal to them. And already for over a century by the 1930's, Prometheus had been a favorite symbolic figure in the West. The question as to how this re-invention of man was to be brought about remained open. Sartre had his own answer. It was to be his task in his role as philosopher.

The very earliest of Sartre's writings, whether philosophy, literary criticism, or literature, aggressively challenged some of the assumptions upon which French social and cultural life rested. Sartre was still attacking these in the sixties. But with a difference. The purpose of his description of his childhood "conditioning" was to lay bare a fundamental limitation in his own outlook; to touch intellectually, one might say, the mental walls that, unknown to him, had determined his manner of thinking. To denounce the mental universe of the bourgeoisie had already been one of Sartre's intents in writing *Nausea*. But the "walls" there under attack had been the mental walls of "others."

The shift in focus from "others" to Sartre himself was indicative. Hence, the concluding pages of *The Words*: "At the age of thirty, I executed the masterstroke of writing in *Nausea*—quite sincerely, believe me—about the unjustified existence of my fellow men and of exonerating my own. I *was* Roquentin; I used him to show, without complacency, the texture of my life. At the same time, I was *I*, the elect, chronicler of Hell, a glass and steel photomicroscope peering at my own protoplasmic juices . . ."[2] Sartre here, as elsewhere, is dramatizing, easily "bewitched," to use Wittgenstein's terms, by "words," even as he deplores their hold upon him. One can hardly take the satanic image seriously and Sartre is, no doubt, laughing at himself. But the undertone of bitterness reveals his fundamental seriousness. Sartre has always been plagued by the "spirit of gravity" that Nietzsche diagnosed as the mark of the "believer"; even when he attacked it, as "l'esprit de sérieux," as a specifically bourgeois ailment. But his effort to define techniques of analysis that would allow him to establish a critique of his own mental processes, quixotic though it be, has its value independently of the techniques he uses and of his belief in the validity of a psychoanalytic case history—his own—undertaken and carried out by the subject himself.

Sartre, as he readily admits, sought over the years to write his way out of intellectual confusion. Not for himself alone. His purpose was to bring about a shift in the awareness of his contemporaries so total that it would indeed "transform" their lives. The intellectual confusion of the time has often been compared to the confusion caused in the Renaissance years by the Copernican revolution. Sartre first thought, in order to bring order into our confusion, in terms of a Cartesian provisional suspension of all a priori notions, but essentially in the realm of human psychology.

For over ten years, he tells us, through the thirties, he worked on *Being and Nothingness*, a treatise which he wanted to be as deliberately radical with regard to the past as Descartes' *Discourse on Method*. Sartre's ontology was not merely speculative. It was meant to act upon his readers' understanding of themselves and upon their way of life. Existential psychoanalysis, Sartre concluded in a surge of optimism, could be the salvation of men.[3] It is this didactic intent and sense of urgency that distinguished Sartre from the many scholars—philosophers and psychologists—upon whose work he abundantly drew and who were not, as he was, intent on "saving" humanity as well as describing it. And, on the whole, the men with a message of redemption—Nietzsche or the Surrealists for example—do not turn, as he did, to the terminology and demonstrative methods of abstract philosophers.

In the thirties, Sartre had joined the ranks of those Western philosophers who were not satisfied with the traditional images of man and his condition, whether Christian or rationalist, nor with the pragmatist approach. He wanted to recast that image in a new intellectual mold that tallied more genuinely with his own experience of life and the more recent trends in philosophy. He sought his method in Germany, outside academic France, where, despite Bergson, the Cartesian tradition still predominated and Kant was the recognized philosophical master. In the ten years he worked on *Being and Nothingness* he characteristically absorbed large doses of Husserl—under whom he worked in Germany—of Heidegger, and finally, and in the long run most important of all, Hegel—forging his own methodological and linguistic syntheses as he worked.[4]

For his part, until the war years, Sartre had considered only the autonomous individual; his work, literary and philosophical, was oriented toward the probing of the individual psyche and he synthesized his conclusions in *Being and Nothingness.* Without going over the now well-known ground of Sartrean argument and existentialist definition, I shall briefly recall those elements that most directly led Sartre in the forties to confront a question left unanswered in his treatise: the question of criteria for gauging "right" from "wrong" actions. In his treatise, Sartre assumed that all human beings share certain basic characteristics—givens that they cannot change—and an agent of indeterminacy, consciousness. He globally subsumed under a single term, *situation*, all the "givens" he did not wish to examine: biological, physical, social conditioning, and the pressures of the past. Sartre argued that the capacity consciously to transcend those givens was the characteristic human mark. The distinctively human trait, in Sartre's terms, was consciousness, the agent of human freedom apparent in all forms of human creativity. Sartrean man, in brief, could lay claims to humanity to the extent that he emerged out of his "condition," a continuous process. Inevitably, Sartre implied, modern minds would have to come to terms with that open-endedness. Men, consequently, were seen as "virtual," self-propelling creatures, answerable to themselves alone for what they made of themselves. And, accordingly, they confront full responsibility for what they become and full awareness that the process of choice and decision is never final, ending only with death. The alternative for the human being is to remain "walled in," "caged in," "imprisoned," "trapped" in those "given" images of the self proposed by others or by society. "In a sense, each situation is a mouse trap. Walls everywhere."[5] In another sense, for those people able to make a lucid use of their freedom, the situation delimits the field of their possibilities. One "invents" the way out. But most often Sartrean man is a self-deceiver, who likes to overlay his freely chosen modes of existence with a false righteousness and justification that exonerate him from responsibility for his decisions, giving him the sense that his life is patterned according to a higher purpose and transcendental dictates. Sartre's purpose was to unmask this self-deception so as to induce the move from false to authentic awareness, thus preparing the advent of fully conscious, therefore "free," human beings.

Sartre's enterprise was not in any sense the enterprise

of a rebel, as has been repeatedly assumed. His language with its built-in dualisms—essence and existence; being and nothingness—reflected the fundamental dualism underlying the mainstream of Western philosophy. He was, philosophically speaking, the legitimate heir to a respected intellectual tradition, and, in fact, from the point of view of French cultural traditions as a whole, he has been a typical and favorite son. A "normalien," young Sartre, *ipso facto*, belonged to the elitist intellectual establishment, and was well satisfied with the fact. As a beginning author he was sponsored by the most prestigious publisher, Gallimard.[6] And so it was to remain to the end. His philosophical work and moral preoccupations were well within the main current of Western thought. In no sense could he be seen as a revolutionary thinker, except by the philosophically naive or in a parochial academic setting. Nor is he a literary rebel. If, as is generally recognized, we are going through a "major mutation of society"[7] then it is probably the traditional cast of Sartre's initial thought that best accounts for its appeal. For all its stress on the future it is solidly dependent upon the past. One of its basic themes, the most dynamic in Sartre's work, is also the most traditional: the distinction between social—inauthentic—and individual —potentially creative—modes of being. Transform life, the Surrealists had said, by enlarging human awareness; change the world, Marx had written, addressing himself to philosophers.[8] Transform life by knowing yourself and thus the human condition in its totality was young Sartre's approach. But the human world he knew was narrowly circumscribed to the French intelligentsia, and his knowledge of it was largely theoretical.

To the individual he first assigned full sovereignty and power in shaping his future; and built an ontology in proof of it, putting his premises to the test of theoretical argument; he then used fiction to put his theory to the test of imagination, a curious form of solipsism already inherent in the childhood fictions of his imaginings. This was the early Sartre, determined to leave no questions unanswered. Though Sartre later denounced his early stance of intellectual detachment, it gave his work an intellectual dimension and an authoritative tone that carried conviction. Sartre, besides, was convinced. Although, by temperament, Sartre tended to treat his methodological frame as incontrovertible—and this it plainly could not be—none the less his critical technique was valuable as an instrument for looking at one's life in a new way. Sartre's immediate appeal was perhaps to minds in quest of certainties; his more enduring value, obversely, was to minds he awakened to the need for just such a critique of accepted patterns of thought as he exemplifies. He himself progressed from critique to systematic expository statement; thence to a new critique and the new systematization announced in the *Critique of Dialectical Reason.*[9] He progressed from one to the other in a slow but sustained motion; the systematizations, whether partial or—in intent at least—total, are what Sartre in the sixties called "totalizations," temporary summings up. What counts is not so much the result as the process and the discipline. Sartre in effect is, paradoxically, doctrinaire at each step on the way but fully committed only to the way. This is a rather disconcerting feature for would-be disciples and temporary opponents.

This Hegelian disposition became apparent over the years as Sartre made his mad but heroic bid to encompass within the theoretical frame he had proposed the vast sweep of knowledge and the greatly broadened experience of human life that time, events, work and fame

brought him. If as Camus once remarked, "every philosopher . . . is a creator [who has] his characters, his symbols, his secret action [and] his solution," then Sartre's
are all involved in his paradoxical struggle to contain the
open-ended reality of his initial definitions within a single
mental frame.

Being and Nothingness had provided the frame of just
such a Sartrean creation. As Sartre made new discoveries
concerning the network of forces that encompassed him,
he fitted them, retrospectively, into that frame: the "characters, symbols, action and solution" remained the same.
What they designated changed. From Sartre's ontological
patterning a guideline for political action emerged. Just
as in the interplay of "being" and "consciousness" a man's
freedom becomes manifest in his ability to transcend the
limitations of a given situation, so in political action existing circumstances must perpetually be questioned and
surpassed in order to make way for the surging forward
into freedom of ever larger masses of men. The *status
quo*, in institutions, social habits, and organization is then
a form of "being," the endangering morass into which
men sink who refuse, in Sartre's terms, to assume their full
human stature. The larger implications of this social pattern were exhilarating—they had a tremendous advantage
over the rather claustrophobic modalities of Sartre's initial
depiction of each man's unceasing solitary conflict with his
"situation," with "others," and with his perpetually alienated and alienating freedom. Outer circumstances seem
more easily open to appraisal and attack than inner walls.
That the framework he had initially built to deal with the
forces shaping an individual life was inadequate, Sartre
quickly came to realize, and he became obsessively involved in the problems of methodology this raised.

His concern with the social and political realities that

were revealed to him was profound and lasting, and his
consequent decision, as philosopher, to heed Marx and
help "change the world" became almost an obsession to
"save the world" singlehandedly. Yet not one of Sartre's
positions in matters of public interest was to prove surprising, nor in fact intellectually audacious. And they are
only very distantly connected with his treatises. They
were and continued to be the positions of the leftist-lib-
eral intellectual Sartre always had been, positions ever
more peremptorily stated and exhaustively analyzed. We
need not here be concerned with the specific positions
taken, but rather with the changes in Sartre's intellectual
attitude as they appear in the rhetoric he put to work in
order fully to explicate in all their inner and outer intricacy his routine interventions in French political life. A
particularly interesting example of this rhetoric is the
meditation he wrote in 1961 to account for his 1952 break
with Merleau-Ponty. Because of the solipsistic turn the
meditation takes, centering, as it develops, more on Sartre
than on his friend, it clearly reveals by what inner mechanisms Sartre's specific commitments are arrived at. The
case in point is Sartre's political alignment with Moscow
in the early fifties, during the Stalinist era. More than any
other, this essay discloses the complex problems at work
in the dialectic of freedom and commitment as Sartre
worked it out for himself in particular instances. And it
illustrates the process whereby Sartre replaced a personal
Promethean myth by a political one.

The essay covers a hundred pages in the somewhat
blown-up format of the Gallimard volume of *Situations*. I
shall consider one short passage only, a crucial passage:

> After ten years of rumination I had reached the breaking-
> point and needed only a fillip.[10] In the language of the

Church, this was a conversion. Merleau too had been con-
verted: in 1950. We were both conditioned, but in opposite ways. Our disgust had slowly been accumulating
and it suddenly made clear to one of us [Merleau-Ponty]
the horror of Stalinism, to the other [Sartre] the horror of
his class. In the name of the principles my class had
inculcated in me, in the name of its humanism and hu-
manities, in the name of liberty, equality and fraternity, I
dedicated to the bourgeoisie a hatred which will end only
with myself.

So wrote Sartre in 1961 as he retraced the course of a
friendship born during the Resistance years and killed,
ten years later, by postwar politics. The semi-ironical,
semi-self-justificatory outburst shows that as late as 1961,
and even in the shadow of a friend's death, Sartre's emotion still stirred at the thought of what was—for him—a
momentous event.

The occasion of the "conversion" was itself in appearance trite. In May, 1952, General Ridgway had arrived
in Paris from Korea to take command of SHAPE. The
Communist Party had called for an anti-Ridgway demonstration which was not an unmitigated success. In the
course of the demonstration, French security forces
stopped the car of Jacques Duclos, one of the Communist
Party leaders. They found two pigeons in his car, charged
him with receiving orders from Moscow by carrier pi-
geon, and arrested him. The pigeons, it was eventually
found, had been destined only for the Duclos dinner
table. Sartre himself was in Italy at the time. The violence of his anger, roused by the indubitable ineptness of
the police intervention, calls for some clarification. For if
1952 was indeed a crucial year of political commitment
for Sartre, one can hardly impute to the May demonstration and routine police action, however reprehensible,

Sartre's hatred of his "class," clearly apparent since *Nausea*, his first work. By 1952, Sartre's "bourgeois-phobia" had long been notorious. Nor can the incident explain the passing crack at the well-known "liberty, equality, fraternity" motto of French republicanism. Still less can one understand the sweeping subsequent indictment with which the paragraph ends. "An anti-communist is a dog. I shan't change my mind on that score, I never will."[11]

There is, clearly, an element of bravura in Sartre's account of his 1952 reactions, and some ambivalence with regard to Merleau-Ponty. The issue at stake was no doubt of consequence in revealing the course political events were taking and it raised problems of political judgment for the two intensely concerned left-wing intellectuals, Sartre and Merleau-Ponty. Yet Sartre centered his 1961 discussion of the incident uniquely on its parochial repercussions: the realignment along Communist lines of the policy of *Les Temps modernes*, hardly a world-shaking nor a particularly significant decision in a country where the Communist Party was both legal and articulate. The moralistic overtones and violence of Sartre's rhetoric hardly seem warranted.

The conflict, however, had broader implications. The outbreak of the Korean war, coming on top of disturbing revelations concerning Stalin's rule by terror, had led Merleau-Ponty scrupulously to reassess his position with regard to Russia and the Marxist theory of dialectical history. In a first phase, when the outcry against the Siberian camps first arose in a France still shaken by the horror of the Nazi camps, the French left was deeply divided. Capitalist propaganda, argued the orthodox communists; while others, like Camus, read into the facts the proof that Stalin's rule had become dictatorship, as fero-

cious as any, and which as such must be exposed. Merleau-Ponty had argued at the time and convinced Sartre
by his arguments, that within the context of the Cold
War, an ethical option could be made between the two
super powers. Considered within the perspective of the
Marxian dialectic, Stalinist terrorism, which Merleau-
Ponty did not deny nor condone, could be seen as a
transitory phenomenon within a society fundamentally
oriented toward the end that both men subscribed to:
social justice for all in a classless society. Whereas, in
contrast, in a capitalistic system, the use of force would of
necessity be directed, however surreptitiously, to the
maintenance of the inequities embedded in the *status
quo*.[12] Communism then had a privileged position in
view of its historical role. Consequently, on the political
front, in the either-or atmosphere of the late forties, *Les
Temps modernes*, although it voiced disapproval of the
camps, had refused to commit itself to the prevailing anti-
Russian mood, in spite of the virulent Communist attacks
which it inspired. The Korean war later convinced Merleau-Ponty of his error; whereas it reinforced Sartre's earlier conviction. Sartre's 1961 description of the respective
evolution of the two men does not attempt to come to
grips with the actual weight of evidence, nor does he
concede that a mind as acute and rigorous as Merleau-
Ponty's when confronted with new facts might have
worked out an acceptable critique of a former position. In
the mid-century years the "paths of freedom" for Sartre
pointed only in a single direction.

By 1952, then, commitment for Sartre had come to signify one thing, mandatory alignment in political issues on
the side of Communist Russia, with a proviso: the right,
from that position, to criticize Communist actions. How,
starting from his initial definition of human reality as, in

essence, freedom, had he within a short half-dozen years, reached so trenchant a position? The question is of some consequence and has often been discussed. Swung by the momentum of his 1952 "conversion," he often in the next few years struck a defiant pose, making obviously irresponsible statements. Once, in a 1954 interview (*Libération*, July 15) concerning his impressions of his first visit to Russia, he flatly stated that in the USSR writers were unconditionally free to speak as they saw fit. "The freedom of criticism is total in the USSR," he declared. Earlier, he had similarly argued that the incarceration of thousands of innocent people in Soviet camps, deplorable as it was, was less reprehensible than a single lynching in the United States; and he found it later possible to approve, with a doubly irresponsible complacency, Frantz Fanon's contention that, for a black, every white man he killed was double profit: the act brought a black man to the awareness of his manhood and rid the earth of another racist. Sartre's moral outrage at injustice sometimes rather easily finds assuagement in irresponsible rhetoric.

Despite a reputation to the contrary, Sartre has been generous with interviews and the interview is the medium that most clearly reveals the spontaneous Sartre, ready like the rest of us on occasion to fly in the face of common sense and overlook undesirable evidence in the defense of his positions. He has admitted that he is a highly impulsive person who may subsequently correct, contradict, or forget what he wrote or said on the spur of the moment. When he retrospectively accounts for the ideological disagreements and consequent breaks with friends like Merleau-Ponty, he is not averse to shifting the ground from actual facts to massively deployed socio-psychological explications that give the incident an awesome aura of importance and inevitability.

The breaks were many in the fifties. "It was nobody's fault," he concluded, looking back, at the time of Merleau-Ponty's death, upon other broken friendships. "It was they, it was I:[13] circumstances had shaped us and drawn us together; circumstances separated us. That is how people live in our times; that is how they love, badly." This rhetoric leaves one with a sense of uneasiness: the jump from the individual to the general, the shift of responsibility from the personal to vaguely objective factors; the speciously aggrieved bitterness of tone. Twenty years before, any such recourse to "circumstances" to explain one's reactions would have drawn Sartre's ire. Such entities as the law of God, human reason, fate, custom, nature, Freudian complexes, and circumstance were then all ruled out, clearly examples of "bad faith." Sartre, in the Merleau-Ponty article, seems to be making a strangely personal use of the dialectic. But what is most surprising is the target of his anger: "my class." Even in Marxian perspective, the alleged motivation for Sartre's option seems curiously abstract and more than a little vague.

In 1961, Merleau-Ponty's death, though it moved Sartre deeply, had in fact served Sartre as a pretext for a foray into his own psyche, an opportunity to pursue the reassessment of his thought and life that he had undertaken in the mid-fifties. The 1952 "conversion" of which he speaks was, he tells us, the final stage in an inner dissatisfaction, a "disgust" that had been accumulating for the past ten years. He refers us back, thereby, to the early forties, to the time when he was finishing *Being and Nothingness*. Under German rule, in the expectation of a new future for France, he was elaborating with Merleau-Ponty his vision of what their part was to be in shaping that future, in part through the review they were jointly to direct. One cannot take too literally Sartre's approximate and sometimes contradictory statements on the chronological development of his thought. The publication of his notebooks may eventually clarify how it actually evolved and the recent bio-bibliography of his work has been of great assistance in this realm.[14] But Sartre's statements do throw some light on his evolution and on the shift in connotation certain fixed terms in his vocabulary acquired in the process. Freedom and commitment are two such terms and their impact is considerably altered by the insertion into Sartre's vocabulary of other terms previously absent. Not the least of these is the word "circumstance," reiterated and quasi-personified. In the essay on Merleau-Ponty for instance, "circumstances" can "shape," "draw together," and "separate" two close friends. The tense hairsplitting on theoretic points which Sartre's essay evokes, involving a small, tight group of intellectuals, recalls the Russian revolutionaries, although the "conversion" pattern seems more specifically Sartrean. However impulsive Sartre's reaction to the Duclos incident may appear, behind it indeed lay a troubled intellectual evolution of which Sartre's political polemics are only the most apparent facet.[15]

The "conversion" pattern, so inimical to rational decision, appears from time to time in Sartre's own life and quite characteristically in the life of his characters. *Nausea*, for instance, is purportedly the journal of a young historian, Roquentin, who, when his story begins, has seemingly been working contentedly for some time on a research project in a French provincial town. The journal is the account of a crisis, a "conversion" that completely changes the pattern of his life. "I must recognize," writes Roquentin in one of the first entries in his journal, "that I am prone to sudden transformations . . . a mass of small metamorphoses of which I'm unaware accumulate inside me, and then, one day, a real revolution occurs; that's what has given my life its spasmodic incoherent aspect." He describes one such "revolution," in the past. In Indochina a friend of his, Mercier, had suggested that he join him in an archeological mission: "Suddenly I woke up from a six-year slumber . . . I felt terribly, deeply bored. I couldn't understand why I was in Indo-China. What was I doing there? . . . I pulled myself together, convulsed with anger and answered curtly: 'Thank you, but I believe I've done enough traveling: I've got to get back to France.' Two days later, I took the boat back to Marseille." Roquentin, to be sure, is not Sartre. But, like many of Sartre's characters, he shares the conversion pattern that Sartre so vividly describes in his account of his own 1952 crisis: a slow inner revolt accumulating under the pressure of outer circumstances, erupting in a sudden break with routine. Sartre's characters often describe their lives in terms of periods of somnolence, broken by these brusque, Nietzsche-like[16] awakenings which end in flight. The link is close that binds Sartre to his characters, even the most apparently alien, though not necessarily to their actions; but no single one of them is closer to him than was Roquentin: "I *was* Roquentin," as Sartre says in *Words.* And it is rather interesting to note that "revolution" is Roquentin's word, like Sartre's, to designate a sudden though subterraneously prepared shift in point of view and brusque disengagement. This metaphor is one of several that over the years allowed Sartre to bridge the gap between the private and public realms, as well as between the microcosm of his subjective situation and the macrocosm of his ideological designing.

A focal experience, it would seem, for Sartre, this inner

process of "slumber" and abrupt awakening, entailing a sharp break with the past, had its counterpart in the dynamics of the "human situation" as Sartre described it, impersonally, in *Being and Nothingness*. Throughout the thirties, under the influence of Husserl, and before Hegel in turn became a dominant influence in his thinking, Sartre, like a number of his colleagues, was examining from the phenomenological point of view such fragmentary and standard problems as theories of perception, imagination, and emotion. The connection is close, in those years, between his fictional works—*Nausea* and the short stories of *Le Mur*[17]—and his scholarly papers. When Camus, then an unknown young man in Algiers, detected in Sartre's early fiction, which he admired, a morbid attraction for ruins, he was only partly right. Sartre's stories are, in fact, carefully constructed and have a positive intellectual intent. It is the imaginative orchestration of Sartre's themes, not Sartre's themes themselves that suggest a mood of despair. From the outset a recurrent Sartrean imagery introduces into his work a dramatic—even melodramatic—tone which cannot be accounted for in terms of the underlying theoretical patterning. It is, in fact, antithetical to it. Even in his ontology, where Sartre uses it more sparingly, this imagery introduces an emotional note with ominous implications. The abstract "being-in-itself" (all that is not freedom and hence a verbal symbol for all that is included in a man's "situation") is endowed by Sartre with a powerful though surreptitious antihuman malevolence: viscous, petrifying, encircling—a morass, a trap. Consciousness, though abstractedly defined as a "lack," is equated with light, transparency, flow. Barred from Sartre's universe of philosophical discourse, good and evil creep into it in the guise of images. Thence, perhaps, its particularly unsettling appeal.

When Sartre used the word "revolution" to describe what was in fact a change in a man's inner relation to his world, the word carried no political overtones. But it was accompanied by images of destruction, terror, and flight from the ensuing chaos. Sartre had based his discussion of human freedom on the basic premise that man is unique in the universe through the power of his consciousness, an intellectual power. But he senses it imaginatively as perpetually threatened in a deliberately hostile world. The threat of engulfment is consistently at work in Sartre's imagery. A gigantic and malevolent power manipulates the reality Sartre contends with. He personifies it in the malicious *on*—they, people—to whom Sartre attributes so many misdeeds in his polemical writing, a power that lies, betrays, constrains, sets traps for the unwary. It can, like Proteus, take many shapes, all inimical. History, the French Communist Party on occasion, or Sartre's grandfather, loom over him, alienating figures out of whose power he must wrench himself and all humanity. Perhaps the most arresting of these incarnations are the "masked men" of the future, those judges from the centuries to come, whom Sartre imagines passing judgment on our twentieth-century crimes. The exciting world of his childhood fantasies then structures his apparently objective political analyses.

The dramatic, myth-making character of Sartre's language is revealing. "Creeping up" on him "from behind," the war "stole [his] future"; the bourgeoisie "sequestered" him, as a helpless child, behind its mental grills. And it was his fate, as a white petit-bourgeois French writer in the mid-twentieth century to be placed "on the wrong side of history," that is, within the establishment, a situation which in his eyes could only be negative. Sartre has long held, it would seem, a latent image of himself as victimized. In his day by day polemics he equates the coercive collective forces that he denounces—his class, colonialism, capitalism, racism, anti-Semitism—with the dangerous and threatening "being-in-itself" of his ontology. And, conversely, their "opposites"—the proletariat, the socialist states, the black militant, the student dissidents, are all successively seen as emanations of the liberating "being-for-itself." They are in his eyes the temporary incarnations of the creative and moral component of "human reality." This polarization and mythical reduction of complex political situations are essentially emotional and irrational in their workings and explain Sartre's "conversions" and his rhetorical excesses.

Sartre's fundamental political stance, generous though it be, is thus emotionally conditioned, yet abstract. "I don't communicate emotionally," he once remarked, "I communicate with people who think, who reflect . . ."[18] in other words with intellectuals like himself. He is emotionally and imaginatively involved with abstractions. They take on for him concrete, autonomous, personified shapes and enter into conflict with one another. They are Hugo-like figures, whose gigantic duels are always about to seal the fate of the human race. And from period to period each hero turns into villain. Hence, for many years, the excitement any Sartrean intervention in a debate was likely to generate. Hence too, when under the impact of the French defeat he felt called upon to move out of his "bourgeois" life, his obsession with what he and Simone de Beauvoir like to call, in Marxian terms, a praxis, a science of action that would allow them to bridge with some security the gap between their mental world and the real world outside themselves. "Commitment," as Sartre understood it, required of the writer that he be in possession of what amounts to an ethic. Here he and

Camus could meet on a common ground. But if *Being and Nothingness* started from a "lived certainty" the certainty was intellectual and had been lived within a traditional mold. The need for a praxis arose from a "lived certainty" of another kind, deeply engaging Sartre's emotions. It was bound to a national disaster and resurgence. In a sense the 1944 "Paris insurrection" remained for Sartre the archetype of what he calls "une fête," a spontaneous fusion of individual freedoms into a collective and definitive assertion of collective freedom requiring no compromise or long-term discipline. He was always to seek some re-enactment of it: in the political demonstrations in which he participated, and more particularly in the 1968 student manifestations where he felt most happily at home. So much so that he misread their implications.

> Sartre's philosophical position . . . is founded on no postulate. It is based on the lived certainty that man is that privileged being who is the author of his modes of behavior and actions; that being the author he *understands* them perfectly; that they are "explicable" by nothing except the ends they are directed toward, freely, starting from a given situation. . . . Consciousness (being-for-itself) is of necessity responsible for all its attitudes and modes of being. If it were not so, if man was governed from outside or from behind by some extraneous will or by some determinism, an ethic would be impossible.[19]

"In 1944 he [Sartre] thought that every situation could be transcended through a subjective movement. In 1951, he knew that circumstances steal our transcendence, that there is no possible individual salvation, only a collective struggle."[20] Later still, Sartre was to say that there was no "salvation," no possible redeeming ethic, at least not until "circumstances" brought a radical change in society. And he saw change only in the guise of a nine-teenth-century type of revolution. This was a paralyzing situation. Thence the successive disillusions and the final stasis. For a stasis it has been, the bursts of energy notwithstanding.

It was the earlier Sartre then who had written what a critic has described as "the jubilant and apocalyptic passage that ends *Being and Nothingness*": "Existential psychoanalysis is going to reveal to man the real goal of his search; existential psychoanalysis is going to acquaint man with his passion. In truth there are many people who have not waited to learn its principles in order to make use of them as a means of deliverance and salvation." This was the Sartre who, Merleau-Ponty tells us, felt at that time that he "could understand the human condition in its totality" and was sure he could lay the basis for an "absolutely positive ethics and politics." But it was the later Sartre who—praxis notwithstanding—bitterly chalked up his political defeat at the hands of "inhuman powers that steal our acts and our thoughts"; and finally resigned himself to "do their bidding." Freedom, Sartre now seemed ready to conclude, was limited to the first gesture whereby one engages oneself "in the mesh of action." After that a man, he suggests, plays out a preordained part.

That Sartre is a man of strong convictions, capable of brusque and sharp emotional responses, violent opinions, and brashly intemperate judgments, his own account of his "leap" in 1952 makes clear; and also that he has an immense capacity for uncritical self-dramatization in spite of his belief that he is particularly endowed for self-criticism. He views himself alternately or concurrently with the self-pity of the bourgeois, self-defined, excluded by fate from the "public garden" of the freer proletarian

life. Or with bitter self-satisfaction he sees himself mirrored in a satanic image: "I'm twice a *traitor*, a *traitor* in
the conflict of generations and a *traitor* in the class war";
"We were recruited [by History] according to our apti-
tudes, Merleau [Ponty] when it was the hour of nuances;
myself when the time required *assassins*." Traitor, assassin, bastard, Satan, monster. One could list many such
examples of Sartre's mythical projections of his role that
have little in common with the realities of his quiet, hard-
working, respectable, and respected existence. These
projections all partake of a double life within a double
linguistic network. And the excitement Sartre's rhetoric
generates, the sense of urgency he creates, come from the
interaction of one with the other. "Traitor" can be fully
explicated in a simple Marxian context: in the "class war,"
I who belong to the bourgeoisie side with the proletariat.
It is a metaphor itself drawn from the initial Marxian use
of the "war" metaphor and it dramatizes a not unusual
situation. Or again it could be translated as follows: "Although I am over sixty, I side with the young, and I join
in the students' indictment of their elders, myself being
one of these elders." "Assassin," coupled with the image
of a personal "election" by a force as vast as "History,"
transforms the secure humdrum existence of the *grand
intellectuel* into a melodrama of awesome proportions;
sometimes with unexpected, comic effect.[21] But the
dramatization, the emotional excitement and scandal
generated by Sartre's language have brought to life for
his contemporaries issues of moment that otherwise
might have remained undefined.

In her *Memoirs*, Simone de Beauvoir describes Sartre's
propensity to build a myth into their lives, starting from
his own fierce convictions, those "lived convictions" upon
which, as André Gorz states, his ontology also rests. "Sar-

tre built his theories from certain positions to which we held stubbornly." Combining the theoretical with the visionary, he was thus the demiurge of a world which, for him, for a time, superseded any other.[22] This propensity plunged him into the contradictions and confusions his doctrine of commitment entailed. But it is because Sartre was willing to put himself personally on the line, to discard the myth of the philosopher's detachment and rational "rightness," that the immensely garrulous, slow-motion process to which his works—thrown like huge, hastily erected and heterogeneous signposts along his path —bear witness, reveals something beyond itself and beyond the changes in meaning the word "commitment" acquired.

Sartre's unabashed use of rhetoric to establish certainty in the absence of facts coerces us into following his "search for a method" from outside and so to participate in his struggle to integrate into a single pattern of meaning the flow of events crowding in on him from all sides. Or, we might say, more imaginatively, he draws us into a participation in the Promethean rebellions of an exceptional mind confronting our twentieth-century realities and gives us a sense that we too live its rebellions, its victories and ultimate defeats. Hence his appeal for a number of intellectuals. This, of course, is only possible if we take Sartre on his terms, seriously, and share his belief that human beings can, within limits, create and control the future. Sartre is nothing if not serious about a man's responsibility for the manner in which he lives his life; he himself wanted to live responsibly and in the service of other men. From the first he meant as a writer to work in the service of freedom. But the sense of the word "freedom" changed for him over the years and the path was long that led from the metaphysical freedom of the "being-for-itself," through the definition of freedom as commitment, to the blunt "freedom consists in having enough to eat and a pair of shoes." This sounds singularly like Camus's basic position, although Camus would reject its exclusivity: enough to eat and the possibility to "live, think and be a man." Shoes, in certain climates, are perhaps secondary.

In the thirties, in articles of literary criticism, Sartre had implied that the writer was responsible to the reader for the vision of the world he communicated, whether indirectly or directly; the aesthetic commitment of writer and reader called for a judgment metaphysical in kind; metaphysical failings had moral connotations as well as aesthetic ones, leading to the judgment one passed upon the writer. The reader's commitment entailed moral judgment. *Being and Nothingness* broadened the writer's case to include all human persons. To exist is to be "committed" and entails judgment. The gauge in both cases was the degree of compatibility of the writer's vision with Sartre's model of "reality," and rested on Sartre's use of the word "freedom." Sartre's vision then was the gauge of right and wrong. His confidence in his own intellect seems overwhelming.

As the world changed for Sartre, so Sartre's understanding of his own responsibility changed; and so the question of his actions came up for scrutiny again and again. Sartre really welcomes the idea of being scrutinized and exposed. When asked whether he did not apprehend that someone might analyze him as he was analyzing Flaubert, he answered, "To the contrary. I should welcome it. Like all writers I conceal myself. But I am also a public figure, and people can think of me as they wish, even if they are harsh. Not all writers are as serene on that score"; and to the follow-up question, "Have you no apprehension as to the judgment of posterity?" he answered: "None. Not that I'm sure it will be favorable; but I hope it will take place."[23] Sartre, unlike Camus, has always been fascinated and horrified by himself.

Self-justificatory, yes, and self-exhibiting. But only if one lays aside the basic assumption—the bravely taken position that every human life in all its details has human significance in terms of the history of all men. We are, said Sartre in an interview in the sixties, "shipwrecked animals" (des animaux sinistrés); perhaps at that moment and temporarily the "sense of the absurd" had caught up with him. His faith in the power of the mind to extricate men from the morass of being that they might achieve freedom may have wavered. Nonetheless he had in fact put up a long drawn-out, rear-guard battle in thought and action against this postulation of man's futility. In this sense he was indeed playing all or nothing for high stakes. One needs to follow Sartre's erratic course through some of the many labyrinthine intricacies in which he became engaged during those years in order to grasp more clearly the mechanisms whereby he attempted to reduce the initial paradox that would make of an "option" a mandatory commitment, and of the exercise of freedom the manifestation of a preordained fate.

Notes to Chapter 4

1. Madeleine Chapsal, Les écrivains en personne, "Jean-Paul Sartre," (Julliard, 1960), pp. 203–33.
2. The Words (New York: Fawcett Books), p. 157.
3. Being and Nothingness, translated by Hazel Barnes (New York: Philosophical Library, 1956), p. 626.

4. Sartre read Hegel, he says, in depth only after Hegel was published in the scholarly annotated translation of Hippolyte, a Hegelian specialist. Sartre's critics, in the various fields of philosophy, psychology, and sociological sciences he has attempted to encompass, have examined the sources of both his method and language, the traditional and original uses Sartre puts them to, and have defined the positive and negative aspects of his syntheses. That Sartre's originality lies in his power of synthesis is generally recognized. But there is a weakness and some pedantry in the rapidity with which he assimilates new—to him—vocabularies: dragging in Chomsky's terminology for instance, quite gratuitously, in the preface to a novel—A. Piug's *l'Inachevé*—because, one feels, he has just heard of him.

5. A trap of course does not necessarily have walls. It is not my intention to pick quarrels with Sartre's eloquent images. It is clear that for Sartre to be "shut in" and immobilized is disaster. The room is a constant motif in his work, and immobilization or "petrification," a basic image. For a thorough analysis of the motif of sequestration in Sartre's work see Marie Denise Boros, *Un sequestré: l'homme Sartrien* (Paris: Nizet, 1968).

6. Sartre is, in a sense, an establishment figure if ever there was one. Wherever he travels, he travels as the most representative of France's intellectuals, an "official" figure, though not officially sponsored, whom no government is likely to hound, least of all his own, which Sartre has always, ritually, opposed. Yet Sartre's style of life is not traditional for the successful writer he is. It is still patterned on student modes and stubbornly recalcitrant to any form of government patronage.

7. Raymond Aron, *Marxism and the Existentialists* (New York: Harper and Row, 1969), p. 146.

8. "The philosophers have merely interpreted the world differently, but what matters is to change it." *Theses Against Feuerbach XI.*

9. This is a traditional procedure in philosophy typically il-

lustrated in Sartre's early work on the theory of emotions and of the imagination, the critique of existing theories preceding Sartre's own accounting of these phenomena.

10. Benita Eisler in *Situations* (New York: Braziller, 1965), gives a more idiomatic translation: "and only needed that one straw" (p. 269). I prefer the literal translation, simply because Sartre uses it several times when reviewing decisive moments of option: the "chiquenaude" or fillip is his image for whatever circumstance precipitated the "leap" or "choice." "Sauter le pas" (to jump the jump) is the rather trivial expression he also uses to describe the passage from one intellectual position to another, a "conversion."

11. Here too, I prefer the literal translation to the more vivid and equally appropriate "rat" of the Eisler translation (p. 287) with its recall, for us, of the Joe McCarthy years, that coincided with the Korean war, and of which Sartre was aware. "America has come down with rabies," he wrote a year later (*Libération*, June, 1953). The "mad dog" image, if not flattering, is consistent with the one above. Sartre also applied it with fine impartiality to France, comparing France's actions, during the Algerian war, to those of a dog with a saucepan tied to its tail.

12. The position was set forth by Merleau-Ponty in *Humanisme et Terreur* (Paris: Gallimard, 1947) and combated in *Les Aventures de la dialectique* (Paris: Gallimard, 1955).

13. This is a typically Sartrean use of a quote, Montaigne's "It was he, it was I"; through the context Sartre reverses the sense of Montaigne's words. Montaigne was speaking of his unbroken friendship for La Boétie. Sartre is here retreating from personal responsibility in these broken friendships by invoking the "force of circumstance," the conditioning that in a reprehensible social setting makes conflicts in human relationships unavoidable.

14. Contat and Rybalka, *Les Écrits de Sartre* (Paris: Gallimard, 1970).

15. For a sympathetic though simplistic account of Sartre's successive political positions as reflected in the editorials of *Les Temps modernes* see Michel Burnier's *Choice of Action* (New York: Random House, 1968). The book suffers from the lack of the broad perspectives in Raymond Aron's short chapter on Sartre in his *Marxism and the Existentialists* (New York: Harper and Row, 1964). Useful in assessing Sartre's position in the early sixties are the little-known essay "Ideology and Revolution" included in the rather poor translation of the articles Sartre wrote for *France-Soir* (June 28–July 15, 1960) during his 1960 visit to Cuba in *Sartre and Cuba* (New York: Ballantine Books, n.d.), and Sartre's preface to Frantz Fanon's *The Wretched of the Earth* (New York: Grove Press, 1966), first published in Paris in 1961.

16. See also Sartre's first stage hero, Orestes (*The Flies*), and his abrupt decision to kill Egisthes and Clytemnestra; and the upsurge of revolt that in *The Roads to Freedom* drives Mathieu, one of the main protagonists, to sudden violent action after a period of confused indecision. In the chaos of the 1940 defeat, Mathieu, seemingly on the spur of the moment, joins a group of combatants making a last desperate stand.

17. Entitled *Intimacy* in the translation. "Le Mur" ("The Wall") is the title of the first story in the French edition. "Intimacy" the title of the fourth.

18. In an interview with Madeleine Goberl. *Vogue*, July, 1964.

19. André Gorz, "Jean-Paul Sartre: De la Conscience à la Praxis," *Livres de France*, January, 1966. It should be noted here again that the French "conscience" designates either "consciousness" or "conscience" in the moral sense. For Sartre it has both meanings. It is for him, as Gorz clearly states, the agent whereby man creates himself as a moral being.

20. Simone de Beauvoir, *La Force des choses* (Paris: Gallimard, 1963), p. 280.

21. For instance, when Sartre abandoned his single attempt at

political action via participation in a political campaign in 1947. The platform proposed was a program of social reform presented by a union of the non-Communist left, the "Rassemblement Démocratique Révolutionnaire," (RDR). Fearing it would turn into an anti-Communist front, Sartre withdrew. As he puts it, "We assassinated the RDR, and, reassured, I left for Brazil."

22. In his account of his dispute with Merleau-Ponty, Sartre makes a disarming statement that shows how completely he can be immersed in abstract constructs. "At that time I was studying the dialectic and the word 'nature' for me referred to the ensemble of our knowledge in physico-chemistry." It did not then occur to him that Merleau-Ponty was referring to the more immediate "world" where "one meets things and others, our body and others."

23. "Un entretien avec Jean-Paul Sartre," *Le Monde*, May 14, 1971, p. 21 (with Michel Contat and Michel Rybalka).

5.

Point of Departure: Political Actions and "The Field of the Possible"

Individuals always did and always do take themselves as points of departure.

KARL MARX

Freedom in thought has only pure thought as its truth which is without fulfillment of life and therefore only the concept of freedom, not living freedom itself.

HEGEL

In December, 1938, following an unsuccessful strike in France, Camus wrote a "Dialogue Between a Prime Minister and an Employee at 1200 Francs a Month." It was a bitterly caustic little piece which he addressed to Edouard Daladier, prime minister of France at the time, a man more preoccupied with the Nazi menace to France at that juncture than with the economic difficulties of the working class. "I merely want to point out," Camus wrote, "that politicians do not imagine how hard it is to be a man, just a man, and without oneself being unjust, to live a life shot through with inequities on 1200 francs a month, with a wife, a child and the certainty that one will die without being mentioned in any history book" (*Essais*, pp. 1317–1318). Camus, who was twenty-five years old at the time, was alive to the Nazi threat, but he was also alert to the malaise of the working class whom, in the interest of national defense, the government was asking to sacrifice the long overdue and hard-won reforms instituted by France's first Socialist government in 1936. He did not think the government should forget that critical social issues subsisted: abuses of power, economic exploitation, poverty, and such things as the endemic famine among the Kabyles upon which he was soon, as a journalist, to report. What the French worker was asking for, he claimed, was the freedom to "think, live and be a man," a freedom denied him if all he could look forward to was the same grim future.

Ten years later, at a time when postwar inflation had sent the franc spiraling downward, Camus reiterated the same point: "15,000 francs a month, life in a factory, and Tristan will have nothing more to say to Isolde. Love too is a luxury and that is the condemnation" of the economic system responsible for the lot of most workers (*Essais*, p. 1115).

Even during the short period of his activity within the Communist Party, Camus was not primarily concerned with ideology. He was concerned with the actual difficulties under which men labored and endeavored to subsist. His political or social interventions were concrete, directed at specific ills and specific cases. It would be tedious to enumerate them; they have been carefully recorded in the abundant notes, commentaries, and appendices to the critical edition of Camus's essays.[1] In the early years of his apprenticeship as a journalist writing for *Alger-Républicain*, when reporting on such cases Camus always applied the same method. He marshaled facts, presented as dispassionate an appraisal as he could, and suggested a relevant and practical course of action. Whether he was seeking redress for an individual unjustly condemned by law, retribution for workers arbitrarily dismissed from their jobs, or exposing the glaring inadequacies of colonial policy in Kabylia, he shied away from wholesale denunciations, ideal remedies, theory, and rhetoric. What urgently mattered to him was to reach those responsible and move them to act. He appealed to their sense of equity and to current moral principles, using as unweighted and plain a vocabulary as possible, presenting the issue in terms familiar to the man in the street. He did not make a literary use of the case. He never would.

As one leafs through Camus's articles and notebooks one becomes aware of his instinctive dislike for the political or ideological rhetoric that trades on the plight of human beings—whether for political, ideological, or religious ends, or to illustrate a man's high-mindedness. The Sartrean doctrine of personal salvation through social commitment was unlikely to hold much appeal for him. He was on his guard, like many workers, against professional politicians and the theorizing of middle-class intellectuals whom he once described as "abstract and logic-chopping gentlemen." In his articles he wasted no time on argument about the origin of the situation, on considerations concerning his own relation to the principles involved. His approach was direct, his style and arguments were realistic with a streak of tough ironic humor; a superb example of this is the series of articles on the Kabyles.[2] His formulation of the right of the worker—"to think, to live and be a man"—might make political men smile, but the naïveté was deliberate and not without its ironies. It undercut the pious abstractions of the politi-

cians and threw into the balance those imponderables—
love, friendship, access to sun, sea, and sky—that most
political theoreticians consider as superfluous. Camus is
more often cryptic than simplistic.

When he addressed the letter to Daladier, Camus was
already at odds with the Communist Party;[3] and with his
reportage on the endemic famine among the Kabyles he
was soon to draw the ire of the colonial administration
already alerted by his activities in the social and political
sphere. He was young but not a novice, nor was he simply
a dynamic and idealistic young man; and he did not hesi-
tate to challenge accepted attitudes and stereotyped
arguments.

The young Camus had an acute sense of social in-
equity. It sprang from a personal reaction to his upbringing. Certainly the young revolutionary who joined the
Communist Party was a militant, bursting with energy,
who wanted to "change the world." Action did not really
pose problems for him. As a young man he seems to have
enjoyed measuring swords with the authorities. Nor did
he question the ends to be attained. He was and remained
a socialist who favored syndicalism and who, until well
into the postwar years when he reformulated his position
in *The Rebel* and indirectly in *The Plague*, seems to have
accepted the axiom that the economic and social changes
for which he worked would come through a political revolution which, he hoped, would not be of the Stalinist
brand.

After his break with the Communist Party he did not
again work from within a political machine. Nor did he
give the bulk of his time to political activities. When he
was deeply stirred by a political issue, as in the case of
the Algerian war, he spoke and wrote and intervened. But
he spoke as Albert Camus, not as the representative of a

group or an ideological trend. Journalism, in which he engaged more and more sporadically, was only one of the channels he used; and he seems to have entertained real doubts as to its efficaciousness. He could be relied on to write articles protesting against major political scandals, or supporting causes sometimes as quixotic as Gary Davis's solitary and now forgotten 1948 crusade for world citizenship. But he was not a propagandist, nor a crusader, and he propounded no theory or system to which he sought to convert the world. In fact, he preferred face to face confrontation and discussion; of these there are few traces.

He was, in a personal way, a man who did not lose sight of his political responsibilities, but a man who fought tenaciously against the tendency of the leftist intellectuals to become engulfed in them. If "commitment" means, as it seems to in certain circles, the willingness to adopt a doctrine once and for all, single-mindedly, sacrificing all other interests to the cause, and acting in conformity with it in all circumstances uncompromisingly, then Camus was not a "committed" writer. He was unable to accept the disjunction between political and personal morality and discipline. His political actions were uncompromisingly anchored to his moral principles in spite of his working-class cynicism concerning the working of political institutions under whatever regime. His literary work in its entirety is an elucidation, reasoned out in essays or imaginatively projected in fiction and drama, of what he had experienced, what he was seeking. It is the expression of what the American poet Hortense Flexner described as an "unseen and personal" universe which he could not elude, often found difficult to elucidate, and which shaped his options.

Camus's earliest writing—the sketches in *L'Envers et*

l'Endroit (*The Right Side and the Wrong Side*)—discloses the degree of his sensitivity to the hardship, nar-
rowness, and insignificance of the lives to which the
working class was condemned. He himself had by chance
and will escaped them. His concern for the deprivation
suffered by people from whom he never cut himself off
was not merely economic. It touched upon the quality of
their lives and their possibilities. When he broke with the
Communist Party, it was because he had found its Mos-
cow-directed policy disheartening. And indeed, in the
thirties, from the point of view of the young militant who
had been charged with the politicization of the destitute
Kabyles, it could hardly have been more equivocal. The
fate of the Kabyles did not weigh much in the game of
power politics being played presumably to ensure the vic-
torious march of humanity toward the classless society.
In the meantime, they had to live.

Camus may not then have questioned the plausibility
of the belief in the advent of the free, classless, and just
democracy of which Russia was the harbinger, a belief
which automatically justified tactics that did not seem
consonant with it. But he was not ready to take it on
trust. When Camus spoke of the worker's right to "think,
live and be a man" the wording was deliberate. He was
not speaking of the "mission" of the proletariat, nor of the
needs of what we now call "the disadvantaged." He was
speaking of individual men and of aspirations not defined
in terms of a "class." That the social stratum in which
they happened to be born should exclude men from certain essential joys was the major injustice he saw; and
among these essentials he ranked access to the life of the
mind, which would give them a chance to become, in a
certain degree, "free" men. Collective abstractions had
their utility, but in Camus's eyes, they easily acquired an

aura of condescension and unreality, downgrading, however imperceptibly, living human beings, their passions, problems, and egos, locking them into a mold, turning them into passive entities to be bartered, used, and otherwise manipulated. In the process, the individual dropped out of sight and resumed his ignored life.

"To be a man" meant many things in the working-class milieu of Belcourt. At bottom, the words referred to the plain facts of life which Camus had learned to confront as a child: one was born, one worked and died. Against this reduction of human life young Camus rebelled. His political militancy was one of the forms of his revolt. Yet in the preface to *L'Envers et l'Endroit* he noted that for him poverty was a privileged experience; not in itself, but because it allows for no evasions and "judges what a man is." Unshielded, anonymous, poor people, however crudely, know their vulnerability, and counter with a certain stoical way of meeting life which Camus prized and which he sometimes referred to as constituting their "dignity." Illness, fatigue, death are seldom a matter of choice and they are not the prerogative of a class. But prosperity acts as a buffer, offering many avenues of escape. In contrast, "death and poverty together form so desperate a combination that, it would seem, no one could speak of them unless he were a Keats who, it was said, was so sensitive that he could have touched suffering with his hands" (*Essais*, p. 1112). The respect is unconditional. The poor live in a form of truth. They are a form of truth. To "be a man" in a broader sense is to confront that truth; and its denial is a form of injury.

One of the writers Camus most admired in the thirties was André Malraux, then reaching his zenith as a spokesman for the left against the rising fascism and as a "new" novelist who appealed directly to the sensitivity of a new generation. In his novel, *Man's Fate*, a young militant, Kyo, tries to define the reasons for his revolutionary action. He speaks of men's need for dignity and of his own revolt against the forces that work toward their humiliation. Camus's revolt was of the same kind. At its core was a revulsion against attitudes, words, actions which implicitly or explicitly humiliate men, attacking them in their self-respect. It is easy to surmise the kind of humiliation that had plagued him in childhood.

He detected the latent contempt of the privileged for the uneducated in the functional political lie, in the fraudulent evasions and fake solutions of bureaucracies, behind the false alternatives of theoretical expediency, and in the pious moralism of officialdom. There is no instance in all his writing of an efficient public administration: the court in *The Stranger* is grotesque; in *The Plague* the city services are impotent; in *State of Siege*, the establishment is cynical, cowardly, and corrupt. "Which of the two do you prefer, man," a voice queries in a dialogue in the early notebooks, "he who works to deprive you of bread in the name of freedom, or he who wants to take away your freedom to assure your bread? Answer: on whom to spit first?"

It was probably Camus's ingrained antipathy to manipulating human beings that prompted his early withdrawal from political action within a political machine. He had a natural flair for leadership and for teamwork, a personal charm and authority that endeared him to other people. The "team" with whom he worked in his amateur theater in the thirties in Algiers, those at least who are still alive, recall those days with unusual pleasure. And he established lasting ties in those years with many different people, not least among them Muslim friends, some of whom were to be among the future leaders of the Algerian independence movement.[4] His activities were various and successful, deployed simultaneously on several fronts.

He was director of a cultural center; organized Muslim-European student work groups; initiated and actively directed a worker-student "Workers' Theater"; and undertook the politicization of the destitute Kabyles. But he was not drawn to the practice of power. He left the Party, but not the social arena. He took with him the social consciousness that had brought him into the Communist ranks and the willingness—if circumstances made it inevitable—to "put his body on the line." But the decision would be his. If the decision led to inner wrestlings and outer conflict, he fought it out with a kind of fierce stoicism. The accounting he kept to himself. Even before the war it was clear that the public commitments of Camus would be personal affairs. He would keep to himself the inner tensions they generated.

He spoke of himself as a "man of passion," and there was certainly in his instinctive way of life a streak of the Spanish "point of honor," of the independence subsumed in the Spanish "hombre," which echoes in the Algerian worker's "to be a man." The answer he gave when asked why he joined the Resistance is genuine: he couldn't imagine himself on the side of the concentration camps. This is an instinctive reaction. He found nothing exceptional or heroic about it. Camus's aversion to the heroic stance was real. He would have understood the contention of the generation of 1960 that what matters is that "you do your thing," ride out the consequences; and let other men do theirs. But within limits. What the limits were he spent his life trying to define, for himself as well as for others. Struggle was built in to life; it would never end. It was a fact, not an end in itself. It involved uncertainty and risk. In the thirties already, Camus was caught

in a cross fire: between the Party and the colonial administration. The mature Camus found the perpetual contes-
tations of the postwar years wearying even as he took
part in them.

His friend and editor, Roger Quilliot, has described the
Camus of the postwar years, when the bravura of his
youth had disappeared: "Albert Camus never ceased to
react to the issues of his time. He did it in his own way
with an often exacerbated sensitivity and an intransigence in tone that masked deep uncertainties; once he
had taken a position on things and people, behind the
courtesy which he seldom shed, the combatant appeared;
he fought without hatred or joy, but if things went beyond certain limits, he fought without pulling his punches
and with a quasi-desperate violence" (*Essais*, p. xiii).

It is curious to note how closely this profile recalls another by Jean Grenier, a professor of philosophy at the
lycée of Algiers who, after Camus's death, described his
first encounters with the seventeen-year-old Camus, the
year he fell ill with tuberculosis.[4a]

> I shall always remember the interview I had with Albert
> Camus when he was just seventeen. He was a student in
> the philosophy section [of the *lycée*] in 1930, the year I
> had been appointed as professor at the *lycée* of Algiers.
> He was one of a large number of students who crowded
> in at the opening of the school year. Was it because he
> looked like a natural rebel? I told him to sit in the front
> row so that I could more easily keep an eye on him. A
> month or so went by and I noticed he had not turned up
> for a rather long period of time. I asked about him; I was
> told he was ill.

Grenier then describes his visit to the boy in the poorer
sections of Algiers where he had never been before. "Albert Camus . . . answered my questions concerning his

health only in monosyllables . . . Silence fell between
each remark. . . . Was his attitude a sign of revolt and
hostility?" The hostility, Grenier surmised, could hardly
be directed against him personally, but rather at society
as a whole. Whatever the motive, he concluded, "the will
to refuse was characteristic of the young man's attitude. . . .
For reasons I did not clearly distinguish, the man [really
still an adolescent, he comments in a footnote, in a kind of
afterthought] I was dealing with refused the hand I was
holding out to him. . . . I could see him, in my imagination, putting his hand behind his back . . . I could see him
refusing by anticipation any help proffered by others."
His was no adolescent revolt, Grenier judged; the taciturn
young man he confronted had, he felt, "the makings of a
revolutionary."

   In part, perhaps, Grenier had mistaken the nature of
the boy's unresponsiveness: the pride, so strong in Camus,
that Grenier himself diagnosed as "castillanerie" (i.e., a
deep-seated hostility to condescension in any form), may
have been in part responsible, or an adolescent unwillingness to betray emotion. But in part Grenier's diagnosis was
exact. "I have no vocation for illness," Camus once remarked. He had no vocation, either, for a mediocre life.
His attitude was linked to an inner revolt against the insignificance that threatened him. To reduce a man to insignificance is the ultimate indignity in Camus's world:
"Every man," he said in his Nobel Prize acceptance speech,
"wishes to be recognized." Grenier's visit was a recognition
and it initiated one of the lifelong friendships that Camus
prized. A single friendship of this kind—and there were
to be many others—was enough to move the young
Camus beyond what he called the "Robinsonism" of the
poor, the temptation to circumscribe one's life, like Crusoe,
to one's own island, to shut oneself into one's caste. His
initial conflict was real: to confront a world that relegated

him to insignificance, or to let the insignificance close over him. He chose the confrontation. What he wanted—from the age of seven, he once said—was to write.

Camus noted in his early Algiers years that, in France, most of the writers who have spoken of "the proletariat" were born in the middle class and dealt with the question of social injustice from outside. Not that what he called "the chance of birth" was necessarily incapacitating. Birth he firmly claimed was "neither good nor bad." He was not prepared to make a case for or against his own. It seems likely that he felt some ironic discomfort, if not disdain, when confronted by Sartre's long complaint on the disadvantages of being born a "bourgeois." But, in order to speak of poverty without sentimentalizing or degrading "the poor," the well-to-do lacked, in Camus's eyes, an insight into the real effects of poverty on those who live it: "I'd always rather a man should bear witness, so to speak, after his throat has been cut," he wrote with the deliberately provocative dead-pan causticity of his youth. "Poverty, for instance, leaves in those who have lived it an intolerance that makes it difficult to hear people speak of certain forms of destitution who have no experience of them at first hand" (*Essais*, p. 1111).

The exigency is of course excessive. But it is not only a question of concrete experience—upon which he always put a premium—that Camus was raising. His remark is connected with Camus's revulsion against a certain tone of condescension which he found intolerable, and detected for instance in the following aphorism by the seventeenth-century moralist, La Rochefoucauld: "The work of the body liberates from the sufferings of the mind, and that is what makes the poor happy"; the work of the body, Camus countered, can kill the mind and, simultaneously, the possibility of happiness. It "shortens the memory, weakens the spontaneity of friendship and love," and so excludes human beings from "the few perishable and essential things that give meaning to our lives: the sea, the sun, women in the sunlight" (*Essais*, p. 1108). The images, simple and elementary, are carefully chosen to reverberate in our imagination. They evoke a climate of warmth, color, and space which suggests a certain atmosphere of plenitude. To be deprived of them is to be dehumanized. Beyond the barriers that separate men— segregation and ostracism—Camus was reaching for those barriers that cut men off from the sources of vitality which give their struggles meaning, from "the unseen and personal universe that the finest hand shall never have the wit to demonstrate."[5] Of this universe most human beings are only dimly aware. It is the domain of artists. As an adolescent, Camus recalls, he felt that he had "infinite forces" but did not know "where to apply them." As an artist he would apply them to the elucidation and objectification of that universe; and increasingly as the years went by his artistic and his social consciousness merged, defining his personality and stature. It was for the preservation and development of that inner life that he fought, for himself and for other men. He had first encountered the forces that jeopardized or destroyed it through the kind of destitution suffered by the people he saw around him, victims of an injustice that acted upon them with the force of fate. It prepared him to a certain extent for the confrontation with the major negations of concentration camps and purges. And it is in that confrontation that Camus made a further option that guided his action during the Algerian war.[6] The years between 1943 and 1947 were crucial years of a personal reassessment that he attempted to clarify and communicate in *The Rebel*. The reassessment centered on Camus's position in regard to violence, and it involved the process

whereby Camus set his course firmly against the revolutionary romanticism and Hegelian dialectic of his generation.

In the thirties Camus had taken position in the world
of practical politics. He knew something of the constraints of action. He had not spoken of commitment. He
addressed his literary work to those who shared with him
"a certain taste for life." His own zest for living was apparent in the roster of his activities and the contagious
warmth and vigor that bound him to his friends. He liked
to work with a group, whether professionally in putting
out a newspaper, or spontaneously in a project like his
amateur Workers' Theater. The epigraph he chose for
The Myth of Sisyphus aptly describes his own dynamism:
"O my soul, do not aspire to immortal life, but exhaust
the field of the possible."[7] The "field of the possible" was
the realm within which he intended to limit and contain
his own thought and action. A letter he wrote to one of
the readers of *The Myth of Sisyphus* who had raised some
questions regarding the point of view developed in
Camus's essay, clarified the frame and mood of his essay.[8]
Camus, in the *Myth*,[9] had set out to counter what
seemed to him a mood of the times, the least conducive to
action, a neo-Nietzschean nihilism, which Jaspers has
succinctly described as the sense that "the world as it is
ought not to be and . . . the world as it ought to be is
nonexistent. . . . Accordingly existence is meaningless."[10]
But, Camus noted, there is a fundamental contradiction
in the position since in itself it gives a "minimal coherence" to the incoherence of existence and introduces a
minimal logic, hence already a systemization, into that
experience. Perfect "absurdity" would enjoin silence. But
silence would "remove from the world what is worth-

while" and "there are things which are worthwhile, whether art or friendship." Camus had shifted the ground of the debate, as he did in the *Myth* itself, from logic back to life by recourse to the most commonly recognized experiences. Furthermore the absurdist point of view, he claimed, errs because it eliminates "all judgments of value in order to substitute judgments of fact." Yet, Camus argued, it is a fact that we inevitably make judgments of value. Even if we place ourselves beyond good and evil— that is beyond the accepted moral code—certain acts seem to us good or bad, certain spectacles beautiful or ugly.

The basic contradiction, then, in the "absurdist" point of view is that it "incites us to live without making value judgments and to live is always, in a more or less elementary way, to judge." In any case, Camus continued, "these are problems that one must first live." For what is first given us is indeed "not value, nor even being, but the world, the frame, the setting . . ." His own essay, he claimed, sought to describe that setting but "did not take up . . . the question of what one can do within this frame"; a question which he hoped to turn to later. But, he insisted, "The idea underlying the book is that metaphysical pessimism does not entail that one must lose hope for man, quite the opposite." And Camus stated his conviction that one could link to a "philosophy of the absurd a political viewpoint concerned with human betterment, and whose optimism would be grounded in the relative"; since "the absurd is more closely related to common sense than one thinks." Common sense is something Camus prized. Under its armature of logic, *The Rebel* was to be an appeal to common sense against the excesses of logic.

But he understood the drives that underlie the instinctive human need to establish satisfactory patterns of belief that account for all the conflicting facets of experience and so allow the mind to rest in peace. To his reader's remark that he had sensed in *The Myth of Sisyphus* a certain nostalgia, "the taste for lost paradises," Camus acquiesced, but added that he saw no incompatibility between nostalgia and lucidity; he could not think that in the realm of metaphysics the fact that one felt "the need of a unifying principle" proved the existence of that principle. *The Myth of Sisyphus* was, in any case, only a "preface," a description of a "point zero," a kind of threshold.[8] Camus, who, like Sartre, was reacting against "laissez faire," or a cynical way of life, had started by relinquishing what Sartre sought: a single unified frame of understanding.

Camus, it is clear, had taken his bearings directly from experience: "one must live" the problems one attempts to elucidate; and the view he adopted deliberately was the view of pragmatic common sense. This clearly puts him on a different plane from Sartre. He was not concerned with the traditional vocabulary and problems of philosophy. He started from the "givens" of life as they appear to the great mass of human beings. When he spoke of "the world," he meant the concrete, physical world which he elsewhere called our "common homeland." And he accepted with it the men and women who inhabit it. Beyond all distinctions, in his eyes, they shared certain common traits. They were united by the "common homeland" they inhabited and which at least in one sphere defined "the field of the possible" for them all. They shared certain human needs; among them the need, however elementary, to introduce some kind of conceptual order into their existence; and the need to communicate with other men through art or friendship.

These were only fragmentary remarks, and in no sense did they cover the range of experience which *The Stranger, Caligula,* and *The Myth of Sisyphus* explore. But they do make quite clear that it was Camus's intent to reason like the ordinary run of men and in simple, direct language. Living, as he saw it, is an active process that includes judgment. It normally contains the "good" or "bad," "ugly" or "beautiful" labeling which more or less obscurely defines an inner field of preferences. To prefer is to evaluate, to consider "worthwhile." To the proposition "the world as it is ought not be and . . . the world as it ought to be is nonexistent," Camus obviously preferred the proposition that from a human standpoint the world exists both as it is and ought to be and as it is and ought not to be. Among the things that are and ought not to be, some are beyond the scope of any human action, while others are subject to choice. *The Myth of Sisyphus* explored the "walls" that limit human enterprise: death; the bounds put upon men's understanding of their own existence; the discrepancy in their own vital drives. These in his eyes are not "traps" but facts. His purpose was to define an area where human preferences have meaning and where choice is possible, as against an area where preferences are of no avail. Where men have no choice, their freedom is not in question, nor their responsibility. Camus here accepts the common attitude toward responsibility. This preserves him from the assertion of total responsibility and guilt that accompanies Sartre's assertion of man's unconditional freedom. Human beings for instance are not free not to die; but, like Sisyphus, who preferred life to the dictates of the gods, they can act to delay that fate or conversely to hasten its consummation. The question for Camus was, then, a question of power and direction; that is, control. He is concerned with the use a man can make of his life within the range of possibilities open to him.

A few years before he wrote this letter, in 1938 and 1939—at a time when he was working on his "cycle of the absurd"—he had briefly reviewed Sartre's first novel *Nausea* and his collection of short stories *The Wall*.[11] His admiration was warm and genuine; in Sartre he hailed a master. He also raised certain questions concerning Sartre's position.[12]

The article reviewing *Nausea* did not question the validity of Roquentin's experience, although Camus tended to place it in a Camusian context and summarized it in terms *The Myth of Sisyphus* was later to make familiar to many readers. There are effective moments, he agreed, even in the best-defended lives, when defenses are down and the "why" of it all surfaces: "Why this or that, this woman, this job and this appetite for the future? And why the urge to live in legs that will rot?" *Nausea* as he saw it described one of those moments. But whereas Sartre in the novel had divided his human world into two camps, the "cads" who are contemptible because they choose not to confront that "why," and those who do, Camus made no such differentiation. The moments when the "why" arises he saw as common to all men. But he, whose mother "almost never thought," was not inclined to pass judgment on anyone's intellectual passivity. Although the moments when the "why" arises are common to all men, all men are not equally equipped to articulate and cope with them. "For most men the approach of dinner, a letter received or the smile of a passing woman" suffices to get them over the passing hump, until the bleak solitude of old age overtakes them. It is the intellectual's attitude he considers and the dangers of intellectual narcissism—not the least of which is impotence. Camus was temperamentally opposed to the Romantic fascination with defeat. A more mature Camus raised the question again when he was reading *Being and Nothingness*. He

found Sartre's thought strangely closed to the practical
question of how a human being can in fact live without
evading the truth. "Can we," he queried in his notes, "accept despair and do nothing about it? It seems to me that
no honest person can answer yes" (*Essais*, p. 1617). The
question for Camus then is only secondarily the question
of "bad faith." Primarily what solicits his imagination are
the positive reasons men recognize for living: love, happiness, friendship, beauty. What he objected to in some
forms of existentialism was that it made of anguish "a
summit" that could not be transcended; the experience of
anguish seemed to him no more fundamental than a
number of other experiences—"happiness, patience or
self-interest or satisfaction" (*Essais*, p. 1670). Roquentin's nausea he sees as a genuine but typically intellectual
illness, the sign that mind and life are working at cross
purposes. One dies, or one finds a reason for living. This is
of course what Sartre's Roquentin does: his purpose at
the end is to justify his existence by recreating it in a
work of art.

Camus questioned the appropriateness of the novel's
ending. To write a novel seemed to him a trivial resolution incommensurable with the real issue at hand, literature being no panacea either for the ills of life or for those
of the intellect. He questioned too the fictional terms
through which the philosophical question was raised. For
insofar as he was concerned, Sartre had confused the
issue. The revelation of the gratuitousness of life did not
entail its repulsiveness. Life could be gratuitous and yet
in "love, beauty and danger" appear "disturbing and
magnificent." Roquentin's confusion of the metaphysically disturbing with the derisory was then a personal
and not a necessary reaction. What is clear in any case is
that, for Camus, from the outset, writing was no substitute for action.

Reviewing *The Wall* one year later, Camus centered his comments upon a specifically Sartrean theme, human freedom.[13] He defined the kind of paradox in which Sartre imprisons characters, destroyed by that very freedom Sartre's Roquentin had discovered; and he discerned Sartre's taste for the "boundary situation." Sartre, he pointed out, depicts characters "without ties, principles or Ariadne's thread . . . deaf to the appeal of action or creation . . . and who, deprived by their creator of any human diversions such as the movies, love, or the Legion of Honor,[14] stumble over their own lives as it were because of an excess of freedom." They "are free, but their freedom is of no avail." It is purely temporal and negated by death. They have no issue but to precipitate themselves into "an inhuman world where . . . they will create their own chains, dementia, sexual frenzy, or crime." Freedom, then, in the "intense and dramatic universe" of *The Wall*, leads paradoxically to self-annihilation, realized or subconsciously desired. And Camus, while praising the greatness and truth of a writer who "in two books has gone straight to the essential problem and made it come to life through his obsessive characters," discerned in Sartre's choice of boundary situations "a certain predilection for impotence in the full sense and the physiological sense" of the word; a lucid nihilism which left the impression of "a man sitting surrounded by the ruins of his life."

The analysis, from the point of view of literary criticism, was somewhat simplistic. Sartre's characters in the short stories are quite distinct from Sartre—far more so than was Roquentin. They are in some respects closer to case studies. But there is a contradiction in those years between the premises upon which Sartre based his criticism and the fate he meted out to his characters in the short stories. They are all indeed trapped, whether by chance or out of what Sartre calls "bad faith." Sartre allows them no exit; and no moments of grace. Whether from inside or out: no "passing smile," no word from a friend, nor any passing intimation of beauty. If Camus's characters are shut in, it is in a very different sense from Sartre's. They can draw on all the resources of their humanity.

The discussion is revealing. It was a first Camus-Sartre confrontation and adumbrated the divergence in orientation of the two men, both at the time newcomers in the ranks of the literati, although with these two volumes Sartre had taken the lead over the younger man. What Camus distinguished in Sartre's "universe" was that he had isolated from the substratum of life certain modalities of feeling or being and, within the bounds of fiction, had allowed them to become dictatorial. Each separate narrative gave shape to the unitary and selective universe of an emotion—such as Roquentin's for instance—which in life is balanced and modulated by others. At certain moments in any life one such modality may temporarily eliminate all others, become obsessive and "totalitarian," stunting all other relationships and modes of feeling. But normally such moods are qualified by others experienced as vividly. A writer who isolates these modalities of feeling or being from the uncharted, unsystematized flux of human life, can give them full sway while yet containing them within a form that bounds their development. Form gives the virtual world he creates its validity by setting limits to that validity, thence qualifying it as relative. *Nausea* and *The Wall* in Camus's eyes then had isolated and developed to their limit certain modalities of human existence, not the full possibility of human life. The potential for good or evil of these modalities in terms of individual destinies was open to scrutiny, but they did not give a full accounting.

Sartre would not have agreed. For Sartre, Roquentin's revelation of the contingency of all existants, consequently of his freedom, was the discovery of a truth that was not open to qualification. He did not recognize the relativity of his theoretical constructs. His fictions were "real reflections of life."

"An intense feeling," Camus remarked, "carries with it its own universe, magnificent or wretched as the case may be," a universe organized according to its own unitary logic.[15] In his early works, whether fiction or drama, he put some of these feelings in command of imaginary figures who live them out single-mindedly "to excess." "Impossible" figures he called them, who create "impossible" situations. And among the common stock of human emotions he chose the emotions he thought were most deeply stirring his age and which as a man of his time he shared. They were linked to his neo-Nietzschean belief that life was, at its root, positive desire and energy. Like Sartre's characters, these fictional characters reach limits where existence in human terms is no longer possible. Unlike Sartre's early characters, however, they set their own course, and to some extent, at least, determine their own fortune. Camus does not regard them as "real" but as mythical. The worlds they inhabit mirror our daily world only in part. They mirror the emotional texture and the distortions of the diverse, individual, inner worlds men live in. It is helpful to recall these fictional worlds, if only cursorily, for the light they throw on Camus's own progress through life and on the emotions and thought that oriented his understanding and manner of commitment.

Of all Camus's works *The Stranger* has been the most widely read and the most diversely interpreted[16] and yet has remained enigmatic, with an ambiguity which is a mark of major literary works. It would be singularly audacious to claim one could formulate its total purport. We shall consider here only one of its many facets. Camus himself once said that it had been his intent to create "a character without a conscience," leaving it up to us to wonder what exactly the French word "conscience" meant, whether the English "conscience" in the ethical sense, or "awareness," and if the latter what kind of awareness the protagonist, Meursault,[17] lacks. This raises the much debated question of Meursault's "innocence" or guilt, and so of the novelist's intent.[18] Meursault, at first glance, does seem, as Sartre suggested, to be an "absurdist" character; one who, in Camus's own terms, notes facts, and makes no judgment of value. Unquestioning and unspeculative, he recognizes all facts without subterfuge or mitigation, giving a meticulous account of what he did, the people he encountered, the incidents that took place. He puts no interpretation upon them, draws no inferences, and a couple of times only proffers a bewildered explanation: he starts to explain why his mother was in an old people's home, and stops. And asked why he shot the Arab he says it was "because of the sun." How he reached this state we are not told. One could surmise that Meursault was born in Camus's imagination at the limit of that nostalgia previously mentioned, in a mind that had left behind it the speculations of philosophy and the overall views of religion.

Meursault is a man born into a society, and aware of it. He is not antisocial and shows no trace of hostility toward others. Throughout the book he is aware that something is expected of him that he fails to accomplish but he does not see exactly what it is. The first words he says, in the book, concern his mother's death and express a vague irrational sense of unease: "It is not my fault . . ."[19] And he has a tacit, but genuine and equal acceptance of other people, a kind of respect: for his mother, about whom he remarks at the time of the funeral when he learns that she had had a sentimental attachment for one of the old men, that he "understands" her; for old Salamano and his dog; for the disreputable pimp Raymond and his difficulties with his woman; for the people he sees in the parlor of the prison on visitors' day. He is in every respect a contemporary "everyman" who reacts to events as they occur and implicitly he lives as if he would continue to do so undisturbed. The revolver shots upon the beach bring about the collapse of that everyday life. They are as startling to the reader as to Meursault. Paradoxically, the innocuous life Meursault was leading reveals malevolent potentialities. Striking apparently by chance, from outside, a kind of fatality turns him in one unexpected second into a murderer. He confronts violence within him and without, in nature and society. "Ecce homo," Camus indirectly seemed to suggest when he sardonically remarked that Meursault was the only Christ we deserved. But how?

It is obvious from Meursault's account that there is indeed, as he vaguely suspects, some insufficiency in his way of life, although, the trial makes clear, not in terms of the social conventions he is accused of flouting. At the time of the shooting he feels instinctively he has transgressed some deep-seated, cosmic law. For a few seconds when a compulsive force, "the sun," takes control of his body he commits an act for which an exorbitant price is paid. We are not far from incidents such as My Lai. Camus, in his first novel, stripping away certain layers of assumptions concerning the nature of human existence, exposes the naked violence at its root, in the most apparently innocuous of men. By his willingness to accept life as it comes, and by his absorption in the present, Meursault had implicitly given a practical assent to a life controlled by chance, from outside. It is his misfortune, as a fictional hero, to have the real implications of his way of life thrust upon him from outside. His awakening too is conditioned by the dead-end situation into which he has been thrust. Only his condemnation to death brings him the physical sense of his mortality.

Young Camus, himself ill, often spoke of death in his early works; however, death was not the issue, but rather human mortality: that is, the sense of the temporal and finite personal existence and personal death of each human being. Insistently in the book, Meursault returns to his mother's death. When, at the end of the novel, in a surge of passion he consciously assents to the knowledge, to the whole truth of life, it is again of her he speaks. It is through his understanding of her that he makes the final and unconditional assent: to the violence and to the rest. The rest, that is the beauty of the earth, of Marie; the give and take of everyday life with its rhythms, sights, sounds, snatches of conversation, human faces that are also a part of the truth of life. Their value is borne in upon him by his mother who, at the threshold of death, was ready "to begin again." What he finds out is not merely that life comes to an end but that living is an end in itself, for the temporal, finite human being.

The novel of course raises many other points of debate. But what concerns us here is the light it throws on the sensitivity of the young Camus, before the war years, on what lay behind his activism. For, as readers, we can look beyond the fiction to the vision it embodies. There is, first of all, the pre-eminence Camus gave the human body itself. He eloquently described its moments of harmony with the natural setting, the physical joys of "the lived body." In a slim volume of lyrical essays, *Nuptials*, Camus had expressed his acute enjoyment of certain moments when he felt the strange happiness of just being in the world,[20] out of doors, alone, or, like Meursault, with other people. And Camus, by choosing to connect Meursault's final awakening to his mother's death, again chose the most physiological, quasi-animal bond that links human beings to each other. The body then is the source of truths and certainties, purveyor of a knowledge that does not concern the intellect alone. These certainties take on their meaning, not in abstract formulae, nor in terms of a supra-sensible reality, but in terms of a human being; for Meursault in terms of his mother—where thought and flesh are one. If the earth is our common homeland, so the body is our common bond. It endows life with value, contains and bounds all a person's possibilities.

Meursault, in his short life, via his physical person, spans life and death, violence done and suffered, understanding, love, delight, solitude, joy, and suffering. The body limits and defines a man's freedom, the feel of his options, and the nature of his relations with other human beings. Social conventions are secondary, and subsequent. All options people make in life are of consequence because they concern finite human beings. Meursault is not responsible *for* the world given him nor *for* the people he encounters. He is responsible for the manner in which he acts in it and upon them; neither his initial "innocence" nor his awakening can change his act. Remorse would not change it either; Camus does not fall into that trap. If Meursault is our "Christ" it can only be because, in his author's eyes, he has lived out to the full, for our benefit, the illusions behind our own assumptions of "innocence," of disengagement from the violence of life. Meursault's initial blindness is clearly not the option Camus proposes.

Limited in his freedom, bound to the earth and to others by a "human nature" and condition, Camus's man can realize within these limits a range of possibilities, all of which are incipient in Meursault's life. A man can not substantially change the curve of his destiny, nor the precariousness of life, nor his basic human needs. His choices lie in the manner in which he relates to what he has been given. But he first must know that he has been given "truth before fable, life before dream," and accept it before he can make any options. A global "yes" precedes the selective "no" of dissent.

"We possess and we acquire," Jean Grenier wrote. "One can say that Albert Camus possessed violence and acquired measure." *The Stranger* may seem to have no bearing on Camus's socio-political commitments in the thirties. Yet it was one of the disturbing strengths of *The Stranger* to make the act of violence on the beach emerge from the most apparently passive of men. Camus's sense of the violence, wildness, and brutality surfacing everywhere in the thirties was not unique. What was more exceptional is that he sensed it in himself. It was through his writing that he sought the self-knowledge to curb it. As he understood it, he was engaged in a social struggle to achieve a greater measure of justice for all men; but injustice was built into the natural world and insofar as men partook biologically, or at least physically, of that world, they necessarily participated in that injustice. Meursault's self-awareness, acquired too late, is the measure of Camus's acute self-consciousness. Camus would never, like Sartre, line men up as good or bad according to his own standards of measurement. He knew he was as prone to injustice as any other man.

Caligula[21] was born of a further meditation on violence. Caligula is the obverse of Meursault. He is a man committed. To his fictional character Camus arrogated absolute power over men, and freedom from the constraints of human law: Caligula *is* the law. Known to his familiars as an amiable and idealistic young man, Caligula is awakened, like Meursault but more dramatically, to the awareness of his own mortality by the death of someone dear to him, his sister and mistress, Drusilla. He is seized by a ravaging sense of the intolerable human condition in a world where "men die and are not happy." It suddenly discloses to him how little human beings and their activities matter in the flux of being. Obsessed by his mind's vision, sure of its truth, he resolves to impose it on his entourage by applying to them the same ruthless measures as the invisible natural law that governs their destiny. They will then see, as he does, that life under such conditions is intolerable, will be shaken out of their acquiescence, and pressured, through terror, into a common insurrection against their fate.

Caligula's crusade against a common evil ends indeed in an insurrection, but the insurrection does not change the human condition. It merely starts a cycle of terror and retaliation, temporarily increasing the pointless violence loose in the world. To prove that human existence is intolerable, Caligula first acts to make it so; and he can make it so only by destroying the human beings themselves who make the earth habitable by men. Caligula is an ideological terrorist.

Camus was obviously marking his distance from all doctrinarians and from the neo-Nietzscheanism of the Nazis in their attempt to revitalize society through violence. He was alert to the destructive potentialities of totalitarian views of human existence and totally skeptical of their claims to infallibility. It was clear that the man who wrote *Caligula* was not prepared to give his adherence to any large abstract overview of life, nor to arrogate to himself the freedom of a Caligula, attributing the responsibility for his acts of violence to external circumstances and to his concern for humanity as a whole. It is not surprising, therefore, that Camus could not work within the Communist Party, unable, as one Party member who knew him at the time put it, to speak its language.

As a young man he had known many forms of freedom: freedom felt in the well-being of a body at home in its world, which had brought him hours of happiness; freedom in human dealings in the give and take of everyday living in the poor sections of Algiers, a human world where conventions are simple and men more prone to look squarely at the essential facts of existence. He had come to know other social spheres too, and their freedoms, the freedom of speculative thinking, the freedom of the artist, the freedom of friendship. He knew their constraints and that each set its limitations upon the others. And he was aware that every form of freedom, finding its object, secreted its own violence. Work itself, the work of the writer to give form to his conceptions was, he once said to Grenier, a form of violence.

By his own account, as an adolescent he had lived with his peers in one only of these worlds "on the surface of the world, among colors, waves, the good smell of the earth." He would then have jeered at prophets who "proclaimed anathema against the world" (*Essais*, p. 1151); "the world" was his world of sensuous delight. His gods were "gods of voluptuousness." Awakening to consciousness, through the mediation of Grenier, he learned to take into account other things: "mystery and the sacred, man's mortality, impossible love," and a "doubt" or questioning that "would not let him rest." The doubt was the key to his own literary undertaking. In his writing he could do what he could not do in his life without stunting his own development: pursue one aspect of his experience at a time to the exclusion of all others.

In the sphere of practical politics it affected his understanding of action. He could not anchor his decisions in any certainty concerning the meaning of the human enterprise as such. He did not intend to duplicate Caligula's revolt against a condition that no revolt could change. He could not then set his course and justify his action in terms of some projected "end" such as the Marxian just and free classless society—a utopia in the eyes of a man who put facts before dreams. But he was not a Meursault, to be manipulated by circumstances, and he harbored within himself a revolt so wild that Grenier sensed it as "frightening." Physical and moral destruction he saw all about him and it was against them his anger was roused. He did not wish to be either a Caligula or a Caligula's pawn. Behind the alleged selfless concern of a Caligula to bring others to the truth, Camus had shown the histrionics, the self-pity, the bloody-mindedness of a tyrant; and also the less noble and more human but equally dangerous wish to see that hypocritical, vain human beings— cheats, liars, panderers—get their deserts. The judge could be as pitiless in him as in any one of us, and he had the artist's eye for fakes.

But he also had the conviction that nothing would greatly change our over-all human failings. As he cryptically said and would maintain, he did not hope that the "human lot" would basically change. But within the range of possibilities, men could select one way of life rather than another, weighing the scales toward greater justice or happiness. He had sensed in these early years what he called, in the rather stilted vocabulary which now seems to us dated, the "world of violence and death" that men were preparing in the name of future utopias.

For him, in all matters of action, the *end* was not in question, but the choice of means, *which in itself was the end*. Self-scrutiny and discipline, the resistance to emotional and ideological inducements, would be part of his way of life, and uncertainty. Independent by temperament, Camus would have to make his decisions in action as best he could. His uncertainties were not uncertainties as to his purpose. "As a very young man Albert Camus knew what he *could* do," writes Grenier who knew him well. "It was what he must do. His obligation was to exploit his possibilities" (*Essais*, p. ix) and he had the will so to do. Whatever the circumstances, but not at any price. His goal was to enhance life, not to destroy it. The same creative urge lay behind his political commitments and his work, however much they might on the surface appear to run counter to each other. He could not be an absolutist; nor a "judge." He would make his mistakes and live his own passions. And he would struggle to realize in himself the goal he hoped might be reached by all men. He "possessed violence" in a time of great violence, and so strove mightily "to acquire measure." By the late thirties Camus had rejected the role of revolutionary, but not his original premises. There are rights and wrongs in human affairs; the wrongs can be intolerable. He was committed to fight against them, as he encountered them in their immediacy here and now according to his own views and capabilities; and, as far as possible without losing sight of his goal, to develop all his possibilities, not least among them his possibilities as an artist; for in the discipline they required of him was a source of equilibrium for him and a way open to understanding. Throughout the war it helped him maintain his sanity; and throughout the years the balance between his public and his personal life.

Notes to Chapter 5

1. Admirably edited by Roger Quilliot, a scholar and a friend of Camus's.

2. Camus's reticence in this respect—in regard, for example, to his action in the Resistance movement and the Algerian war—explains the questionable, though sympathetic and refreshing, interpretation of his attitudes such as is given in Conor Cruse O'Brien's *Albert Camus* (New York: Viking, 1969); but it does not excuse the lack of serious documentation, the faulty quotations, erroneous statements, and arbitrary inferences that seriously mar an essay in which the author is anxious only to bring his interpretation of Camus into line with his own rather schematic view of Western guilt.

3. Camus, as we have noted, had been shocked by the equivocal policies of Moscow, in the thirties, uncritically endorsed by the Party hierarchy in France and applied to the Party's policies toward the Algerian Muslims, for example, with no respect for local needs.

4. O'Brien states erroneously that Camus knew practically no one among the Algerian Arabs. To the information given by Quilliot, one should add the well-documented account by Yves Courrière in the second volume of his *Guerre d'Algérie*, pp. 239–64. Camus was in touch with many Arab Algerians and with the very small group of European Algerians who frequently worked with them and acted in their behalf.

4a. Jean Grenier, *Albert Camus* (Paris: Gallimard, 1968), pp. 9–12.

5. Hortense Flexner, *Selected Poems* (London: Hutchinson, 1963), p. 36.

6. I regret that I must take exception to O'Brien's sketchy view of Camus's position. In his book, *Frantz Fanon* (New York: Viking Press), p. 56, David Caute sums up the results of the Algerian war briefly. "By the end of the war,

the FLN (Algerian Liberation Front) estimated Algerian deaths, including victims of starvation, at over one million out of a total population of nine million. The majority of Europeans fled, and by the end of 1962 Algerian industry was at a standstill, the harvest had not been brought in, two million were unemployed and four million others were declared 'without means of subsistence'; the Algerian government had no alternative but to remain dependent upon French economic and technical aid." One might envisage the possibility that had the escalating violence of the war been stopped, as Camus and a group of his Algerian friends—European and Muslims—had attempted to do in 1955–56 in circumstances of great personal jeopardy to themselves, the blood bath of the Algerian war might have been mitigated. It is hardly proven that efforts to stop such blood baths in the process of decolonization were of necessity "colonialist." Quoting Camus's remark, in answer to a militant, that if he was forced to choose between his mother and the revolution he would choose his mother, O'Brien makes the further inference that thereby Camus had "chosen" to be on the side of the special forces of the French Army. The misinterpretation is obvious. Camus was speaking in specific terms. If a man came at his mother with a gun, whoever the man was, he would, of course, defend her. Terrorism, in other words, creates primitive conditions of self-defense, instigating a violence that has nothing to do with the issue at hand. O'Brien further contends that for Camus, Algerians were European Algerians. "For the millions of Algerians who are suffering from hunger," Camus wrote in 1945, when no one else was concerned about the problem, "what can we do?" (*Essais*, p. 947). I could line up other examples. He was certainly not thinking then in terms of the European Algerians. It is perhaps too early to evaluate Camus's position fairly. At worst it might be judged utopian, but only in the distorted vision of political passion could it be judged reprehensible. Facts do not bear out the dubious image of Camus as a "poor white" type of liberal, a colonialist under the skin, that some critics have tried to perpetuate.

7. From a translation of Pindar's *Third Pythian Ode*. Paul Valéry had used it as epigraph for one of his best-known poems, "Le cimetière marin" ("The Cemetery by the Sea").

8. Lettre à Pierre Bonnel, *Essais*, pp. 1422–25.

9. Camus's description of the "absurdist" viewpoint has been so widely discussed that it does not seem necessary to go over it again. The best quick summary is no doubt Sartre's, which distinguishes two meanings of the word: one, designating a "state of fact" and, two, the "lucid awareness" certain people have of that state of fact: "What is meant by the absurd as a state of fact, as primary situation? It means nothing less than man's relation to the world. Primary absurdity manifests a cleavage, the cleavage between man's aspirations to unity and the insurmountable dualism of mind and nature, between man's drive toward the eternal and the *finite* nature of his existence, between the concern which constitutes his very essence and the vanity of his efforts. Chance, death, the irreducible pluralism of life and of truth, the unintelligibility of the real—all these are extremes of the absurd." (*"An Explication of The Stranger"*; in *Camus*, a collection of critical essays, Prentice Hall, 1962, p. 109.) *The Myth* argues against the conclusion that the state of fact and the awareness necessarily make man's efforts vain.

10. Karl Jaspers, *Origin of European Nihilism*, p. 243.

11. The collection is titled *Intimacy* in the American translation. "The Wall" is the title of the first story, "Intimacy" of another. However, the substitution is unfortunate since the central motif concerns the walls—death, madness, bad faith—that hem men in. For Camus's reviews see *Essais*, pp. 1417–22.

12. *Nausea* is so widely read that I shall merely outline it here: it is the account in diary form of the experience of a young historian, Roquentin, who is carrying out research in a small provincial town in France. Roquentin, in flashes first, then overwhelmingly, is overcome by a feeling of

anguish and disgust as things and people lose their re-assuring daily aspect, break loose from the words that label them until in a moment of panic Roquentin confronts the monstrous, purposeless, and inchoate proliferation of existence, even in himself. He becomes aware of the contingency of all existants concomitantly with his own freedom. The revolt that sweeps over him leads him to abandon his way of life and to envisage the creation of a work of art—a book—as a possible exorcism against "l'absurde."

13. *Being and Nothingness* was still four years from publication. But Camus may well have taken his cue from Sartre's critical articles published in the *Nouvelle Revue française* in those years.

14. The enumeration here is again deliberately cryptic and not without its dash of humor. Camus's manner sometimes recalls the Zen Koans.

15. Camus seems never to have dug deeply into Freud. He was well acquainted with those facets of Marxian thought currently accepted by the Party militants in the thirties, but was never versed in the exegesis of the Marxian texts. But he had read Nietzsche whose "vitalism" echoes in his early writing and was familiar with the questions raised by Nietzsche's equation of life, violence, and creativity. It was probably Nietzsche who reinforced his sense of the irrational assumptions which underlie the most apparently rational logic. Camus quite naturally belongs to the "era of suspicion" in which the constructs of the mind are regarded with a critical eye, a post-Nietzschean, post-Freudian, post-Marxian era.

16. Sartre's brilliant explication of *The Stranger* is well known and has set the horizon for many others. It is, of course, valid only within certain limits. Characteristically, it systematizes the book and intellectualizes it, missing, it seems to me, its human dimensions and appeal.

17. *The Stranger*, like *Nausea*, needs no introduction. I shall merely recall the outline: the protagonist and narrator, Meursault, a white-collar worker in Algiers, relates the events. The first part of the novel is an account of

the events which, in a brief set of days, started with the funeral of his mother and end with his unpremeditated shooting of an Arab on a beach. The second is an account of his days in prison, his trial, and condemnation to death.

18. Much of the discussion has been beside the point: Meursault killed a man and is condemned to death for his action. He is clearly not innocent of his act, makes no excuses for it, and faces the consequences. He is neither a Raskolnikov nor a Billy Budd. He is innocent perhaps in the sense that "he had no evil intent or motive"—to quote one of Webster's definitions of the word. What is more interesting is that it is he himself who, accounting for what happened, links the incident on the beach to his mother's death. His "innocence" may then also be connected to "a lack of knowledge," a "fault" in his relation to human existence as a whole, which his fate dramatically illustrates. His initial "innocence" then would be akin to that of the young Oedipus.

19. This raises some rather serious objections to the incisive interpretation offered by Robert Champigny who sees in Meursault "a pagan hero," in a kind of "state of nature."

20. Camus's "Mediterranean" sensibility has often been mocked. In his support Virginia Woolf can here be quoted, speaking of Greece: "We must sharpen the lines of the hills. We must imagine the beauty of stone and earth rather than woods and greenery. With warmth and sunshine and months of fine weather, life of course is instantly changed; it is transacted out of doors. . . ." *The Common Reader*, p. 25.

21. It is not my intention to fully explicate *Caligula*. But it is clear that Caligula generalizes a *partial* truth and makes of it an absolute. Men die and they are *often* unhappy, but they also know those respites and joys and the comfort of familiar faces that Meursault comes to value so highly, and which make the world inhabitable. To oblige men to live by his truth, Caligula must first make the world seem to them uninhabitable; he can only do it by destroying human beings.

6.

The Political Imperative and the Conundrums of History

Progress, when optimistic, always promises some form of exodus from history as we know it, some emergence onto a new plateau of life. Thus the Marxist revolution promised deliverance from history as history had previously been, a series of class struggles.

NORTHROP FRYE

"If a man is to have a history, it is necessary that he change, that the world change him as it changes and that he change as he changes the world"[1] (*Saint Genet*, 1952). Movement was built into Sartre's image of the lucid man, consciousness spiraling on itself to smash former patterns of compliance and leaping thence into a kind of spatial void, a "new plateau." This is the "conversion" scheme latent in the story of Roquentin's life. The crisis he describes in *Nausea* is for Roquentin only one, the most recent in a series of similar "passages." A man, for the early Sartre, was not so much a problematic individual as a problematic future. *Being and Nothingness* is still essentially a reasoned theory of this pattern compulsively enacted by Sartre's protagonist, Roquentin, at the author's bidding. But there is a gap between the pattern of change schematized in *Being and Nothingness* and the complex interaction of "world" and man defined in *Saint Genet*. There is little sign in *Being and Nothingness* that Sartre saw the problems of his human being in a perspective reaching beyond the limits of a circumscribed private life. As Frederick Hoffman has said, Sartre "developed a cosmogony, an eschatology, an earth and a hell—solely along lines of the immediate issues of existence in space and endurance in time that emerge from the abandonment of immortality."[2] At that early stage he cut these to fit the patterns of private modes of behavior in a static middle-class society.

By the time *Being and Nothingness* came out in 1942, Sartre's point of view had already begun to change under the pressure of exceptional circumstances; and it was to continue to change in major ways during the next years. During the thirties, the direction of Sartre's thought was still situated within the mainstream of French thinking since the 1890's. In reaction against positivism, which they conceived as mirroring a kind of "scientific fatalism," French thinkers, according to H. Stuart Hughes, had shown a common concern "to restore the freely speculating mind to the dignity it had enjoyed a century earlier."[3] Sartre had pushed the trend to its limits and put his own personal mark upon it, reinstating the "free mind" as the dynamic agent of all worthy human projects. In the forties, the inquiry turned again to a confrontation with the events and enigmas of history. Sartre's postwar declaration of confidence in the ability of each human being to act upon the course of collective events, corresponded to a general need, shored up by the memory of the shared emotions of the war. It had been, for Sartre, a new departure. It was then that he reassessed his positions.

Sartre has consistently pointed to the war years as the crucial years in the reorientation of his thought: "It was the war which made the obsolete frames of our thought explode, the war, occupation, resistance, the years that followed."[4] And he has himself emphasized two major factors in that change. One is personal in nature, his experience as prisoner of war; the other is intellectual in kind, his confrontation with a power he had not previously recognized, the force of history.

History is a word he was long to capitalize, personify, and endow with those human faculties that make for allegory. Sartre, the philosopher, confronted the complex impact upon him of a vast network of events within which he had been, somehow, "situated." "We have learned History and insist that it should not be forgotten." What Sartre learns, he seldom pauses to consider that others may have learned before him. He universalizes his own position immediately; thence his urgent desire to "enlighten others," his haste in joining issues in the battle of ideas.[5] He has described his own mental progress as "crablike," moving obliquely in a direction toward which it does not seem to be headed. This is particularly true of the dozen odd years that followed the war. History, the "making" of History, the developing patterns of History, their meaning and relation to the individuals and groups that "live" them became the central object of his meditation as philosopher and of his political actions as a citizen of France and the world figure he rapidly became.

"When I was a prisoner during the last war, I got on admirably with the workmen and peasants who were with me. If I had gone to speak with them in their factories or farms, in my overly abstract language, they would have turned their backs on me. But in the camp we spoke the same language because we had the same things to do and reacted in the same way."[6] Thus Sartre, when he recalled his nine-month stay in the prisoner of war camp (1940–41), while discussing the 1968 May "revolution," triggered by student unrest, and the short period when students and workers had coalesced. It is no secret that Sartre sees himself as an "intellectual," that he is an "intellectual's intellectual," ill at ease with nonintellectuals of whatever kind. The prisoner of war camp seems to be the first instance when he felt he had broken through the barriers that separate him from the "masses."

He came back to Paris in 1941 with the nostalgia for direct participation in a communal life. In the tiresome Marxian jargon they later adopted to describe their simplest moods, Simone de Beauvoir sums up Sartre's concern. "If they (the workers) rejected him, he would remain shut into the singularity of the petit-bourgeois."[6a] This would have been the ultimate defeat for the writer. Sartre much later defined the writer as the "singular universal," a curiously abstract restatement of an age-old contention that nothing in the human condition should remain foreign to any man, least of all to the one who writes. The concern then is curiously self-centered and asocial in kind.

In the 1930's Sartre had not thought of men in terms of social categories. He still thought in terms of "man," a universal entity. Moreover, he implicitly situated that man within a static and placid bourgeois society whose permanence is not really called into question: it is against that permanence itself that he threw the full force of his hatred. He accepted, for the time being at least, the universal validity and solidity of the society and human being he depicts. His intellectual certainty concerning his own ontology reflected that sense of permanence, in spite of the fact that its aim was to show that human beings cannot

live within a *status quo*. He was entirely convinced of the
universal applicability of his theory, and that it would be
always applicable to human modes of behavior. He was
happy in this certainty except during the period when
he suffered acutely from the aftereffects of an experiment with mescaline, and he observed "contingent" political events with the philosopher's traditional detachment.

The prisoner of war camp, however, modified one important feature in his own experience that affected the
over-all philosophical description of "man" he had been
working out. In Sartre's ontology, each consciousness is
the center of reference, the organizer or "author" of its
world and, consequently, enters into conflict with all others. The passive acceptance of a given order—religious or
social—is a sign of abdication. It is the root of all forms of
evasion and "inauthentic" behavior. Conflict is mandatory.

In the camp, Sartre had, in effect, personally transcended this situation. His "I" had merged into a "we," in
an "authentic" experience. It was for his fellow prisoners
that he had written a first and successful play, *Bariona*,
surely one of the strangest of Christmas plays.[7] The success of the play was probably due to the common emotion
felt by the men in that first Christmas of captivity, and in
their response to the atmosphere of total bleakness and
yet hope Sartre's play managed to convey. Sartre could
rightly feel he had spoken for the group. Author and
audience had shared in a common awareness of their
plight; metaphorically, it was their own "existential" situation reflected in the play that they had seen objectified,
had understood and temporarily transcended. Sartre's
play had fulfilled a social function, and derived its power
from the relevancy of its intent.

The same sense of communion was to color Sartre's
experience of the grim occupation years. In immediate

retrospect, his quasi-passive existence during that period took on a mystic cast:[8] "We were never so free as under the German occupation. We had lost all our rights and first the right to speak; we were insulted every day to our faces and had to remain silent. We were deported en masse as workers, Jews, political prisoners."[9] Neither worker, Jew, nor political prisoner, Sartre furthermore had not lost the right to speak, witness *Being and Nothingness, The Flies*, and *No Exit*. This was, in fact, the time of his emergence as one of France's important new writers. But partaking in the public emotions, he had submerged his own identity in the "we" for whom he now assumed the role of spokesman. It was no longer for Sartrean "man" he was speaking. He was speaking as witness for certain groups of men, victims not of their own "bad faith," but of the brutality of others. He was speaking, as he had spoken in the camp, for a group; but in this latter instance, as one of them only symbolically. The emotional identification was profoundly felt. The torture chamber haunted Sartre's mind, with its embodiment of evil personified in the well-fed, well-clad torturers. Confronting them was their challenger, the victim, a solitary individual physically broken, alone, yet by sheer force of will setting limits to the torturers' power to negate his autonomy as a free man.

There were then, in effect, sub-men and heroes. This image crystallized the abstract pattern of Sartre's ontology, and became its tragic emblem. "Is not the total responsibility [of the victim] in total solitude the very revelation of our freedom?" The dynamic but abstract conflict of the "being for itself" trapped within the walls of a given "situation," when extrapolated into the emblem of the confrontation in the torture chamber, took on an intolerable intensity and a compelling moral evidence.

All Sartrean "free" men, then, had become participants

in a mystic sacrifice. What had been an ontology—a "description" of human reality—now engendered a desperate heroic ethic. The actual victims of Nazi oppression, for Sartre, lived concurrently in three worlds: in the real world where a momentous historical struggle had indeed been played out at their expense; in Sartre's vivid imagination as victims of human brutality; and in the metaphysical world of his ontology, where they played the role of icons illustrating its truth.

Once, at least, in 1960, Sartre looked back with anger at that epoch, lashing out with bitter irony at his past— and, as always, generalizing rather sweepingly: "I seem to remember we had acquired beautiful souls, so beautiful that I blush when I think back on those years"; and when he thought back, too, on the young men and women of the forties now become "forty-year-old carcasses," those "former adolescents" who "for five years" [during the war] had "thought that they would die," and who had lived. As Sartre himself had lived. "Adolescents, the defeat had jolted them; they started to throw their parents' furniture out of the window. . . . Then Marshall came [the Marshall Plan], our hippies (*rats de cave*) turned into stupefied old young men. They had started out. Their train bogged down in the fields. They'll go nowhere and will do nothing."[10]

In her *Memoirs*, Simone de Beauvoir, describing Sartre's delight in building myths into their lives, also notes that intellectually Sartre "built his theories from certain positions to which he held stubbornly," thus combining the arbitrary, theoretical, and the visionary. Emotion, naturally enough, had colored his view of his countrymen and their predicament during the war years. Emotion, again, had colored it adversely twenty years later. An emotion had created and an emotion had destroyed Sartre's sense of identification with his former self and his countrymen. Sartre's disengagements, then, are deeply affective, and anger is often a sign of his frustration at the destruction of a formerly cherished theory or myth. His attacks on "others" are often emotional verdicts on his own past. Sartre, in distributing those verdicts, is verbally murderous on occasion. In the degree that "others" fail to play adequately the role for which he had, in his imagination, cast them, they become objects of his contempt.[11] He then may go to extreme punitive lengths: he will proclaim, as he did in 1968, that his erstwhile friend, the eminent professor of political theory, Raymond Aron, no longer has "the right" to teach, because he ventured to criticize the students and, Sartre arbitrarily charges, never contested his own ideas. Or again, Sartre strikes a whole class of people from the roster of humanity: "my class is the enemy of humanity," a statement which, rhetorically and psychologically, is more complex than may at first appear, but which makes little sense rationally.

Emotion, the manner in which people live their emotions, had been one of the main areas of Sartre's philosophical investigation in the thirties. "For Sartre," Fell, an early critic, notes, "emotion is one mode of that attempt to achieve self-identity which he holds to be the irreducible motivational explanation for all human behavior."[12] Emotions, as Sartre then saw it, were ways of confronting facts that people find too difficult to cope with in a rational manner. "The emotional response is an act, a chosen response which attempts to transform magically a situation which presents difficulties not resolvable by ordinary pragmatic means." In Sartre's original view, people choose their emotions intentionally though not lucidly, to achieve a given end. When the "instrumental"

(pragmatic) world becomes too difficult to cope with, a
"magical" world is substituted that "nullifies" the difficult
situation and at the extreme obliterates it entirely.[13] Sartre's verbal violence in this perspective seems almost entirely emotional in nature, a form of exorcism that serves
until he has fitted the offensive situation into an adequate
conceptual frame. This may account for the contrast between his personal kindness, his hard-working life, and
the verbal tongue-lashings and calls to violence that
punctuate his polemical work and echo in his plays.
There are no such outbursts in his writing before the
1940's. Sartre's brash, witty, and arbitrary attacks, in his
prewar critical reviews, directed against some of the
prominent novelists of the day, François Mauriac and
Jean Giraudoux for instance, only faintly announce his
later bitter acrimony. The acrimony appeared only when
Sartre, the "grand intellectuel," turned from the speculative and fictional interpretation of men and events to the
discussion and evaluation of actual historical events and
opinions.[14] It disappeared when he addressed himself to
the gigantic task of reinventing Flaubert.

In effect, the stories in *The Wall* (1939) were all ironically slanted "cautionary tales" on such "magical" emotional ways of dealing with life. Six small routs Sartre
called them, because, fundamentally, he wished to gear
his own life to reason rather than to magic. "In Sartre's
hands," writes Fell, Husserl's "every consciousness is consciousness of something," becomes "every consciousness is
consciousness of something to be done" (p. 40). Thence
Sartre's early need, as Simone de Beauvoir stated it, to
"build an ideology which, while it enlightened man on his
situation, would propose a praxis to him," man here being
more peculiarly himself. Sartre's early theory of the emotions already states the main thesis of the ontology: that

man is free and defines himself by what he does. And it throws light too, on the rhythms or—if one prefers—dialectics of Sartre's political polemics during the postwar years. Sartre swung between violent emotional responses to events, generally unforeseen by him, followed by lengthy, abstruse, theoretical post-mortems of events already past and done with. And all eventually culminate in a colossal new conceptual structure, the unfinished *Critique of Dialectical Reason,* in which Sartre attempted to "totalize" and order rationally his chaotic experience over those years; and *The Idiot of the Family* whose projected four thousand pages aim at "showing" a man complete, and demonstrating a method in all its intricacy. Sartre's essential commitment, then, does seem to be toward the rational ordering of an experience often lived in an irrational mode. This may prove as disturbing to the onlooker as the unresolved tension between images and intellectual structures in his work.

In the forties, Sartre had continued to think, even though existentially, in terms of a universal Sartrean model of mankind. But his frame of reference had shifted drastically in the interval of the war years. "Man" was still the center of consciousness and organizer of the world, but the point of view as to his identity had changed. It was now, Sartre had decided, from the "point of view of the least favored" that each conscious thinker must view the world. Sartre had entered into battle with himself. For, even in the occupation years, in no sense could he take a place among the "least favored." He now had evicted himself from the center of his world, and substituted the "other's" subjectivity for his own. He had polarized his universe around "the other." He could see himself only negatively. Concurrently, he had lent his consciousness to the "least favored." The "oppressed," the "proletariat," the "blacks," the new "emerging nations," the student revolutionaries, successively took the place of the "we" of the prison camp and Resistance years. The polarization also absorbed the emotional intensity and stark moral absolutes of the "torture chamber" image. It left no room for the perspectives Camus sought in order to glimpse the fellow creature behind the enemy. Sartre had begun to "think against himself."

In the Manichean world of the Resistance, the Hegelian conflict of consciousnesses had taken on a moral cast. The conflict now became broadly politicized. In Sartre's political writings vast entities became engaged in a metaphysical war in which man's metaphysical future was involved. It was not so much a struggle of good versus evil as a struggle between evil—bourgeois capitalism, white imperialism, American racism—a solid, compact, domineering evil, and the challengers of evil. Sartre had previously had no very specific political end in mind, except, in very broad terms, belief in the ultimate emergence of a "socialist" community of "free" men. In the mid-thirties he had taken that long-term evolution for granted. In a general way he had equated its coming with men's gradual awakening to a sense of their powers and responsibilities as they came more clearly to think in Sartrean terms and realized that men and men only made the history men suffered. But he had not attempted more specifically to connect political processes with his view of reality.

There are signs that in the late thirties Sartre's philosophical detachment no longer satisfied him. "Childhood of a Leader," the last of the stories in *The Wall*, a brilliant though schematic example of the introduction into literature of Sartrean psychoanalysis, had clear political connotations: it was anti-fascist and anti-anti-Semitic. Sartre stressed the class conditioning of his burgeoning young fascist, Lucien. True to the pattern of the ontology he was then developing, however, he laid the responsibility for each of the young man's decisions squarely at Lucien's feet. Nothing had fated the boy to become a fascist and an anti-Semite. The "cautionary tale" remained open-ended; other young men of similar origin need not fall into the same trap.

Simone de Beauvoir's *Memoirs* and the first volumes of *The Roads to Freedom* indicate that Munich had shaken Sartre out of his political quietude. Subsequent events then made it clear to him, as he later put it, that in political matters the eventual "triumph of Good over Evil" was not assured. And the spectacle of the rout of the French army which he had witnessed at first hand had alarmed him because of the moral disintegration it revealed. He envisaged a new activity and responsibility for himself as an intellectual. In point of fact, in spite of himself, he had already assumed it; he was no longer an obscure young writer and had become mentor to the young in a time that tried men's souls. Even as he was publishing his ontology, the context and direction of his thinking had changed; it was only through the ambiguity of the word "freedom" itself that the old and new frames of reference could be made to coincide. The process of self-transformation Sartre advocated had turned out to be more complex than he had at first envisaged. Events had changed him and he now in turn wanted to "change the world" and to change it according to a certain pattern. He did not want the evil he had seen to flourish. He now knew *what* it was *right* to "choose"; beyond that he had, in Plato's terms, to learn how to will what he had now chosen: political action. He wanted to evolve valid principles which would define the "right" from the "wrong" use of his freedom.

It had not before occurred to Sartre to "find himself" or others in History. When he confronted this new dimension of his experience, during the war, he had turned anew for guidance in his reflection to the works of Hegel and Marx. The Hegelian dialectic provided a general historical frame for his thought and for his rhetoric. Marx offered a method and language whereby he could gear thought to practical action in immediate political issues. Entirely different in style from the analytical *Being and Nothingness, What Is Literature?* approached the problems of the writer in 1947 from a sweeping historical perspective, and a Marxian view of society.[15] Sartre had entered a new world because he had acquired a new language. The Marxian terminology gave him an adequately rational way of dealing with the emotional discord and polarization within himself: "I still stammered confusedly in that language . . ." It provided Sartre with a method for "situating" himself in the present and within the context, not merely of French culture, but of the whole social and political fabric of European civilization. The 1947 manifesto spoke the "new language" jubilantly, and set in motion, rhetorically, the newly found Marxian historical dialectic of which Sartre was to make abundant use. Concomitantly, Sartre abandoned the novel and turned to drama, a medium suited to the representation of conflict and with a direct impact on an audience. The new language naturally conditioned the direction of Sartre's search for understanding. It led him to the investigation of social, economic, and political facts and their relation to his function as writer.

Sartre's view of his role as writer in the thirties had been Hegelian. He had not formulated it as such, but he had stated it quite explicitly in his critical essays.[16] The novelist, in relation to the novel of which he is the author, is likened to the individual in relation to the world he perceives: he organizes it purposefully. There is a crucial difference between the two. The novelist communicates his world to another; he needs the reader. The reader, through the mediation of the words the writer selects from the common language, lends his own consciousness and time to the author for the duration of the reading and re-creates the novelist's world; author and reader freely engage in the process of creation and communication. The novelist's world is an organized whole, every component of which involves personal decisions concerning the nature of human life. A novelist thus replaces the amorphous world of our immediate percepts by a coherent imaginary world that temporarily "nullifies" the other. He creates a metaphysical order. The reader, who has "lived" the story in its temporal unfolding, must then withdraw from it, and contemplate it critically for what it is, a "world view." He then perceives its explicit and implicit metaphysical structures and examines them in the light of his own understanding, the one reacting on the other, in a movement toward an ever more total, rational understanding of human reality. Novelist and critic, through the mediation of the novel, are then reciprocally engaged in furthering the Hegelian movement of the human mind toward greater understanding at the high level of art and metaphysics. Sartre had felt no further need then to justify his chosen activity as a novel-writer: In those terms there could hardly be a more appropriate example of creative freedom and responsibility than to write a novel. This was what Sartre was doing at the time. But between 1945–1947 he changed his sights.

"I wanted to show," he said of *The Words*, "how a man can move from literature considered as sacred, to an action considered as the action of an intellectual." The 1947 manifesto marks a personal moment of transition in that "passage." And political efficacy takes precedence over literature. A writer no longer "communicates," he "reveals," not *his vision* but the *real* world.

Though Sartre stubbornly opposed the materialistic conception of history, five years after the publication of *Being and Nothingness* little in fact had remained of his ontology. He defined himself now as a man with a social purpose, a function, and, in fact, an essence. . . . He situated himself with some satisfaction as a petit-bourgeois intellectual. His "split consciousness" or inner discord took on a new meaning as an "alienation" for which society could be held responsible. He could then redefine his role as a man whose immediate task as writer was to disclose to his bourgeois readers the truth regarding their social condition and their complicities in the oppressive class structure. He formulated the program of *Les Temps modernes* in this perspective, generalizing it as mandatory for all writers in France at the time, with his usual uncompromising readiness to devise universal principles.

It was clear that a prosecutor had appeared under the mask of the implacable "scientific" analyst of the social scene. Sartre now gave free reign to his moral bent, but he also now applied it to real events and people, fixing responsibilities and defining motivations. He was genuinely, totally involved in a double project: to fight for social justice and simultaneously to deny the narrowly Marxist view of historical determinism. And he had also integrally engaged his own future and personality in his enterprise. The political arena could be, in Sartrean terms, "the instrument of his success" by being the "instrument of his defeat." That is to say that through his action as an intellectual he would prepare the destruction of the social structures that favored his own activity as writer and so pave the way for radical changes in society and in man's psyche; and make the kind of human being Sartre was, obsolete. The sacrificial role now replaced the messianic. It too was to disappear.

"I am an intellectual," he wrote in 1967, "not a politician. . . . My duty as an intellectual is to think, to think without restriction. . . . I must set no limits within myself and I must let no limits be set for me."[17] In the early sixties, Sartre again frequently and almost defensively circumscribed the intellectual to the realm of thought. He was explicit on that point in the interviews he gave to explain why he had refused the Nobel Prize: "A writer who adopts political, social or literary positions *must act only* with the means that are his—the written word."[18] Sartre's "Presentation" of *Les Temps modernes* in October, 1945, and his *What Is Literature?* in 1947, had been rather differently slanted. In style, both pieces fall halfway between Sartre's former analytic-demonstrative rhetoric and the equally demonstrative "progressive-regressive" dialectic he was to adopt in the future. Both, too, are peppered with aphorisms designed to become the passwords which they promptly became. "To speak is to act." "The committed writer knows that speech is action." "I disclose a situation by my project to change it." "Speech is a certain phase of action and is not understandable outside action." In those years Sartre preferred the immediacy and directness of impact suggested by the word "speech" to the reflective distance conveyed in his later use of "the written word." Speech was action.

In later years, at the time of the Merleau-Ponty article, Sartre described his own political thinking in the mid-forties as "confused." This is more than apparent in his rhetoric. "By taking sides in the singularity of our epoch we finally accede to the eternal and it is our task as writers to give a sense of the eternal values implicated in social or political debates." "Man . . . is an absolute; but in his time, in his environment, on earth." "It is not because our words mirrored a few skeletal principles empty enough and meaningless enough to pass from one century to the next that we shall be absolutes, but because we shall have fought passionately in our time, because we shall passionately have loved it and have accepted to perish entirely with it." "In brief, our intention is to help produce certain changes in the society around us" by changing "the social condition of man" and "the conception he has of himself." In 1945, the shift to the "new language" had not quite been completed; Sartre was using it more freely in 1947. But the confusions were still there.

When, in the 1947 essay, Sartre had proceeded to survey whole sections of French literature in terms of a schematic sociological view of the evolution of French society over the centuries—and of the writer's "condition" within that society—it was not clear which of the two, society or literature, was to be held responsible for those literary traits which, though they were presented as "sociological," were obviously unpalatable to Sartre. Upon these he threw a kind of moral onus. The closer Sartre came to the twentieth century the more Sartre's ire rose against those "singing birds," the bourgeois writers, his contemporaries or near contemporaries. Proust, who after all had been a "committed" Dreyfusard, was attacked for his "analytic" approach to his characters; Flaubert, because he had not intervened in 1871 against the murderous repression of the commune, was held responsible and charged with complicity in that event. Voltaire, in contrast, was "saved" because he had denounced the injustices suffered by individuals like the Protestant, Calas; and Gide—though this was only a reprieve—was exonerated from the general indictment because he had taken a position against the exploitation by the French of the Chad and Congo.

Social commitment apparently, but only on occasion, cleansed a writer from the original sin of analytic bourgeois thinking and made his work as writer more valuable. Sartre characteristically paid no attention to the long procession of "involved" literary men that had wound its way throughout history, in France as elsewhere. Since the Dreyfus case they had not been lacking. The Russian Revolution in turn had motivated others, to say nothing of the Spanish Civil War, and outstandingly the war that had barely just ended. Sartre's "singing birds" were then rather elusive though rhetorically amusing beings. But Sartre's intent was clear. In the political postwar chaos, Sartre was asking French writers to take the lead in shaping rational frames of reference that could serve as guides toward critiques of political decision-making. The arbitrariness of his arguments and their pretentiousness could not obscure the timeliness of the appeal.

What predominated in the manifesto was a sense of purpose and exhilaration at the prospect of a collective and dynamic participation in the world of practical politics. What spoiled it was the self-righteousness. But only in the context of the moment and of Sartre's own intellectual history can the belated impact of Marx, and even more perhaps of the Marxian terminology upon Sartre, make any sense. It was, after all, only a few years earlier, in 1941, that in the United States Edmund Wilson's *To the Finland Station* had provided a thoughtful introduction to the nature and development of the revolutionary tradition in Europe and to Marx's contribution to its social themes. To be sure, in 1941 and the succeeding years, Sartre was in no position to benefit from such a book. But the thirties had witnessed a thorough debate on Marxist thought and methods of analysis: its strengths and contradictions; its various interpretations and deviations as Lenin took over and the Russian Revolution followed its course, with Stalin in turn replacing Lenin.

But Sartre in the thirties had been working at the opposite end of the philosophical spectrum. The ambiguities of Communist tactics had not interested him and he had shrugged aside the concepts behind them. The simplified Communist credo he at that time rejected, posited the dependency of mind on matter; this was, for him at that time, the heresy par excellence, in absolute contradiction with his own premises, and he fought it in no uncertain terms; twenty years later, he would still be struggling to discredit it as a misreading of the Marxian text.

But, for the left, in France, as Sartre saw it in the forties, it had become imperative to master the Marxian method of analysis and view of society, if one wished to enter the field of practical politics. With that future in mind, Sartre and Merleau-Ponty had engaged, during the war years, in a study in depth of Hegel and Marx. Sartre has much in common with Marx: the truculence; the passion for vast syntheses; the power to animate abstractions,[19] to personify them and make them come to life; the intellectual intransigence and vigor; the almost frightening capacity to absorb the most arid studies; the tendency to tackle problems on so vast a scale that the work remains unfinished; the superhuman capacity for work, and the propensity that Edmund Wilson pointed out in Marx, to develop minor analyses "to inordinate lengths . . . out of all proportion" to the importance of the topic itself. After 1945, many of Sartre's formulations were almost literal translations of Marx. What Sartre did not have was Marx's insight into the functioning of political and economic institutions or Engels' experience and powers of observation. He remained, essentially, a moralist.

His view of the functioning of society, like his view of the masses, was to remain abstract to the very end, scholastically acquired in intensive reading, strait-jacketed in obsolete language, and immobilized. *Being and Nothingness*, in the phenomenological-existentialist perspective, had brought its share of new insights. In sociological theory, Sartre often floundered badly, caught in the conceptual frame of the past. And his early rejection of Freud was crippling.[20] There was, besides, one vast sphere in which his knowledge lagged disastrously: the sphere of modern science. Many of the questions he raised were real questions; the manner of the asking and the language adopted led to many dead ends.

What Is Literature? in one of its aspects is a hasty transferral to the realm of literature—a field that hardly interested Marx himself—of some of the more sweeping and dubious Marxian concepts. Sartre had welded together two different terminologies, absorbing Marx's sociological concepts within his own elastic frame. Marx had furnished him what he lacked, a link between the cultural activities in which he was engaged and the political sphere which he wanted to penetrate; and Marx offered a justification for Sartre's dislike for bourgeois values and bourgeois ethics.

The basic patterns of *Being and Nothingness* were subsumed in the definition of the conflict that took place in each human being between the static "being-in-itself" and the dynamic drive of the "being-for-itself" to transcend the constraining static boundaries, to manifest itself as freedom. In society, Sartre founded personal relationships on the premise of another inevitable conflict: the conflict of each with all others, arising from "the look" that objectifies and alienates. The dialectical Marxian movement of mankind toward freedom and a classless society could be equated with the ontological freedom of Sartrean man; class and race antagonisms could be understood as collective enactments of the Sartrean drama of the "look." Individual self-awareness could correspond to a clearly conceived class consciousness. The "end" of History would then be the emergence, within a universal classless society, of Sartrean man, conscious of his human freedom and his human responsibility. The "authentic" Sartrean man's options and acts would then, logically, coincide with the underlying dynamic in the dialectical march of History as it moved toward its end: freedom for all mankind. Sartre could then define the establishment of the socialist state as "*the* human project," a neat but entirely verbal resolution of the contradiction between his original view of human reality and the Marxian. What Sartre did in the interest of consistency was to turn Marx upside down again, deriving Marxian conclusions from his own Hegelian-Sartrean view of man as Freedom. What Sartre had thrown together then in *What Is Literature?* was a perfunctory sociology of literature based on Marx; and a moral critique of French writers based on his own ontology. The marriage allowed him peremptorily to situate himself and his "project" within a coherent theoretical frame.

Sartre's decision to consecrate his life to the shaping of the immediate political future of his contemporaries obviously did not in itself need the curious overlay of existential-Marxian rhetoric to justify it. It was more than understandable under the circumstances, and very generally shared. And it was certainly genuine. The sincerity of his dedication is obliquely suggested in the rather puzzling statement whereby the intellectuals of *Les Temps modernes* eloquently asserted their readiness to "perish entirely" with their epoch. Had they then sacrificed some intimations of immortality? Sartre, in *The Words*, speaks of the feeling he had as a child that he had been elected to partake in the immortality of the great writers who live on in men's minds after death. If this was the immortality forfeited, the resolve, in 1945, would seem rather belated. There had been many among Sartre's contemporaries who had in fact forfeited that possibility, with their lives, in battle. One can only take the words, as is often the case with Sartre, in a metaphoric sense. It was Sartre's way of signifying the intent of the group. They had resolved to give their time to the study of "relevant" questions of immediate practical interest which could rapidly become obsolete.[21] Their purpose was to serve the cause of freedom here and now; not to add literary works to a culture about to reach its end, in its present form at least.

Nothing in the project itself made a commitment of this kind mandatory for all writers, except its purely verbal relation with Sartre's philosophical premises, which authorized Sartre's equation of moral integrity with mandatory political positions. One can easily detect here the fallacy of so many Sartrean arguments. Sartre simply overlooked the purely speculative character of his own premises, and the Sartrean "puisque," ("since") was put to work. Thus, "since" freedom is the inescapable human reality and can be achieved for all men only in the classless society, then to oppose the dynamic movement of history toward that end is to be guilty of sinning against humanity. The circularity of the logic is evident. In Sartre's hands the supposedly impersonal dialectical process had acquired personal connotations. Sartre had already described the individual human being as totally responsible for what he made of himself. The individual now also bore the responsibilities for all the injustices perpetrated over the face of the world. It was the intent of *Les Temps modernes* that no one could claim the innocence of ignorance. Sartre had reinvented original sin, doubled in spades, for the middle class at least: metaphysically, and in terms of the class struggle. Hence Sartre's sweeping indictments of others and the contemptuous overtones that so easily mar his polemics. Hence too the shotgun declarations such as: "My class is the enemy of mankind."

Why it was that Sartre so often judged that he and he alone was in possession of the light and in a position to disclose to "others," presumably stumbling in voluntary darkness, the real image of their plight can only be explained by the purely personal idiosyncrasy which *The Words* attempts to explain, the Romantic inflation of the "I." It ultimately limited Sartre's efficaciousness in the practical political sphere where he so optimistically had hoped to make his presence felt. In the long run it was not so much because of his ideology that he was called upon to take sides with many other writers in the innumerable issues that troubled Western consciences in the next years. If he was called upon, because of his status as philosopher and writer, it was because he responded generously whenever he saw fit. At first his determination to effectively influence events gave his literary work a new impetus. His aim as writer had first been to fuse the writer's literary creations with the philosopher's rational view of human life. Although he was not immediately aware of it, his leap into the political arena —with its bitter battles of ideas, the ambiguities of action, and uncertain outcomes—gave substance to his greatest literary achievement—his theater. There the powerful and conflicting images that lurked in the ontology and had come to life in the crucial Resistance years took shape and substance in dramatic stage confrontations. On stage, ideology and imagination were set free from the constraints of reality.

In brief, in the discouraging aftermath of war, Sartre's 1947 appeal had been tonic for himself and for his readers. It was an invitation to leave the past behind and look to the future. It had the ring of the evangelical summons to the paralytic: "Pick up your bed and walk"; and it shook a generation of young intellectuals out of their despair. Nineteen hundred forty-eight and forty-nine are the years when Sartre's influence in France reached its height. But his position soon yielded a crop of dilemmas. The first, for Sartre himself, was Sartre's own inherent distaste of and incapacity for concrete political action. It was one thing to diagnose—with most of the political left—that if the non-Communist French Left were to prove effective it must give up its traditional division and find a common platform. It was another to create the platform and fight for its survival. Sartre had no practical sense of political maneuvering. He was not a Lenin and no match for General de Gaulle in the contest for men's votes. He left the "Rassemblement Démocratique Révolutionnaire" without putting up a fight, in a characteristic mood of moral indignation and ill-concealed relief. And characteristically he explained the failure retrospectively by the iron laws of History. Freedom and necessity had begun to play strangely personal roles in his justificatory system. Always lucid in the long run, Sartre now developed the intolerable unease that exploded in his "conversion."

When and if Sartre's "Notebooks" are published, schol-

ars will no doubt unravel the intellectual crisis that followed the defeat of Sartre's single attempt to engage in
positive political participation on the national scale. If one
can judge from the extracts Simone de Beauvoir gives us,
it is obvious that Sartre must often have been plunged in a
rather equivocal debate with himself and was engaged in
a fake moral dilemma. The formulation of the dilemma is
quasi-religious in its language, starting from premises that
are in fact articles of faith. "I know that there is no salvation for mankind other than the liberation of the working-
class. I know that the interests of the spirit[22] are with the
proletariat, but the proletariat adheres to a doctrine, materialism, that destroys thought. Have I fallen into an unacceptable dilemma: either having to betray the proletariat
in order to serve truth, or betraying truth in the name of
the proletariat?"[23] Sartre was still for himself the center
of reference of a universe he posited abstractly in Hege-
lian-Marxist terms; and furthermore, he still spoke as if he
were in solitary charge of the fate of "mankind" embodied
in a singular passive and gullible "proletariat."

The abstract nature of Sartre's political vision is apparent in his early postwar articles on the United States. In
the first articles Sartre, fresh from the Liberation, sees
America in contrast with Europe and, in terms of his ontology, as a country open to the future. America was then
for Sartre a symbolic America, hence a kind of dynamic
"being-for-itself," in contrast to the morass of French tra-
ditionalism. Within a couple of years, the United States
became, in Sartrean polemic, the evil colossus of North
American capitalism, the single greatest threat to the liberation of the masses. This symbolic activation of vast
entities dramatizes Sartre's political positions and insights. Whole groups periodically pass from a dynamic
liberating role to the negative status of "being-in-itself":
the French proletariat, the French Communist Party, "or-

thodox" Marxism, and even one of Sartre's exemplary men—Castro—in turn change roles as they appear to Sartre to betray the historic role and mission he ascribed to them. With the Korean war, American power became in Sartrean eyes the single greatest obstacle in the way of the "salvation of mankind" and Sartre, in a sense, then wrote America off the map, a curiously unrealistic attitude.

The polarization of "good" and "evil" forces en bloc that animates Sartre's plays when translated into pronouncements concerning the complex, changing course of history, can prove, and sometimes was, misleading. Events have frequently "overtaken" Sartre "from behind," to use his own language. As the Cold War developed, drawing France into the American orbit, Sartre's hope of a socialist revolution in France receded. He had formulated a rational theory of action, logically derived from his premises. In the postwar years he found that the political reality had temporarily blocked the movement of History defined in the Hegelian-Marxian dialectic: both in the West—with its ever more powerful technology—and in the East, with its established dogmatic ideology. Sartre judged that he could not achieve his ends within the French frame and the parliamentary process.

In France his frustration took the form of purely negative attitudes and constant calls to revolution, to the violent overthrow of the existing institutions. Sartre then redefined his commitment in new terms. The key to his decision is buried in the conclusion of his Saint Genet, "A Prayer for the good use of Genet," and the outcome is dramatized in The Devil and the Good Lord.[24] In Saint Genet, at the end of his long and exhausting analysis of Genet's personality and life, Sartre, in an unexpected, dramatic development, recalls Bukharin as the Soviet counterpart of Genet. He describes both men as impotent rebels who pitted themselves as subjects against the decrees of their society and yet had to accept that society's judgment for all time, judging themselves according to the maxims of their society. Sartre's own involvement in this analysis is obvious. The tone of his writing becomes charged with the lyrical eloquence of a Bossuet. He draws up a list of our "derelictions" patterned on the liturgical confession of sins: ". . . since the event transforms, not only in history but even within our family life, our best intentions into criminal designs, since we are never sure of not becoming traitors in retrospect, since we continually fail to communicate, to love, to make ourselves loved, and since each defeat makes us feel our solitude, since we dream sometimes that we shall efface our criminal singularity by confessing it humbly (like Bukharin) and sometimes by asserting it defiantly (like Genet) in the vain hope of assuming it in its entirety . . ."

This rhetoric continues on and on, culminating in an exhortation to consider Genet's plight—Genet, whom he transforms into a Christ figure "tied to the stake" by us, the "just." Here, Sartre absolves himself of guilt and, speaking in the name of History, indicts our age for its incapacity to transcend its contradictions and to create a better future for all men. The religious overtones, the solemn intimations of disaster betray Sartre's distress as the Korean crisis seemed to foreshadow a catastrophic world conflagration. Sartre's optimism had been short-lived. In 1947 he had defined his intent "to act in history and on history to effect a synthesis of the metaphysical and moral absolute with the hostile and friendly world." He now, in the light of the Korean war, questioned the feasibility of his project:

> Today revolutions are impossible, the most bloody and
> inept war threatens us, the possessing classes are not very
> sure of their rights and the working-class is in retreat; we

see injustice more clearly than ever and we have neither the means nor the will to correct it; meanwhile the lightning progress of science gives the future centuries an obsessive immediacy: men will go to the moon, they'll create life perhaps. Those masked men who will succeed us and who will have knowledge of everything, whom we can't even glimpse, we feel they are judging us; for those future eyes, whose look haunts us, our epoch will be an object. And a guilty one. . . . (p. 549)

Sartre now had moved theoretically from "our epoch" into the world of the future, among its judges, their interpreter and spokesman.

As he had done in *Being and Nothingness*, Sartre in 1952 announced in *Saint Genet* a solution which he was to present in the future: "What resource is left us? There is one I see and which I shall present later; but the solution commonly offered is to settle down into this moment in history and to want it in spite of everything with the stubbornness of the vanquished; people invent sophisms to maintain principles they know are about to disappear and truths they know will turn into errors." (p. 549) Sartre has not to date offered his solution; but Sartre's play, *The Devil and the Good Lord*, and Sartre's "conversion" indicate its nature, which is to give up the Romantic stance that makes of the self a center of reference and to merge one's individuality with that of a group in the hazards of a dubious battle on the side of the dispossessed. It is the position taken by Goetz, the hero of the play. Sartre had in fact buried his ontology or at least replaced his central concept: man's total freedom and total responsibility had turned into a horrified sense of the individual's impotence in regard to the forces of History. "One is not saved by politics any more than by literature," Sartre was later to conclude.[24a] Saved? from whom or what?

This is all the more startling since the avowed intent of Sartre in the *Saint Genet* was to "show the limits of psychoanalytic interpretations and of the Marxist explication and demonstrate that freedom alone can account for a human being in totality . . ." The thesis had turned into its antithesis; *The Devil and the Good Lord* possibly pointed in the direction of the synthesis, opening the way, perhaps, for the *Critique of Dialectical Reason* on which Sartre started work in the early fifties. These are the years when the ubiquitous powers designated by the pronoun *On*—"they"—became an active and evil force in Sartrean polemics. In one article after the other "they" impose reprehensible patterns of behavior on the French nation. These are the years, too, when Sartre spoke of "History" somewhat from the same point of view as Trotsky: History acts, selects its agents, its moments, its own path. Sartre's new concern with a "praxis" was preparing a new critical "turnabout" and complexity in his thinking.

With Genet as mediator, Sartre had stepped down from the empyrean in which, intellectually, he had dwelt. Sartre had once rejected Freud because Freud's conclusions concerning the human psyche ran counter to Sartre's premises. He now considered Freud anew and studied his own complexes as a product of social conditioning. "How did I become what I am?"—the question tentatively answered in *The Words* seems at this time to have taken precedence over others in his mind. And, having relinquished all absolutes, he relinquished little by little the overwhelming sense of guilt fostered by his philosophical stance. He had relinquished his responsibility to History. Marxism, in Sartre's version of it, was now accepted as defining his mental horizon. He admitted its relativity. His project in *Saint Genet* had clearly been to synthesize and transcend those two great conflicting modern theories of human reality, Freudianism and Marxism; to fuse them and surpass them in the vast development of an original synthesis. He now reversed the movement: he proposed to insert his "ideology" as the dynamic impetus that kept History moving along its preordained Marxian course. He might, he hoped, thereby succeed in setting up a complete modern anthropology. His *Flaubert* is a kind of trial run.

In this perspective, Sartre's anger at the trivialities and ineptness of French politics and politicians in 1952 is only a minor event, the sudden upsurge of his exasperation at his impotence. Stripped of its portentous language, his subsequent political option is absolutely logical. Given his premises, the only course left open to him was to get the revolutionary dialectic on the move again. He could do this only by becoming not, as heretofore, the "bad conscience" of the bourgeois—which was inconsequential—but the bad conscience of the Communist leadership. Sartre then accepted the Socialist world as the limiting horizon of his action and, in that world, his own role as participating antagonist. He had learned at long last, as he said, that he was inside, not outside society: "In *The Words*, I describe how I have come to realize that I am a member of society, of society in motion."[25]

This takes us full circle back to the question of commitment. In practical terms, Sartre's actual influence on day to day politics in France can be seen as almost nil; the tactics he advocated were consistently ignored by the voting public. On broader issues involving demonstrations of opinion he hacked out his own path, abused or hailed as the case might be. And he made his "errors": "Sartre, 1950, justifying the North Korean aggression, refusing to take a position on the Russian labor camps, assimilating in the proletarian countries opposition to rebellion. Sartre, 1952, leaning more and more toward Stalin. Sartre, 1954, observing in a journey to the U.S.S.R. a 'complete freedom of criticism.' Sartre, 1956, suddenly awakened by the Hungarian revolution"[26]—suddenly and reluctantly. This is a factual but partial summary. For there is also the painful reassessment and rethinking after each discomfiture, the "totalization," as Sartre came to say, and the new leap ahead.

There is also the blazingly angry Sartre of the Algerian War years, whose partisanship knew no moderation; until recently, the almost slavish admirer of Fidel Castro, the defender of Lumumba, and the strident supporter of the call to racial violence of Frantz Fanon. It has been in the sphere of culture rather than in the sphere of politics that he has made his impact. His ventures into the field of actual politics had rapidly taken him into an impasse, a typical experience that men of the Resistance underwent everywhere in Europe:

> The collapse of France [to a whole generation of writers], a totally unexpected event, had emptied, from one day to the next, the political scene of their country . . . and they who as a matter of course had never participated in the official business of the Third Republic were sucked into politics as though with the force of a vacuum. It did not last long. After a few short years they were liberated from what they had originally thought to be a "burden" and thrown back into what they now knew to be the weightless irrelevance of their personal affairs. . . . And if they refused . . . they could only return to the old empty strife of conflicting ideologies which after the defeat of the common enemy once more occupied the political arena to split the former comrades-in-arms into innumerable cliques . . . and to engage them in endless polemics and intrigues of a paper war.[27]

Camus attempted to limit his involvement in the "paper war." Sartre did not escape it, but he fought to give it meaning and to lift it out of its parochial triviality.

This he did for an elite, as the roster of the men he influenced shows: Francis Jeanson, Frantz Fanon, Régis Debray, to mention only a few controversial but respected figures who took the leap from theory into violent action that Sartre himself was never able to take. It is a curious fact that Sartre has seldom detected new trends or initiated actions. They were brought to his attention by others, or belatedly by events. Yet time and time again it was he who brought the question, in its most general implications, out into the open: anti-Semitism, "négritude," the colonial syndrome; the conflicts, contradictions, and evasions of the Western conscience.

Essentially, Sartre's commitment had first been, and remained, to rethink the world in order to reform it. In *What Is Literature?*, with the war just behind him, he had defined as "tragic" the world's opacity to reason: a typically abstract declaration after the turmoil. He wanted a rational reordering and a synthesis of our fragmented knowledge into a single coherent mold: a wild ambition, doomed to failure and which, in the onrush of change, was exhausting. Sartre in this realm strikes one as the last thinker of the nineteenth century, as he is in his view of human time as a vast linear flow directed toward some end; a flow which he struggled to encompass and arrest within a single conceptual frame. He had committed himself in his role as twentieth-century philosopher, to "exist" his time and grasp it fully as he himself experienced it. This involution and intellectual battle blinded him, at times, to the simple necessities, griefs, and joys of human living. He lacked Camus's instinctive sense of the realities at issue, and his healthy cynicism.

It was apparently only in the fifties—if we are to believe him—that Sartre, who had lived through the years
of Occupation, discovered people on this earth went hungry. And it was through a Russian film, Tarkovsky's
"Childhood of Ivan," that he learned, late in life, that the
dialectic of history did not redeem the shattering of a
child's life: "The death of a child in hatred and despair:
Nothing, not even future communism will redeem that. . . .
The society of men progresses toward its goal . . . and
yet the little dead child, a tiny straw swept aside by history, poses a question with no answer."[27a] This was a question Camus had posed in *The Just Assassins*. Because of
Sartre's abstraction from the drudgery and servitude and
limitations of ordinary men, although he had committed
himself to defend the "oppressed," he had, in fact, always
been removed from their way of life, their claim to their
small share of happiness here and now, whatever the
promise for tomorrow.

It was Sartre's dedication to the elucidation of theory
through experience and vice versa that ultimately and
belatedly brought him to diagnose one of the crucial
phenomena—perhaps the most crucial—in our political
history: the breakup of Marxist orthodoxy. Because of his
effort to master Marxian terminology and Marx's vast
body of works, and to engage in strenuous debate with
intellectuals in the Socialist countries, Sartre wielded an
influence in the rising wave of conflict within Marxism
itself. He may indeed in some measure have set the dialectic moving again—although perhaps not according to
the pattern he had thought.

In the last years, Sartre, in France, has been attacked
as a thinker, in particular by the structuralists who study
the relationships established within formal systems, from
pluralistic angles. The student rebellion fascinated him;

and left him behind. He has attempted to catch up with it by giving the prestige of his approval to the extremist group of the "enragés." It was characteristically Sartre himself who, in regard to the students, made the most pungent criticism of his own intellectual odyssey. "What is interesting, in your action," he concluded after an interview with Cohn-Bendit, "is that it puts imagination in power. . . . We were conditioned in such a way that we have a precise notion of what is possible and what is not possible. . . . You have a much richer imagination. . . . Something has surged out of you that astonishes, upsets, disowns everything our society has done and what it is today. It is what I would call the extension of the field of possibilities."[28] This comes as an echo of Camus's earlier words.

Sartre's single a priori projection of the future under the aegis of Marx had indeed narrowed the field of possibilities. In a world recalcitrant to any single intellectual mold, it accounts perhaps for his appeals to violence, his dreams of a revolution somehow modeled on the Terror. Perhaps, too, what his fascination with violence by proxy expresses is Sartre's deep-lying aspiration to wrench himself out of time and its conflicts into the world of absolutes, to stop the process of change even as he grasps it. In the last analysis, perhaps, to escape death. In *Being and Nothingness* he elided the confrontation with death; then jumped beyond it under the severe eyes of the "masked men" of the future, into the mainstream of History. He detests the here and now and he has not as yet completed the movement that, in his terms, will allow his "judges" to grasp his life as a whole. It can be grasped now, in any case, only as a process. No assertion Sartre makes can be taken as final, for it most surely will later appear as the ground for one of those counterassertions that keep his mind working. "Commitment" for Sartre is the commitment to keep abreast of inner and outer change. And there is little point in placing him in contradiction with himself. The contradictions are part of the dynamics of his dialectic.

In the latest phase of his evolution, Sartre gave a new and an old definition of commitment: "The writer is committed when he plunges to the very depths of himself with the intent to disclose, not his individuality, but his person in the complex society that conditions and supports him. That is what constitutes commitment and not the writing of opportunistic works. . . . Art is as always the presentation of the world as it would be if it were taken in charge by human freedom."[29] For the Trotskyite definition of 1947—"literature is in essence the subjectivity of a society in permanent revolution"—Sartre has substituted another: to write is "to disclose and make real the content of the tragic in contemporary life." The "tragic"? The tragic situation is the situation in which the conflict cannot be resolved even by a dialectic. Fate made a belated entry into the Sartrean world.

Commitment for Sartre was a word that like all the others of which he makes use, took on different connotations as Sartre pursued his search for understanding. In each case nonetheless it was *his* task and *his* understanding that were in the balance. That there were other possibilities and other options, Sartre was for many years reluctant to admit. And he only at long last came to terms with his own "historicity." A man in transition from one epoch to another, despite his intransigence and the drastic intellectual games he sometimes played—or perhaps because of them—he carried along with him into a new era the self-questionings and intellectual passions of the past. Sartre's onslaught against tradition in all its forms is itself traditional in all *its* forms. It was not to reality that he looked but to words, and the words often came to him from the past. And that is perhaps why, despite all the effort to define the "praxis" of which he made so much, he could still, in 1960, declare with genuine sincerity: "From my boyhood up to now I have known what it is to be completely without any power of action."[30] And, he added, the here and now was always a condition he wanted to leave behind. But the here and now is the ground of all action. Only in the writing of his *Flaubert* did he seem to reach a kind of serenity. And it involved a retrospective excursion into the past, not the future. Sartre, in 1971, seemed to have taken up with deep satisfaction and was intent on bringing to completion the task of historical biographer which Roquentin, in *Nausea*, had so abruptly abandoned.

Notes to Chapter 6

1. In French, the word "histoire" means story, fictional or real, and history. "L'histoire" of a man is his biography. The interaction of our collective "history" and our individual "stories" became a central preoccupation for Sartre, who has rather freely extrapolated his theories from one to the other, and attempted to rationalize the extrapolation.

2. Frederick Hoffman, "Mortality and Modern Literature" in *The Meaning of Death*, ed. Herman Feifel (New York: McGraw-Hill Paperbacks, 20347, 1965), p. 151.

3. H. Stuart Hughes, *Consciousness and Society*. The Reorientation of European Social Thought 1890–1930 (New York: Alfred A. Knopf, Inc., 1958), p. 38.

4. *Critique de la raison dialectique* (Gallimard, 1960), p. 24.

5. This is the weakness in Sartre's re-creation of such figures as Baudelaire, Genet, and even Flaubert, to whom in various degree he abritrarily "lends" a "subjectivity" and inner history that correspond to *his* psychological theories and turn them into representatives of a Sartrean "species" with a fully explicated, morally evaluated, and "judged" Sartrean personality.

6. Interview in "Le Nouvel Observateur," June 26, 1968.

6a. *La Force des Choses* (Paris: Gallimard), p. 17.

7. Tired of the misery to which Roman exactions have reduced his people, Bariona is in revolt against further submission to Rome, and against the news of the birth of the Messiah which he considers as a further incentive to a slavish acceptance of the intolerable situation. But when he senses the tremendous force of the people's hope as they gather around the child, he accepts it as a potentially liberating force and organizes an armed resistance against the Romans which enables the child to escape the massacre of the Innocents. Bariona already has many points in common with Goetz, the hero of *The Devil and the Good Lord*.

8. Sartre was in complete sympathy with the Resistance and from time to time contributed articles to underground reviews. He was adamantly opposed to the Vichy regime, intellectually, and was a fierce denouncer of the collaborationist intellectuals. He took no active part in resistant activities.

9. "La République du Silence" (1944), *Situations*, III, 11–14.

10. Preface to *Aden Arabie*, *Situations*, IV, p. 133, 136. Sartre frequently passes from the "I" (as accuser) to the "we," thence to the "they," as he does here, an example of oblique disengagement. The phrase "then Marshall came" is a typical Sartrean play on Boileau's "Enfin Malherbe vint" known to all schoolchildren in France. Sartre makes frequent use of this play on catch phrases. His work, literary and philosophical, is shot through with verbal reminiscences, used ironically, directly, or unconsciously, produced from his vast reading. One of the concluding sentences of

The Words, for instance, "rien dans les mains rien dans les poches" (nothing in my hands, nothing up my sleeves) —is a direct quote from a 1945 article on Sartre by Claude Roy. This article appears in *Descriptions Critiques* (Paris: Gallimard, 1949), p. 163.

11. It is curious to follow Sartre's emotional reactions to the masses as these are symbolized in his metaphors: "an enormous somber body which lived Marxism"; a "heavy presence" or "dark ocean" on "the horizon of the mind." And the ironically cutting indignation when the masses failed to act as theory indicated: "the proletariat, the invincible force that pronounces judgment against capitalism, had taken the day off." The French expression "être de sortie" applies to servants. That there is a correspondence between Sartre's feelings about history and his sense of the masses is also apparent in some of his images: "the obscure weight of history," "the ocean of history," "History advances masked." His uneasiness with both is evident.

12. Joseph P. Fell, III, has studied the question thoroughly in his book, *Emotion in the Thought of Sartre,* to which I here refer (New York: Columbia University Press, 1965), pp. vii–viii.

13. Emotional behavior in Sartre's terms is one of the modes of action whereby people attempt to bridge the chasm between their subjective wish and the objective situation by negating the second. The short stories in *The Wall* are all descriptions of "magical" Sartrean behavior. The schemas of at least three of these and most ostensibly of the first, "The Wall," were drawn from case histories presented by one of Sartre's professors of psychology, to illustrate his own theories. See S. Braun, "Source and Psychology of Sartre's *Le Mur,*" *Criticism,* Winter, 1965, pp. 45-51.

14. A critic has noted that Sartre "exists"—to use the term in its transitive, existentialist sense—political questions only through the mediation of indignation. This was not true in the early forties; it became ever truer with the frustrations of the fifties. Actually, Sartre's explosions of verbal vio-

lence seemed by the mid-sixties to have considerably decreased.

15. It is, within its context, comparable to Lenin's *What Is to be Done?*, 1902.

16. For a further discussion of Sartre's esthetic theories see Eugene Kaelin, *An Existential Esthetic* (University of Wisconsin Press), 1962.

17. *Playboy* interview, May, 1965, 69–76.

18. *New York Review of Books*, December 6, 1964. The most peremptory statement of this position came in a virulent attack upon a woman journalist who drew Sartre's wrath when she mildly pointed out Simone de Beauvoir's purely cerebral "commitment" as judge and censor of others.

19. Edmund Wilson speaks of the "mythopoeic creations" of Marx and of their hold on the imagination. "The abstractions of German philosophy convey in German, through their capitalized solidity, almost the impression of primitive gods. They are substantial, and yet they are a kind of pure beings; they are abstract and yet they mix . . ."

20. In contrast, within the same conceptual framework, one could quote Herbert Marcuse's observations on present social trends, his up-dating of Marx, controversial though it be, for example, in his *Essay on Liberation*, Beacon Press, Boston, 1969. Sartre's first rejection of Freud is typical: he did not confront the facts described. He disliked a conception that offered no ground for a dialectic: so he rejected it. And, Simone de Beauvoir tells us in *The Prime of Life*, "Sartre forged the concept of bad faith to account for what goes on in the subconscious."

21. The Marxian terminology gave Sartre what he needed, the assurance that his was a rational, not a "magic," emotional decision. And it seemed to furnish a guiding principle for "rational," practical options: in all issues the cause of freedom must be defended; practically, this meant the furthering of the liberation of the proletariat. This was the first level of the "action" projected: to change social conditions. The second was to change the social awareness of the read-

ing public. In both spheres Sartre proposed to apply the critical method of analysis that would remove the uncertainties and hazards of action. A careful sociological analysis of each political issue would lead to the logical inference of the action best suited to promote the liberation of the workers and the advent of a free society. It was the task of the writer to apply the method, diagnose the trends, and indicate the decisions to be made.

22. Clearly the Hegelian "esprit."

23. *La Force des Choses*, p. 280.

24. Although *Saint Genet* was published after *The Devil and the Good Lord*, it was written before the play. Sartre had at the time accepted Merleau-Ponty's justification of the trials of the Stalin regime in terms of the dialectic of History. Sartre's analysis assumes that the trial was fair and the verdict pronounced in good faith. This casts a good deal of light on the theoretical nature of the argument, which is logical within its premises, but nullified by facts in this instance. *Saint Genet*, pp. 548–49.

24a. *Le Monde*, April 18, 1964.

25. *Playboy*, May, 1965, pp. 69–76.

26. Alfred Fabre-Luce, "Un barbare parmi nous," *Aurore*, March 21, 1964. This is a typical rightist position. But the facts remain. Sartre's 1954 position was even stronger and typically Sartrean in its abstract doctrinairism: "The freedom to criticize is total in Russia. Contact is broad, open and easy as possible. In Russia a man is aware of the constant progress of his own life as well as social life. Intellectual and collective interests coincide." *Libération*, July 20, 1954.

27. Hannah Arendt, *Between Past and Future* (New York: Viking Compass Book, 1968), pp. 3–4.

27a. *Lettres françaises*, Dec. 26–Jan. 1, 1964.

28. *Le Nouvel Observateur*, Lundi, May 20, 1968.

29. *Clarté*, No. 55, March–April, 1964.

30. *The Reporter*, September 1, 1960.

7.

The Designs of Violence: The End and the Means

In the confusion into which life was now thrown in the cities, human nature always rebelling against the law and now its master, gladly showed itself ungoverned in passion above respect for justice, and the enemy of all superiority.

THUCYDIDES

My world is an apple. I cut it in two: good men-bad men.

THE JUDGE (*The Balcony* by Jean Genet)

It was not by chance that Camus's first two fictional characters bring violent destruction down upon others and eventually upon themselves: Meursault because of his initial passiveness, Caligula because he deliberately apes the random violence of the cosmos. At one level, Caligula and Meursault are obviously surrogates for Camus, who indirectly reflect his inner tensions and uncertainties. They carry to extremes some of his own impulses and so put them to the test. *The Stranger* and *Caligula*, in good literary tradition, contain their own implicit critique. They seem to have not the slightest bearing on Camus's socio-political activities. Yet there is a connection; they place the same emphasis on the value of everyday life and of those personal, physical joys and human pleasures which Meursault in his prison discovers, and which keep Cherea and Scipio from giving way to Caligula's nihilism.

In those early years Camus's uncertainties, as reflected in his literary work, concerned his own way of life rather than the nature of society and how a man should act to change it. In the social sphere his position was trenchant and he felt little need to justify his actions. But in different ways both his private world, as mirrored obliquely in his literary work, and his socio-political activities were rooted in a concern not so much with metaphysical speculation as with an ethic: how can a man win or keep a certain balance and the control of his life while not denying his experience, knowledge, mind, and feelings.

Commentators have pointed out how much Camus's political outlook had in common with the view of the anarchist philosophers who have always attracted a substantial following among workers in the Mediterranean countries.[1] This is more particularly true of Camus in the thirties, although he never spelled out his position. Like the anarchists, he linked social protest to the metaphysical theme of man's insurrection against his condition, his refusal to submit to "necessity," and his urge, like Sisyphus, to cheat the gods. Like the anarchists, Camus was fiercely antiauthoritarian and disdainful of the machinery of government. He mistrusted all forms of political power and prestige and scorned abstract bureaucratic systems. And, like the anarchists, he much preferred syndicalism —the trade-union formula—to the hierarchized and centralized workers' organizations of orthodox communism. In all spheres of activity, cultural as well as political, he favored action through freely constituted groups such as his own Workers' Theater, groups which spontaneously defined their own concerns and forged their own discipline in their common endeavors.

His own personality was far from submissive and his sensitivity and background had made him aware of the variety of needs and values by which men live and which cannot be defined in terms of "economic" man. Two of the most fundamental in his eyes were those which the existentialist philosophers either overlooked or failed to take into account adequately when they made their staunch attempts to deal with the contemporary mood. The "man" Camus spoke of and worked for could not be, like Heidegger's or Sartre's, cut off from nature; Camus could not, like Sartre, concentrate all his attention on strictly interhuman relations and historical fate.

Nor is Camus's man reduced to total solitude. He does not confront, like Sartre's, only hostile and threatening "others." True, one of the dominant themes in Camus's early sketches is indeed the solitude of human beings, particularly of the old and poor, and their groping dependency on others. One remembers old Salamano in *The Stranger* and the dog he mistreats and weeps for when he loses it; and Meursault's mother who, in the old people's home when she found a friend, was ready to start life over again. For Camus's human beings, bounded by death, the only real recourse against panic is the presence of others. If human solitude is one of his themes, another concerns the moments of understanding, the bonds, the fleeting moments of insight. They clearly function in counterpoint to the plague in Camus's novel and furnish the elusive substance of some of the more striking stories of *Exile and the Kingdom,* such as "The Guest" and "The Silent Men."

Camus had grown up in the seaport of Algiers, and had

not known the solitude of the dreary working-class suburbs in large industrial cities. He had been in contact
with the variegated and colorful population that filled the
streets of Algiers in the twenties and early thirties, a population not as yet profoundly polarized by the political
tensions which were later to surface so violently. Camus's
sense of human needs and ways of life was shaped in
part by the distinctive character of that population, in the
artisan enterprises and commerce that throve on person
to person relationships and, as often as not, out in the
streets: rivalries, conflicts, alliances, loyalties, idiosyncrasies. Tempers were hot, violence quick to erupt, but feelings were spontaneous and direct; and there were simple
codes which he spelled out with a good deal of humor.
There was, too, the bond between that way of life and the
land, of which most were more or less aware. These were
the concrete human beings that the abstract word "man"
evoked for Camus. And his familiarity with them was one
of the factors that heightened his distrust of such quasi-
allegorical or sociological abstractions as "the proletariat," or "the masses." It was also from his personal experience that he had drawn the universalizing image of "the
man sentenced to death," an image that qualified his own
mental attitudes toward such existential themes as man's
confrontation with the "nothingness" of human life. The
mother he described in his early sketches "almost never
thought"; and the friend of the narrator drinks when he is
thirsty, eats when he is hungry, makes love when he feels
like it, and says "I feel better." It is the rare man, Camus
knew, who confronts that "nothingness" of human life *consciously*, although many have mute intimations of it. The
people he describes sense it only as something lurking in
the back of their lives. But the image of "the man sentenced to death"[2] is understandable to all and counters the

Caligula-like indifference of human beings to the lives of others.

At the outset, Camus proposed a way of looking at one's fellow man that minimized the differences of class, race, or whatever, something quite different from the Sartrean alienating "look." In that perspective the joys and pain of a person's life take on a kind of value and each human being is seen in his vulnerability, uniqueness, and similarity to all others. What happens within the span of each life, however trivial, counts and counts absolutely. Hence Camus's outcry against all that mutilates human beings, and that outcry establishes the link between his fictional work and his socio-political actions. It is from that view of man that Camus postulated an ethic of commitment rooted in human emotions and solidarity.

In *The Myth of Sisyphus* Camus had argued that the most lucid appraisal of the human situation was also the most likely to inspire a passionate desire to enhance life rather than to devalue it. His "absurd heroes," Don Juan, the conqueror, the actor, the creator, all live their lives with passionate single-mindedness. Passion, in a sense, is the driving force behind much of Camus's creation—the passion of Caligula, of Martha in *The Misunderstanding*, of the terrorist group in *The Just Assassins*; the passion of the rebels and revolutionaries in *The Rebel*; the dark passions of Clamence and of the "Renegade" in *The Fall* and *Exile and the Kingdom*; the murderous passion of Dostoevsky's "possessed," that so long fascinated him. Disaster, in Camus's fictional worlds, always attends the single-minded being "possessed" by a passion which develops its own irrefutable logic of unreason.

He was, Camus noted, living in a time of collective passions and implacable logic. Totalitarian in intent, both are inimical to a personal life and a free exchange between men, and, when given full rein, murderous in their effect. Camus himself was a "man of passion." One can say, I think, in brief, that it is the man of passion who, in Camus's world, is the active force, but he is also the most dangerous. Schopenhauer is not far in the background. The force Camus proposes that can best mediate between the devouring logic of passion and its destructive acts is a heightened sense of men's vulnerability and the respect for their personal sphere of life. The denial of that personal sphere, or the contempt for it, was one of the things Camus found intolerable whether in private or in public affairs, and fast developing in our society. In one of its facets, *The Plague* describes just such an invasion of all the aspects of an ordinary life by an abstract totalitarian organization—whether we see it as ideological, political, or military does not really matter. It makes little sense to object to Camus's symbol. He had not proposed to show a combat between "good men" and "bad men." He had proposed to show the gradual poisoning of the human atmosphere, such as we ourselves in the United States have lately, to some degree, been experiencing. Camus's plague awakens its rats wherever individuals become officially suspect and unacceptable to the governing powers because of their opinions on issues such as Vietnam, law and order, capitalism or socialism. We need only recall the era of Joe McCarthy, the Third Reich, and Stalin's Russia. The plague is not merely a symbol of the 1940–44 occupation. It is any slide into collective repression and regimentation. Regimentation, computer-like and abstract, was one of the threats to personal fulfillment Camus detected beneath the surface of the immediate political issues which his contemporaries and he joined in battle over. In that context, man, in Camus's eyes, might fight in a worthy cause and nonetheless be a plague-carrier. That it was hard to make that distinction in the immediate post-World War II years the various interpretations of the novel show. A "résistant" was unconditionally worthy. But a man could fight out of a Caligula-like contempt for life, or in order to impose another way of life, and not because of his opposition to a systematic reduction of human freedom as such. Historically and practically this might seem immaterial. To Camus it was a distinction that had to be made. And it was germane to his attitude regarding the question of ends and means, and of the use of violence in achieving those ends. A man in Camus's eyes might fight in the Resistance ranks while pursuing the same ends as his opponents. Hence the symbol he chose, which in itself defined the kind of commitment he wished to describe. Whether he succeeded, of course, is a matter of understanding and aesthetic taste.

"Dreams change with men," Camus noted, "but the reality of the world is our homeland." Men's dreams between 1939 and 1945 turned that reality into something grimmer than a nightmare. The words Camus used to describe it express his revulsion although their very intensity, outside the emotional ambience that inspired them, makes them sound somewhat banal. Europe became a "prison," "hell," a "charnel house." It was not to this reality that his first works had belonged, although they came out during the occupation. Sartre saw this immediately. "Amid the literary productions of its time," he wrote of *The Stranger*, "this novel was in itself a stranger. It came to us from the other side of the Equator, from across the sea. In that bitter spring[3] of the coal shortage, it spoke to us of the sun. . . ." Meanwhile, except as the deadly sun of *The Plague*, the sun had disappeared from Camus's world. It was the period when Camus really entered the political arena on the national scale. By 1944 he was no longer an unknown young man. He had participated actively in the Resistance movement and in the insurrection of Paris, and had become one of the directors of a nationally distributed paper, *Combat*, still carrying the aura of its clandestine years. In his editorials, and as one of the most prominent intellectuals in Paris, he was now called upon to take a position in the innumerable political issues—national and international—that arose in the wake of the war.

It was in this milieu that Camus met and later crossed swords with Sartre. "Jonah," one of the stories of *Exile and the Kingdom*, gives a sardonic little parody of the writer's existence—crowded out of his own life.[4] Camus deplored the almost total politicization of life. It, too, was a form of the plague.

It was then that he reached certain convictions that culminated in what was to be an unshakable commitment. They are his answer to the question of the legitimacy of political violence, whether individual or state-initiated. These are the years when, concomitantly, Camus brought out three plays—*The Misunderstanding*, *State of Siege*, and *The Just Assassins*, as well as his well-known *The Plague*, and his essay *The Rebel*; each of these works explores some facet of the question.

Camus spelled out his commitment explicitly in the first of a series of articles entitled "Neither Victims Nor Executioners," which he wrote in 1946 (*Essais*, pp. 333–31). "Having said one day that, after the experience of the last two years, I could no longer accept any truth that would put me under the obligation, direct or indirect, to condemn a man to death . . . I was told that this was Utopia; that there was no political truth that might not one day lead to that extremity, and that we must run the

risk of having to confront it and must accept the world as
it is."

Taken at its face value the commitment does appear
both utopian and irrelevant, in fact, rather unreal. In the
political atmosphere of the period, it was quite the opposite. Camus, as was his habit, sometimes to his detriment,
was practicing the drastic reduction to concrete terms of
the implications hidden beneath current political language. He was looking back two years, to 1944, the year
of the great euphoria at the time of the liberation of
France. But 1944 was also the year that had produced the
outburst of hatred which had exploded in a vast lawless
purge, only too slowly brought under control by the
courts, supported by de Gaulle's provisional government.
By conservative estimates, in 1944 alone, approximately
40,000 Frenchmen were killed and some 400,000 sent to
jail by their compatriots.[5]

Camus, a "leftist" intellectual, had shared the mystique
of the Resistance, its hopes and passions. Vichy was a
symbol for him of the deepest betrayal of all he believed
in. And he had supported the policy of the purge as necessary and just. He knew what the collaborationist collu-
sion with the Nazis had cost the underground fighters. If
a renovated France, so the argument ran, was to emerge
from the catastrophe, it must first "purge" the rotten elements that had dishonored the country. The excesses of
the purge and the blatant political use made of the
"martyrs" of the Resistance in the petty postwar tug of
war of the parties soon inspired some intellectuals to protest: Jean Paulhan, the powerful "gray eminence" of Gallimard, and François Mauriac, among others. Camus was
slower in reacting; but by 1946 he too was shocked by the
ugly business. His declaration of principle was a rejection
of what he had condoned. But it also had a bearing on his
political position in regard to Algeria.

It would be tedious to spell out the situation in detail. The question Camus now raised affected all the French left. As the war receded, the cold war was taking shape. For the French the international situation reverberated upon the national. In the split between right and left, the left was fragmented and weakened by its ideological dissensions. Strengthened by the stubborn and well-organized stand they had made in the underground and the heroism of their militants, the Communist Party was a most powerful bloc. Under the leadership of Maurice Thorez, who had spent the war in Russia, it was unwaveringly Stalinist; and it thought in terms of a revolution that would do away with its "class enemies." Europe was just emerging from a blood bath and French intellectuals took the question of more bloodshed seriously. These were the years when the philosopher Merleau-Ponty was working on an essay justifying the use of collective violence for political ends. His *Humanism and Terror* (1947) had an immense impact on Sartre, whom it convinced, and led to a rift with Camus which was never bridged.

Accepting the fact that violence is inherent in political power, Merleau-Ponty sought to establish a distinction between forms of violence, and in practical politics, according to his own Marxian view of history, the end did, in a sense, excuse if not justify the means. Since the creation of a socialist France was a desirable step toward establishing social justice in France, then the requisite violence must be accepted, ethically speaking. In these terms, the spectacular trials and the massive deportations characteristic of Stalin's Russia were seen as inseparable from the positive movement of a society headed toward the ideal social future. Whereas violence perpetrated by a capitalist country—whether colonial or racist—was absolutely evil. In practical terms, this meant that in the cold-

war struggle between the two superpowers, only one
choice was ethical: to support Russia. The subtle mind of
Merleau made the argument plausible. But it was in essence a justification of the means by the ends and an
example of the kind of desperate sophistry the political
chaos called forth at that moment. Europe was emerging
from a war in which Russia had suffered heavily, millions
of the people having died in the fight against the Hit-
lerian war machine. But Russia had not been vanquished.
The ruthlessness of the regime was thereby exonerated.
The image of Russia as a country building its future deliberately and rationally was a heroic and exemplary
image. But in the postwar years the purges in Russia and
the growing mass of information concerning Stalin's tyran-
nical government were beginning to cause considerable
unease. The image was being drastically retouched, but
some found it very hard to relinquish.

Camus's political position had not changed. His experience in the Resistance had not affected his dislike of
the political and repressive machinery of the Russian
state. He thoroughly hated the maneuvers of the French
Communist leaders intent on co-opting the whole heroic
legend of the Resistance for their own political ends. Immediately after the war, in the interests of political unity,
he voiced his opinion only with great moderation. It was
not for him a question of setting a new course of action.
Camus's opinion was formed. Although a man of the left,
he considered Russia to be no longer in fact a socialist
democracy. It had become a police state, a tyranny. In
terms of the cold war it seemed to him that neither what
he called the "merchant," "bourgeois," or "consumer" society, nor the Russian police state, was geared to the
needs of the present; nor to a desirable future. There
were, he thought, other paths to be explored. What ex-

asperated him was the unwillingness of the leftist French intellectuals to face the Russian reality and their haste in labeling "bourgeois" and "reactionary" any attempt openly to confront the facts. His exasperation sometimes made of him a poor polemicist; his habit of thinking and acting in terms of facts and possibilities made him an easy target for minds geared to the complexities of dialectic argument.

It was from this position that he had defined his commitment in 1946, and he defined it more and more explicitly in the turmoil of the next ten years.[6] In 1946, he had bluntly rejected on humane and ethical grounds the kind of argument developed by Merleau-Ponty in his *Humanism and Terror*, an argument with which he was familiar, since at the time, without belonging to the inner Sartrean circle, he frequented the group: he would not accept the computer type of argument, that is, the justification of a policy of terror and mass repression as a necessary stage in the march of humanity toward its ultimate liberation. One may feel that this position hardly needed justification beyond the pile of corpses and the blight of concentration camps.

The documents gathered by Roger Quilliot disprove the image of Camus as a man who in those years floated above reality, in the pure realm of the ideal. This was the image which the critic of *Les Temps modernes*, Sartre's disciple, Francis Jeanson, pinned on him at the time of the controversy concerning *The Rebel*. Whatever his limitations, Camus was not a sentimental idealist. That version of his position masks the real sense of his commitment and consequently also blurs the line of action he took at the time of the Algerian war. It created the image of Camus as a utopian dreamer, a man who refused to confront the fact of political violence; a man who confessed his own impotence in *The Fall*. Yet Camus did attempt, in his own context and outside the Marxist frame, to "think out adequately" a situation that "so many people were living badly."

The best statement of his position occurs in the letters and interviews collected by Roger Quilliot and which followed the publication of *The Rebel*. Camus was concerned by the decadence of the French left, by the loss of the generous "spirit of liberation and justice" that had in the past inspired its political vision and made it politcally efficacious. This was the spirit which the Resistance had inherited (*Essais*, p. 1753). He diagnosed the source of that decadence: the fascination exercised by the Marxian millenarianism, which he considered at best dubious, and in any case "unreal" and dangerously stultifying. His objection was not original but it was clear. What he most questioned was the effect of the Marxist view of history upon practical political decisions. "When I criticize twentieth-century Communism for judging everything in terms of the future, it is because that future is presented as certain and the happy outcome of history then authorizes any excess." For Camus, "The future in terms of history, when we estimate it, is only a collection of possibilities and, in order to determine an attitude, we must consider each one of these eventualities. The historic future does not vindicate any kind of dogmatism, but it does imply risk." Hence the chance of error or defeat; hence the willingness and need of open dialogue and the personal burden of responsibility. Hence his support of a multi-party democratic system, however faulty. "One has to define oneself in terms of all the eventualities and so lay down the limits within which to clarify one's commitment and option." There is no rule of thumb whereby one can decide the right and wrong decision since no direction is necessarily set. And there is no room for "situational" guilt. In Sartre's scheme of things, in contrast, a person's situation can be a source of guilt. A bourgeois who belongs to the governing class is, *ipso facto*, doubly condemned: for his complicity in the established scheme of things and by the future verdict of a History that postulates the destruction of his class; and so, in regard to racism, is the white man. For Camus, in politics and history there were no certain outcomes; there were rights and wrongs and no guarantees that "History" gave a correct verdict in terms of human ethics or rational patterns.

To his Marxist opponents, Camus's position smacked of bourgeois moralism and concern with personal righteousness, however genuine his outlook. It limited his commitment in their eyes to the preservation of a certain image of himself. Yet, in the forties, more particularly in the polemic following "Neither Victims Nor Executioners," he had attempted to clarify his point of view by arguing it, as a concession, from within the Marxist frame.

He accepted, for the purpose of argument, the thesis that revolutionary violence could be considered a necessary phase in the movement away from the bourgeois toward the classless society. And he granted that, in all good faith, the aim of the Marxists was the establishment of a just and free society. He argued that under the circumstances in which France found itself, this goal was incompatible with the means proposed. His reasons were not startling nor farfetched and they are familiar to most of us. The cold war, he contended, had set up two competing superpowers, each one persuaded that its system alone could bring about a desirable organization of society. But the economic fabric of society was so closely interwoven on an international scale that a local revolution in France would only bring about an apparent, surface change; furthermore, the concentration of modern arms in the hands of the government made problematic any chances of revolutionary change through mass insurrection. Under the circumstances, a real change on the socio-economic level could be brought about in France through violent action only if one of the two superpowers eliminated the other. This entailed war and, for France, the external imposition of a political organization by the winner. "On the theoretical level," Camus continued, "one could admit that dialectical materialism could justifiably exact great sacrifices in order to establish a just society, whose probability [of coming into existence] was high." But in view of the realities of modern war what would "those sacrifices mean, if that probability were reduced to nothing, if the society in question writhed in agony on an atomized continent?" (*Essais*, p. 359). And if "in spite of the sacrifice of several generations and a few values, our grandsons, supposing they should exist, found they were no closer to a just society?" No Marxist theoretician, he had rejected as dubious the Marxist postulate of the final outcome of history. He saw it as one possibility; examined it in the light of present circumstances and the proposed course of action; and rejected the course of action as inadequate to and indeed in contradiction of the ends.

But this was a form of reasoning as circular in its way as the current Marxian, and Camus knew it. What he wanted to emphasize was that his refusal to accept violent political action went beyond moral scruples or humane concerns, although these were important to him. It took into account the practical outcome. It was his conviction that both what he called the "liberal imperialistic" system and the Marxist system were "obsolete and in their present form unable to resolve" the problems of the time. Hence his call to caution, to the setting of "modest" and attainable political goals within the frame of parliamentary democracy, the "less bad" in his eyes of the prevailing systems, until new solutions adequate to the times were forthcoming. His repudiation of "murder" in the service of political truth was consistent with his view of history. He could not on the strength of a "gamble" give his support to "privileged executioners" against their "pre-condemned victims." And he rejected the either-or mentality of the debates: that "either" one must be *in toto* for socialism and Russia "or" for the United States and capitalism. In his eyes these were artificial dilemmas that masked realities and blocked the future for the political left. He rejected the charge of utopianism on still another count. What he saw as the greatest threat to human beings in the mid-century was a new form of oppression: violence itself and the widespread suffering it caused. Again, the attacks of his opponents obliged him to spell out his position. "I never argued in favor of [nonviolence] . . . I don't think one answers blows with a blessing. I believe violence is inevitable, the years of occupation taught me that. I admit that in those years there were terrible instances of violence that cost me nothing. I shan't say therefore that one must suppress violence, [a solution] which would be desirable but utopian indeed. All I say is that we must refuse to make violence legitimate, whether as an absolute necessity of state or in the interests of a totalitarian ideology. Violence is both inevitable and unjustifiable, I think we must continue to see it as exceptional and contain it within whatever limits we can. I do not preach nonviolence. . . . But in a world where people apply themselves to justifyng terror by contradictory arguments, I think we must put a limitation on violence, confine it within certain sectors when it is inevitable, assuage its terrifying effects by preventing it from going to the limits of its rage" (*Essais*, p. 356). His targets were more particularly what he called "comfortable murder," that is, the violence of the intellectual who calls for blood while comfortably ensconced in his study; and what he called "institutionalized" violence—state violence—the kind of violence he described in *The Plague*.

The commitment is clear. It was rooted in Camus's experience, his reason, and his acute sense of the depth of the physical suffering political violence generates. Time and time again he returned to that point. In practical terms it inclined him to support all attempts to create what he called an "international democracy"; and to refuse to take part indiscriminately in the attacks of the left on the United States, of the right on Russia. It inspired his indefatigable and often successful interventions on behalf of individuals unjustly condemned by dictatorships right or left: of these, his editor, Quilliot, in the two-volume Pléiade edition of Camus's works, gives an astounding record; it explains the steadiness of his political course as "historical" incidents rolled by. It would be tedious to go over his many political acts. But a brief review of his position during the Algerian war is revealing. It has often been discussed and diversely interpreted. He has been vociferously attacked and impugned because of it.

I shall only briefly refer to the long list Quilliot gives of Camus's many interventions on behalf of Muslim militants unjustly imprisoned. They often involved something beyond mere protest: Camus's willingness to testify in person, hence to take the time to travel from Paris to Algeria where militant supporters of the status quo were hardly favorable to his presence. He willingly intervened, up to the time of his death, for men whose political affilia-

tions with the extremist branch of the insurrectional liberation forces he opposed. He was himself, as an Algerian-
born European, more in sympathy with the moderates in
the Algerian movement for independence than with the
extremists. But he did not vilify the extremists.

Beyond this, from 1945 to 1958, there are his articles on
Algeria, which, with the early 1939 report on the situation in Kabylia, were collected and published in 1958
under the title *Algerian Chronicles*.[6a] One finds it hard to
understand how, in the light of those articles and the
accompanying documentation, Conor Cruse O'Brien can
so readily argue that Camus had only the vaguest suggestions to make. In fact, the articles contain, besides factual
information on the situation in Algeria as it was evolving,
definite warnings and suggestions, both economic and
political. In 1955, more particularly, Camus returned for
a while to active journalism in order to support Mendès-
France, who had negotiated the Tunisian settlement earlier and was determined to do the same for Algeria.[7] And,
simultaneously, he wrote four vigorous articles on Algeria.

Since the thirties he had been one of a small group of
European Algerians with friends among the Muslims,
who, over the years, had defended the Arab cause, supporting the reforms initiated by the French government
and regularly countered by the colonial administration
and the small and powerful group of wealthy European
settlers. In 1939, his articles on Kabylia had led to the
suppression of his paper and consequently his livelihood.
Colonial exploitation was a form of "institutionalized violence" which he and his group of friends absolutely opposed. Camus described it as operating with the bill of
rights in one hand and a club in the other. He and his
friends wanted the bill of rights for all Algerians, he re-

marked, whereas the ruling clique wanted only the club. What he and his friends sought were specific measures that would give Algeria a representative, democratic mode of government. They actively supported all political measures that pointed toward the outcome and attempted to open the European settlers' minds to its necessity. Theirs was a tough and unpopular job and they knew it.

Camus was aware, as early as 1944, that a crisis was rapidly gathering momentum in Algeria, compounded by the changes the war had brought and the near-famine that existed. He immediately undertook, as a journalist, a campaign of information. *Combat*, his paper, was then the only French paper concerned with the Algerian question. When, in 1945, insurrections broke out in the region of Constantine, and were followed by a murderous repression, Camus's reaction was violent. He denounced the viciousness of the repression, just as he had protested against French violence in other cases, in Madagascar for instance, when, a lone voice at the time, he had excoriated the use of torture by the French forces.

In 1945, he traveled through Algeria, talking with the Arabs and Europeans, gathering the facts and assessing the realities of the situation, the near-famine and the Arabs' deep dissatisfaction with the political statute under which they lived. From that moment on, Camus's articles reiterated three themes. First, he stressed the gap between the tardy and never genuinely implemented reforms initiated by the French government and the rapidly evolving demands of the Arab leaders, which he spelled out. Then, he indicated in no uncertain terms what the outcome would be—war—and stigmatized metropolitan France for its indifference and irresponsibility with regard to Algeria. Third, he took a position against repression in all its forms, pointing to the dreary cycle of violence and counterviolence it inevitably generated, and claiming amnesty for the militants who had been condemned on political grounds. It should not be forgotten that well into the mid-fifties French opinion—including the leftist—was still in the main euphorically inclined to accept the official image of France's role in Algeria; furthermore, the French were plunged in the difficult problems of immediate postwar reconstruction. Nor should it be forgotten that, well into the fifties, the Muslim leaders, too, thought in terms of an Algerian nation with federal ties to France. There was no question then in anyone's mind of uprooting the million Europeans living in Algeria.

November 1, 1954 is now the official date given for the outbreak of the Algerian war. In fact, as is the case in guerilla warfare, no one was fully conscious of what was happening, and there was a broad spectrum of opinion among the Arab leaders and even among the Europeans as to the tactics to be used. This was true in particular in regard to the fate of the civilian population, as violence spread and terrorism became rampant, whether it broke out spontaneously or was initiated deliberately as a political weapon used to polarize opinion, spread panic, or bludgeon the population into submission.

It was at this point that the political conscience of the French left began to awaken.[8] It was at this point that Camus, called upon by both sides for support, refused to take sides with either one. His last public intervention took place in 1956. He was a member of a joint European-Muslim Committee which made a final attempt to stem the tide of war. They advocated an immediate end to the colonial status; the elimination of the "gros colons"—the wealthy landowners; and a round-table meeting where the leaders of the diverse Arab groups would meet with French representatives to seek political solutions. Simultaneously, in agreement with some Muslim leaders, among whom, it would seem, were leaders of the FLN—the movement for complete independence—the group proposed a "truce." It was, in fact, a moratorium on terrorism they were proposing, aimed at saving civilian lives, both Muslim and European. Camus was the spokesman who presented the proposal at a meeting which united Algerians—Muslim and European—in a last and generous movement of understanding. Outside the meeting hall, the European extremists had gathered and threatened Camus's life. It was a spectacular demonstration of the reactionary "colons" a few days later that blocked any velleity the administration might have had to consider seriously the moratorium. The inevitable dialectic of terror took over. Camus resorted to silence. He gave his reasons. And only in the dubious light of a grossly simplified Marxian dialectic can it possibly be said that he justified by that silence the brutality of the French military machine. Camus did not think in terms of the dialectic. He had always mistrusted the army, and its tactics in North Africa were anathema to him.

Among the possibilities or alternatives for solving the Algerian problem, one seemed to him the best: the institution of a socialist democracy in which all Algerians were represented. In line with his view of the risks of political action, he was willing to confront the chance of defeat, but ready to try, as long as some chance of success remained, to bring about a political solution to the conflict. At stake were the lives of the million—Muslim in the main, and European—who eventually died; and the suffering of millions of others. One may posit that the conflict in that form was inevitable; one may, too, as does the historian Yves Courrière, see in the history of the war a signal example of inefficiency and "lost opportunities." With deep distress Camus saw it from that angle. It is a curious distortion to read that distress in terms of a "guilt" complex, alien to him,[9] or of a lack of realism.

His stand against terrorism was coherent. There were in his eyes no "privileged executioners," whatever the cause. There were no preordained, "expendable" victims either. As he had defended the hapless Muslim population, so he defended the hapless "small" settlers, on whom the French leftist intellectuals, Sartre among them, so willingly passed judgment: it was too bad, in Sartre's view, if they happened to be standing in the path of History. It made them utterly expendable. In those terms, for Camus, dialogue was impossible and silence the only answer. As we have seen, Camus had long before decided that as an intellectual he would provide no verbal incitations to violence.

His political position, on the other hand, is open to question. The Communist branch of the liberation movement had taken the leadership in the war. Some of its leaders were in Egypt. Camus was opposed to both communism and Egyptian leadership as foreboding a new system of oppression and pauperization for Algeria. One could interpret this view, in Marxian terms, as reflecting a "colonial" consciousness. Nonetheless, when he suggested possible solutions, Camus never insisted on an a priori commitment to his ideas. He always proposed an open dialogue, a round table. Again, the *means* he proposed defined the ends as open, within the limits set by the situation; the intent was to contain the random violence, to have it officially disowned by both sides. By 1956 he was realistic enough to know the actual fighting could not be stopped; he had cast no blame on the militants, only on the terrorists, French and Muslim alike. Nothing beyond the passions of the hour warrants the *ad hominem* attacks his position inspired, except perhaps the constrained tone which in Camus's writing always signals great inner tensions and distress; and the stubborn pride that made it impossible for him to make public many of his actions.

In his political action, Camus had opted for forms of militant nonviolence, putting whatever influence he had behind those initiatives which rested on the democratic principles of open discussion and negotiated settlement. He had no illusions as to their limitations, but he had no illusions either concerning the alternative: the use of violence. In those years, in contrast with the preceding period, his literary work was closely related to his public actions. He lacked the vocabulary of the social historian and he worked from an inner core of intuition, outward, subjectively. But his initial meditations on human limitations and basically unchangeable human drives had prepared him to contend with what he called the "age of fear" that closed in upon the Western world in the midcentury years, more lucidly than had he clung to the optimistic belief in unlimited human perfectibility so characteristic of Sartre.[10] Both Caligula and Meursault indirectly show that Camus had little confidence in anyone's harmlessness; and that he was alert to his own ambivalence. He had a qualified view of the ability of human beings to control their passions and had very early measured their propensity for controlling others. He had not accepted the Marxist myth of the "new man" who would be born out of the revolutionary process. He looked beyond the immediate political ideologies to the violence they engendered. Human violence is the central theme of *The Plague, The Just Assassins*, and *The Rebel*.

Camus's choice of the plague as the organic metaphor for his novel has often been adversely criticized. Yet it was the symbol he needed. In *The Plague*, violence is a deadly faceless presence that works through the social organism, consuming individuals like a monstrous machine, purposelessly piling up their bodies like so much industrial "waste", and silently, relentlessly, invading all the spheres of private life, destroying identities, feelings, hopes, joys. It is an all-pervasive evil, and, even in those who fight it, requires a total subordination to the conditions it imposes. Camus had something in mind beyond the "good" and "bad" dichotomy of the two sides: a new form of tyranny, the totalitarian aspect of modern war itself; the new methods of impersonal organization; the threat to the individual of the police state or, less dramatically, of "the system."

There is nothing glamorous about the small group of men who challenge the scourge, and who are forced to fight it on its own terms, processing, computerizing, coercing. Their activities are an offshoot of the plague. It is clear that Camus made a deliberate and difficult effort to demythicize the legend of heroic armed conflict. The plague is an emergency, a disaster, and the inevitable counterterror it inspires is of the same order. What is obvious when the grip of the plague weakens and the people of Oran can return to the pursuit of their own private concerns, is the horribly useless costliness of the whole affair. There are many facets of the book that throw light on Camus's specific "engagements": his faith, born of experience, that there will always be men who will challenge the authority of the plague, that the drive to total power will eventually be contested and fail. The force that links the men who fight is not ideological in nature. Each has his own realm of concern, his own way of understanding the meaning he gives his actions, which,

in differing degree, each can communicate to the others
because of the mutual bond of respect that unites them.
It is their understanding of the nature of the evil and its
implications that made of them the patient, stubborn, un-
glamorous enemies of a force which intends the destruction of fundamental human ways of life. They do not
engage in dialogue with the plague; they fight it. But
throughout the weary struggle they do speak with one
another openly from that individual inner core of feeling
which the plague attacks. The tactics they use are determined by circumstance, bounded by it; but not the bonds
between them, whose very existence defies the plague.
Another question arises: the scourge as Camus describes
it liberated no one, and destroyed no injustice; it merely
killed. Nothing compensates for the suffering it caused. It
is a sterile form of violence.

The Plague is a deeply personal novel and it makes a
clear statement. The tactics used to counter a collective
evil are determined by the character of the threat. They
are not in themselves absolutes; they are temporary and
relative, a therapy, not a cure. Dr. Rieux's task is to circumscribe the infection. He and his helpers are on the
defensive; their efforts, the novel suggests, may have had
little to do with the evolution of the situation. If we consider the novel in terms of its social implications, it is
clear that the question Camus was asking is whether
there might not have been an initial way to counter the
plague beyond the ineffectual routines of the past, typi-
fied by the breakdown of the administrative institutions
in Oran and the problematic and uneven struggle belatedly improvised by individual men against their virulent,
faceless enemy. The real question then lies beyond the
book itself. The Oran plague leaves the real problem unsolved.

The play, *The Just Assassins*, raises the question of violence from another, more personal angle. Is a person or a group justified in resorting to murder in the cause of social justice? In sacrificing a human being for the particular objective of bringing about a good society? Camus chose to dramatize the question through a group of Russian terrorists who had answered in the affirmative, and who, in 1905, had successfully assassinated the Russian minister of justice. Their situation is a paradigm of that of the many revolutionary cells blossoming in the world today, in response to whatever form of "the plague" they discern in their society. Camus drew on the actual memoirs of the leader of the group. The circumstances are specific: the institutions of justice had broken down in Czarist Russia; reforms had not been forthcoming. Hence the resort to violent action. The question raised does not concern the tactics; the bomb will be thrown, and the representative figure will be killed. It concerns the motivations behind the commitment, and the dilemma of the revolutionary, who recognizes that his vision of the future is in part myth, for which, nonetheless, he sacrifices his and others' lives. One of the terrorists in the play, a poet, Kaliayev, understands the full significance of his act when he sees two children in the carriage in which his victim, the Grand Duke, rides. He feels he cannot carry out his mission under those circumstances. This brings out a latent conflict between himself and one of his companions, Stepan. Anger animates Stepan, a cold anger against a system under which he was imprisoned and humiliated, lashed by a prison guard. Beneath his allegiance to social justice is a violent need for vengeance, irrational in essence. He rationalizes it logically: the lives of two children are nothing to him in regard to the future salvation of thousands of others. He levels his accusation against the world unconditionally, implacably, at all who are now a part of it, guilty by the very fact of their existence, and justifiably expendable in terms of a rectified future. Kaliayev confronts injustice out of the fullness of a happy life, and his sense of what all lives should and could be. He sees his act for what it is, an unlawful action, imposed by exceptional circumstances: justifiable in social terms, unjustifiable, humanly speaking. He accepts the covenant: the retribution meted out by law. Stepan's impatient justification of indiscriminate violence discloses the real though unconscious intent beneath the revolutionary rhetoric: ideological tyranny. He recognizes no obligation other than the destruction of all obstacles in his way. In contrast, even in terrorist action, Kaliayev recognizes that his commitment to social justice is binding on himself. He can thus remain a truly human being. But terrorist action is incompatible with the rich personal life he must sacrifice. In the silence of his prison cell the inner burden of the sacrifice is his to bear. But what of the society that brought him to that extremity? Furthermore, Camus's 1949 audience could view Kaliayev's sacrifice in the light of Stalin's Russia. For he had been, after all, a real human being, something more than a character on stage.

It was the identification of violence with social progress that Camus examined in *The Rebel.* He knew he was living in a time of crisis but he had come, as we have seen, to entertain doubts as to whether the nature and development of the crisis could be accounted for by the rhetoric of the revolutionary left. *The Rebel* was Camus's reappraisal of a mythology of revolt and revolution woven into the very texture of Western culture. Its meaning lies in a conclusion upon which much scorn has been poured. Camus had separated the question of social action from the rhetoric of revolt and revolution in which it had been entangled since the French Revolution. In that respect *The Rebel*, however schematic its argumentation, was a declaration of independence. Camus had definitely turned his back on the dialectics of History. In the short fable which concludes his foray into what Camus now saw as a cultural myth, the rebel Prometheus, finding no gods to strike him down, turns into Caesar, a human despot. Against Caesar's tyranny, a new Prometheus then arises, sounding the call for the liberation of men; he too, rejecting all impediments to the realization of his ideal, turns into Caesar. But whether Caesar or Prometheus, he has little patience with the human beings who, on this difficult but desirable earth, attempt to lead their lives as best they can. *The Rebel* restates Camus's dedication to that community of men, in which contention and conflict are qualified and limited by the consent and acceptance of the imperfections, inadequacies, inconsistencies, and never-ending struggles inherent in the human lot, and of men's simple addiction to their happiness.

It is difficult to remember the ideological confusions of the period; the almost impossible task, at the time, of distinguishing between the goals of socialism, its terminology, and the reality of Stalin's Russia. We are actually now leaving that aspect of the question behind. The Greek metaphor at the end of *The Rebel*, with its appeal to measure, to positive values, for concerted action toward an open future and to an end to the endless ratiocination, was more a lyrical expression of Camus's own escape from the prison of radical polemics than a philosophical position. But he had taken the measure of his own limits. He saw his political choices in terms of his major needs as artist. To write, he needed the special freedom to search privately for his own understanding, to sort out the "yes" without which it was impossible to write from the "no" of social conscience; while excluding nothing and no one. This, again somewhat cryptically, referred to a need which he recognized as the driving force behind his work as artist. The need to rise above the zone of conflict, to accede to a larger vision, is a major theme in his work. He needed those moments of perception where he could recover the sense of an essential unity, see his own life from that vantage point, and the face of a fellow creature in that of his "foe." It was the kind of comprehension he admired in Dostoevsky; the understanding needed, for instance, to depict the Karamazovs in their wide diversity, good and evil, known as such and yet known always as human.

This sense of fellowship was what bound him, much as Kaliayev's different commitment had bound him, to stand beside those who were victims of the tragic nature of human affairs. It was his private life that guided his public actions. With *Exile and the Kingdom* he turned to the personal domain in which private options surface in gestures that define the "weight" or "character" of people, their relations with themselves and their fellow men; where, at certain moments, like the "Adulterous Woman" or the workman in "The Silent Men," they confusedly reach that vantage point and, for a brief instant, see more clearly.

Nothing is more illuminating than to put Sartre's *Roads to Freedom* alongside *The Plague*; his *Dirty Hands* and *The Devil and the Good Lord* beside *The Just Assassins*. The rift over *The Rebel* was, in fact, only the culmination of a deeper misunderstanding. The two men had been traveling for some time on a collision course. Though Sartre's novel, *The Roads to Freedom*, was never finished, we know through different sources the ending Sartre had planned, and, through his own explanation, what he had intended to do. He had planned the novel before the war, in 1938; since it deals with the years 1938–1944, it obviously grew with the historical events themselves. Its setting is history itself: 1938 before and during the Munich crisis for the first two volumes; the defeat of the French army in 1940 for the third; and for the uncompleted fourth volume, the years of German occupation up to the liberation of Paris.

The title itself is illuminating. Sartre spatialized history. History is a field of action that offers his characters opportunities, paths to realize themselves, to become, in Sartrean terms, "free men." "My intent," Sartre wrote, "is to write a novel on freedom."[11] The novel was composed to illustrate what freedom was. Curiously enough, one feels that history for a short while played with unusual docility into Sartre's hands. In 1938, he could have had no inkling at all of what was coming. Munich had jolted him out of his intellectual empyrean. Subsequently, events furnished exactly the history he needed. Sartre stated his purpose quite clearly. The characters and "social groups" he describes will emerge out of the pre-1938 world, with its comfortably closed horizons, into the Munich crisis in which those "walls dissolve"; thence into the world of defeat and occupation in which circumstances present "the conditions of real freedom." Before defeat they all embody a "travesty of freedom," false freedoms, mutilated, incomplete, spurious forms of freedom. Sartre characterizes those travesties in terms of Hegel and *Being and Nothingness*. As each character evolves toward clearcut choices he will, he says, become heroic; it is a "novel of heroes [he] wants to write."[12] The liberation of France and the "liberation" of his cast of heroes will coincide. Sartre's confidence, reinforced by events, was so great that his characters, creating themselves in Sartrean fashion by their free choice of specific actions, all found themselves on the "freedom" side of history. All ethical in the degree that they acted as free men, they are justified by history. History too is ethical. Even the collaborationist, Daniel, had Sartre finished the novel, was to "find" his act, blowing himself up in a café with the German soldiers who filled it. The main cast of characters closely resembled Sartre's own circle of friends. The fusion of philosophical demonstration, history, and reality was complete—and exemplary. Thanks to Sartre's optimism, his main characters were all to find what he called "deliverance"; for by their actions they had participated in "making" history, and in making the history of all men they inevitably had taken the "road to freedom." History was Sartrean, not Marxian, in those years.

The mood could hardly be more different from the ambience of *The Plague*, with its total refusal in any way to glamorize war itself. Sartre later accused Camus of remaining the "man of the Resistance." It seems more exact to reverse the allegation. Camus was the man who aspired to "normal" modes of life, for whom modern war was a hideous nightmare. For Sartre the war years were the great years of truth. There was, however, one level where the two worlds met. Sartre had provided many alternative roads to freedom for his characters, personal modes of commitment that corresponded to the circumstances that had fashioned each character's psychological "situation," thus the modality of his choice: joining de Gaulle's Free French, or the internal Resistance movement; or like the collaborationist, Daniel, choosing a last and deliberate act that "redeemed" his whole life. Within the common "field" of historical circumstance, the private preoccupations and former orientation of the characters limit the area of their action within the wider configuration. For each one the Occupation is a situation in which the private and public spheres merge, determining which among the limited number of options open to all Frenchmen he will choose.

It was the total disengagement in his own life of the private from the public sphere that had troubled Sartre, a condition he had wanted to remedy and to which his doctrine of "engagement" was an answer. It posited a man working for all men and himself free; thence eventually a society both socialist and free, the advent of a fully "human" existence. Similarly, no two characters in Camus's novel fight the plague for quite the same reasons. But Sartre in his novel implicitly rejected one position, the Communist, shown as a typical example of "bad faith." And that rejection proved to be the obstacle which blocked the completion of the novel. In fact, it put an end to Sartre's novel-writing days, at least so far as we know.

The example is typical both of Sartre's intellectualization and schematization of so vast a reality as history, and the dangers to the writer who so confidently disposes of the future. It also shows Sartre's intellectual haste in discarding outworn schemas. When Sartrean history turned into Marxian history, the novel ground to a halt. The passion to "understand" immediately and to demonstrate that understanding instantly, outstripped the slow imaginative shaping of art. It is clear that when he planned *Roads to Freedom*, Sartre had known what he wanted history to say. It spoke like the Jean-Paul Sartre of *Being and Nothingness*.

With *Dirty Hands*, Sartre structured a dramatic universe in which there is "no exit" in terms of a man's unconditional freedom. There is an exit into the reality of collective history, a single exit. The situation is political. The characters are revolutionaries, the question raised, as in *The Just Assassins*, is the question of murder. Also, as in *The Just Assassins*, Hugo, a young bourgeois revolutionary in revolt against his milieu, has chosen to work within a Communist cell. And he has undertaken to kill a political enemy, allegedly a "traitor" to the Communist cause. Hoederer, the "traitor" in question, is the head of the Party. Here Camus's play and Sartre's part company. The play is set in 1944, in central Europe, in a country under German occupation, as the Russian armies of liberation approach. It is in essence a "trial." The man on trial is Hugo, who many months earlier shot Hoederer upon the order of his cell. The trial takes the form of a flashback, reconstructing the events. Two attitudes are contrasted: Hoederer's, who in Sartre's terms is the real hero; Hugo's, who misses his chance.

If Hoederer is condemned to death by the cell, it is because in the absence of direct orders from Moscow he has devised, in Machiavellian terms, the political tactics of compromise with other parties in order to put the Party in the strongest political position at the time of liberation. The cell leaders are "pure" doctrinaires. But Hoederer's decision, based on facts, turns out to be correct. He dies, but what he planned lives on. He becomes a Party hero. The "truth" of the murder must be forgotten.

Hugo confronts two alternatives: death or a break with the past. He can assume a different name, forget the murder, and continue to militate in the party. Tied to the past, to an image of himself, to "truth," to "his act," Hugo refuses that alternative and so must die. He is "nonsalvageable." The plot is ambiguous. *The Devil and the Good Lord* provides a context. It is set in the turmoil of a chaotic Germany in which the old feudal alliance of church and aristocracy is breaking up. Goetz, the hero, is a rebel, a bastard, neither aristocrat nor peasant, the lawless captain of a band of mercenaries. He sees himself as Lucifer, the anti-God, and he cruelly decimates the land. Challenged by an alter ego, Heinrich, a priest, he decides to change his role; so he plays the role of saint, with the same disastrous result. Finally, consenting to play his role as a man, a particular man with a particular skill as military leader, he consents to take his place as general of the peasant army in insurrection against its feudal lords.

In the secular world in which Goetz acts, the play demonstrates that what counts is the future of the masses fighting to wrest their freedom from their oppressors. For Goetz, personal and collective salvation coincide. In the light of that future, his acts—even the most violent—futile heretofore, acquire their significance and his existence its justification. They make sense. In this perspective, Hugo is an antihero, a bourgeois, intent on keeping his own personal image of himself, just as he never discarded the photographs of himself as a child. He is no revolutionary. He cannot make the passage Goetz makes from the individual world of moral uncertainties into the objective world of historical judgment.

Sartre had by now thrown out Hugo's preoccupations. The "boundary situations" he projected on stage in the two plays are rife with violence; in each, violence is both a fact and an issue. The issue was no longer, as it had been in *The Roads to Freedom*, the nature of the commitments whereby individuals make history while making themselves. It is history which confers upon Goetz's choice the aura of authenticity. The "apple" of the Sartrean world, to use Genet's image, is cut in two; good acts, bad acts. In terms of the future of all men, the stern Sartrean judges, the "masked men of the future," have appeared. In that perspective all human beings are expendable, those who "make" history and those who stand in its path. Ethical standards and scruples have become bourgeois alibis and, like Hugo, are expendable. There is no "inner world" of belief and aspiration, no inner cogency to maintain. As men change the world, so they change, neither subject nor object, but agents of a force working through them.

Sartre had recast his early image of the unconditionally "open" future. The two plays reflected Sartre's own intellectual evolution.

In practical terms, at the level of everyday reality, he had qualified his initial view of a world open to an infinite choice of possibilities. They all now flowed into a single one, politically defined. Goetz's situation at the end of the play was both didactic and symbolic. It is interesting to follow Sartre's own passages from one crisis of choice to another, and to examine the question of commitment within his dialectic of oscillation between decision and rupture so antithetical to Camus's sensitivity. It underlies his increasingly intransigent political commitments, his subordination of art to politics, and his justification, in fact his fascination for certain forms of extreme violence, while sternly reproving others. In *The Plague* and *The Just Assassins*, Camus had questioned that very fascination for violence, and had sharply delineated its disastrous human effects, showing that in the counterviolence it generated it perpetuated itself.

By 1952, when the Camus-Sartre controversy broke out openly, with Camus's publication of *The Rebel*, Camus had shaken off the obsession with politics into which the Algerian war then threatened to plunge him once again. And, though he suffered through it intensely, he refused to consider political partisanship as a mandatory action, and to see life, at all its levels, only from the political viewpoint. Art once again claimed his attention: the theater and the work he was planning, which was to be the statement of that larger vision of life slowly reached and fictionally recreated. He had, perhaps prematurely, sensed that the ambience of life in Europe was changing, that a new sensitivity, in some ways more akin to his own, was seeking its expression. He had wished neither to become a political pundit nor the conscience of his contemporaries. As Grenier noted, he had done what he must; the short story, "Jonah," illustrates his rather wry sense of surprise at what had happened to him: Jonah is an artist who has a star—a destiny—and a talent for painting. The two together create his dilemma as a human being. Camus was leaving behind him the tragic vistas of the mid-century and its tense rhetoric and moral escalations. The stories in *Exile and the Kingdom* focus on the joys and sorrows, the errors and awarenesses of everyday life. He was not, as Sartre alleged, "left behind" by the times. In some respects, he had quietly taken his distance in regard to them, and to what in them was irrevelant to his own sense of life. He had something to say about how one may attain some sense of inner coherence and live with some degree of integrity in spite of one's own confusion and the confusion of the times.

Notes to Chapter 7

1. See, for example, Raymond Gay-Crosier, "L'anarchisme mesuré de Camus," *Symposium*, Fall 1970, 243–53.
2. Camus's "man sentenced to death" embodied in Meursault can be contrasted with Heidegger's "being for death," or

"life facing death." See *Heidegger* by Marjorie Grene (London: Bowes and Bowes, 1957), pp. 17–37. Camus's man is a man very much alive and not reducible to his end. Caligula in a sense draws the natural conclusion from the premise that man is a "being for death"; a man's life matters not at all. Camus wants to draw the opposite conclusion.

3. Sartre wrote this in February, 1943; *The Stranger* actually came out in July, 1942.

4. A more recent view of the case applies fairly well to the tempo of that life at a somewhat later date: "Between two trains, between two taxis, beween two doors, between two booking offices, between two offices, between two telephones, between two projects, between two angers, between two depressions, between two drinks, between two wars, between two lives, between two worlds . . ." Jean Moral "Un billet pour ailleurs" (a ticket for somewhere else) in *La nouvelle Table ronde*, No. 1, May 1970, p. 100. Simone de Beauvoir's *Memoirs* give a good idea of the hectic activity and political concern in those years.

5. These are the figures given by the historian Robert Aron in his two-volume *Histoire de l'Épuration* (Paris: Fayard, 1967–1969).

6. H. Stuart Hughes in *The Obstructed Path* (New York: Harper and Row, 1966); and David Caute in *Communism and the French Intellectuals* (New York: The Macmillan Co., 1964), give accounts of that period which Stuart Hughes calls "the years of desperation."

6a. The third volume of *Actuelles*. Quilliot gives a number of other articles in the volume of essays, pp. 1862–1885.

7. Sartre, in the meantime, voted against Mendès-France. He has never to my knowledge supported any political candidate who had the slightest chance of actually winning nor has he ever supported any action taken by the French government.

8. Sartre's *active* concern dates from 1955–56 and his participation in a "Committee of intellectuals for action

against the pursuit of the war in North Africa," which held a meeting in favor of peace in Algeria on January 27, 1956.

9. O'Brien, in the interests of his thesis, misreads the short story "The Host." Camus presents the situation of a schoolmaster on the high plateaus of Algeria, to whom is entrusted an Arab Algerian who has committed a murder. The murder is not political. It is quite obvious that the young Arab is unaware of what is going on outside his village. The schoolmaster treats him not as a prisoner but as a guest. When the time comes to go to the village to face trial, the man asks whether the schoolmaster will come with him and the "gendarme." Mr. O'Brien misinterprets the "us" as referring to the Arab militants—and so transforms the whole meaning of the story.

10. Halfway between the early works and those rooted in the war experience, *The Misunderstanding*, written in 1943, is the most pessimistic statement Camus was ever to make. The basic theme is the perversion of a justified aspiration toward freedom and happiness, that turns into a grim and ruthless mechanism of destruction.

11. M. Contat and M. Rybalka, *Les Écrits de Sartre* (Paris: Gallimard, 1970), p. 113. A large as yet unpublished fourth part of the book will appear in the Pléiade edition in preparation.

12. *Ibid.*, pp. 113–116. One of the misinterpretations of the novel, due to its unfinished state, has been that the intellectual Mathieu, like Sartre a philosopher, preoccupied like Sartre with the problem of freedom, was killed in battle. Sartre had indulged in a technique of melodramatic suspense. Mathieu it turns out was to become a hero, a Resistance leader whose choice of freedom would not be broken down by the torture under which he would die.

Conclusion

And what would be the story? That wanting desperately to become a writer, I became a writer.

H. MILLER

And among all the agents by which the widening of the sphere of human sensibility may be brought, the arts are the most powerful, since it is through them that men may most cooperate, and in these experiences that the mind most easily and with least interference organizes itself.

I. A. RICHARDS

Thirty years after Sartre spelled out in *What is Literature?* his mandate to the French writer, life has changed, in the United States but even more, perhaps, in Western Europe. Violence, it is true, is still with us; famine, war— one need hardly recall Vietnam—oppression, racism. And the specter of atomic havoc has not been laid. Few people still cling to the neatly ordered view of the world Sartre has been at such pains to castigate. But the acute crisis that spanned the half-century between 1914–1960 has subsided; when disorderliness erupts amid the orderliness of our daily routines we tend to speak more of a new era opening in our human history, less of a pending apocalypse. To a certain extent, Sartre's affirmation that men can control their future and should do so in terms of ends consciously defined, has many echoes in the warnings of scientists, more particularly perhaps, biologists and environmentalists.

In the first half of the century when the gaps were gradually opening in the Western world between human knowledge and current views of reality,[1] men of intellectual vigor tended to create vast syntheses that attempted to make sense, or order at least, out of the total human history on the planet, in terms of the record of men's activities—Spengler, Toynbee, Teilhard de Chardin, St. John Perse; in theology, Barth, Bultmann and Tillich; in history of art, Elie Faure, Focillon, and Malraux, one might even add Marcel Proust; in science, Julian Huxley. They often seemed to look back to Hegel, if not Marx. Sartre belongs among them—the last of the great system-builders, the humblest, in a sense, and yet the most arrogant, whose postulations and positions are the most paradoxical.

We are, at present, as a theologian has noted,[2] in a phase which can best be defined by the prefix "post": post-Freudian; post-Marxian; post-Barthian; post-Sartrean. We are drawn to the dangers and excitements of a pluralistic world rather than to sweeping syntheses. Beyond Sartre's unfinished work, no large new syntheses seem to have challenged our imagination. And it is a fact that within our present perspectives Sartre's political positions seem strangely akin to Jarry's *Pataphysic*, a science of imaginary solutions. Camus is a man who laid aside the fascinating quest for a totally coherent intellectual order in the modern world in order to examine how best to live in it.

The writers today must be few who have not meditated

upon the relation of their occupation to the world about them; and in the last years the question has spread well beyond them to all realms of social involvement. We are not living in an age of innocence; when the sense of ambient disorder becomes overwhelming, that concern may become obsessive. Until recently writers have traditionally been involved in giving some kind of unity or shape to their personal experience, working toward an integration through the use of language, of their inner emotions with the world they see around them. If the outer disorder becomes overwhelming, then the natural impulse of the writer may well be to attempt to transcend it by transferring, as did Sartre, his private view of the world to the sphere of ideology, thence to a doctrine of political activism. A personal vision, esthetic in origin, then engenders a political myth. Or, in contrast, as Camus would have it, a collective experience of great magnitude may stir in the artist basic feelings which he shares with a whole community. Artists, then, in their search for expression may transcend the purely personal vision that is theirs and shape what are in essence myths, ways of relating to the common reality which reverberate throughout the community of their readers, helping them to preserve their inner equilibrium. In both cases, the writer may then feel that he is in fact performing an indispensable social function and that he is morally responsible for what he communicates to his fellow citizens.

There is a basic difference however between the two attitudes, though both are hedged with the same kind of danger, for the confusions are many that can arise from the relations unwarily established between the structures of the myth—political or otherwise—and the structures of reality. Political myths imbedded in literary works have often pointed the way to action, appealing to the idealism of the young or of those a society wrongs. But they have seldom worked out according to pattern. Collective apolitical myths, as Sartre had discovered and proclaimed, may lead to a collective "slumber"; civilizations have collapsed when cultural patterns have become too remote from the realities. In a time of chaos, the writer will tender to his readers the necessary patterns only if he can refer them to familiar structures. This both Sartre and Camus did. Most of the writers who won acclaim during the years of crisis—poets like Aragon, Eluard, Pierre Emmanuel—were as intensely involved as Camus and Sartre in the same torment and in the same patterning of a collective myth.

The literary situation in France in the years that stretch roughly between 1940–1960, shows marked contrast with the emerging patterns of the twenties that have of late asserted themselves so triumphantly in America. The assault upon traditional forms and language, upon logic and meaning, was held in abeyance. Writers accepted, consciously or instinctively, their roles as mediators, interpreters of a common experience. And because this was indeed a common experience, the moral tensions, needs, and preoccupations of the community were in turn reflected in the substance and esthetic tensions of the work. A historical situation was being turned into myth, incorporated into the structures of the national past. The literary patterns translated the most immediate modes of a common sensibility. The less palatable facts, the actual directions and significance of the events would wait for less immediate perspectives. In this sense, as today's social or historical critics fail to see—as Sartre himself I think has failed to see—Sartre's substitution of an emotionally charged ideological structure for the world of reality was in fact a desperate and courageous challenge to that reality. And it was symbolic of the need of the moment. It could not be sustained, as Jacques Ellul so clearly pointed out, beyond that moment. It was self-destructive.

Sartre's initial existential view of human reality, with its assumption that the human self, insofar as it is human, exists apart from everything else and in hostile confrontation with everything else—including others—was patterned to fit a climate either of withdrawal or of aggression, not of commitment. An intellectual structure, it was dramatized through an imagery that belied its cognitive patterns. In Sartre's early system, the mind and the mind alone stood between human freedom and engulfment into the chaos. The mind is an instrument of domination. And it was always so to be. It is this intransigent faith in the absolute power of logic—whatever the kind—to dominate reality, in a man as emotionally impulsive as Sartre, that led Sartre rapidly to a couple of dead ends, to his vacillations and confusions concerning the function of literature in our society, and to his most dubious political pronouncements. Among those emotional impulses, as an analysis of his language indicates, fear is dominant; one aspect of it is fear of the "real" as obstacle in the path of thought. The consequent impulse is to do away with it—in flight or, as the child had done, by a stroke of the pen and to rationalize the deal through the working of the dialectic. This has made of Sartre a brilliant polemicist in "right" causes, but not a "committed" man. Real confrontations in human situations take place when a "right" cause, wrestled with, reveals all its ambiguities, and there is no white and black.

Humanly speaking, Sartre's whole enterprise by its dimensions and complexity may deeply engage our minds and it has more than others defined the dominant intellectual climate of an era. But it may also leave us deeply dissatisfied. For it omits too many elements of human experience, more especially those that militate against an obsessive involvement in the political, equated with the human. This drains life of enriching elements and leaves human beings emotionally impoverished. This is perhaps what so drastically curtailed Sartre's literary career, and, in the sixties, spelled the waning of his influence.

From the outset, Camus had known the pressures of reality; not least among them was the illness which confronted him with the fact of his expendability, and the intimation of the unimportance of an individual life. *La Mort heureuse* is the account of his reaction to that experience. Life sets limits. A life that ends in death cannot be wasted. Thence Mersault's deliberate leap out of his daily round of mediocre tasks mechanically fulfilled; thence the pistol shot that jolts the Stranger out of his somnambulism; thence Caligula's furor against the compliance of men quietly going to their death behind the screen of routine tasks. This is the revulsion, too, that Camus felt toward a society quietly submissive to its own destruction, behind its nonchalant façade of routine procedures —a society he portrayed in *The Plague*. This is a reaction others have described before Camus. To Camus it imparted the sense of life as risk. Camus's characters are gamblers, Sisyphus the greatest gambler of them all. Camus's first gamble was to play life against death, to enhance its price; and this is a game played with a man's flesh and blood. "For a man who has something to do," he wrote a young friend who had fallen ill, like himself, with tuberculosis, "a good body is the first tool." Camus's stance was that of the craftsman: he knew his tools. Among those tools were a body impelled by certain drives, already touched by illness; a mind; and the single short appearance on stage allotted a human being. It was the performance that mattered to him. Each man had his

choice of roles in the chaos of existence; various ways of
life, of which some, more than others, enhanced life and
the dignity of the performer. Camus's own choices were
hazardous—most of all the choice to become an artist.
And valid only if a man played them genuinely—committed himself beyond make-believe. This was Camus's
choice of paradox. "I think I really don't mind living in
contradictions," he wrote, "I don't particularly want to be
a philosophical genius. I don't particularly want to be any
kind of genius . . . I want to find some mode of harmony.
. . ." (*Essais*, p. 1612). And it entailed other paradoxes:
options are made at the expense of something else; it was
their impact on that something else which he constantly
reassessed. A man who knows he lives at the expense of
life performs perhaps more warily, and measures the risks
not to himself only, but to others. It is Camus's relation
with others that most clearly differentiates his attitude as
writer and as human being, from Sartre's. His confrontations are with himself; others he may have to struggle
against but he does not "judge." Rare are the *ad hominem*
arguments in his writing. Each man, in Camus's eyes is
his own Sisyphus.

This is a point of view which contrasts with Sartre's
sense, vividly described in *The Words*, that his tasks and
destiny were preordained. His role, from the start, was
the role of guide and teacher. His aim—so clearly stated
in regard to Flaubert—was to force people to see their
lives in clear intellectual perspective, leaving no facet unexamined; in other words, to lead rationally controlled
lives. There was a remedy for human failures and that
was to turn the light of reason on all the obscurities of
human behavior. Evil he once defined as the irreducibil-
ity of life to reason. He had undertaken to fight that evil.
It seems quite clear that Descartes, in the thirties, was
the model he had in mind.

Neither Sartre nor Camus was in fact deflected in his initial orientation by the war. It merely injected into their lives new and serious challenges more disturbing perhaps to Sartre than to Camus.

Sartre's formulation of his doctrine of commitment was a phase in the development of his enterprise. He set two goals for the writer to unveil—disclose—to his readers the developing patterns of the social world as seen through the eyes of the least favored among men; and, personally, joining action to thought, to close the gap between knowledge and practice. Both these aims assume the priority of acquiring knowledge in what Sartre now called "praxis," whether in the practice of writing or of life. One has to discern the directions of history in order to disclose them. Sartrean dialectic was Sartre's tool, a flow of language linking and organizing in its deployment the immense concatenation of facts, theories, conflicts, welding them into its unitary pattern. It was to the corroboration of that pattern and to participation in its unfolding that Sartre was in fact committed. But it was *his* pattern, which accounts for the widening gap between his expectations for the future and the actualities of history; perhaps, too, for his bitter explosions of anger and calls to violence.[6]

It was the ambiguous use he made of the word "action" which created a good deal of confusion, for a while reflecting his own nostalgia as an intellectual. Sartre has his roster of heroes—Castro, Lumumba, Fanon. Although since the fifties he has often specified that action, for the writer, can only be intellectual in kind, his fictional work, more specifically his plays, at one level are imaginary enactments of a lifelong dream of heroic participation in human affairs.

Sartre's greater moments of literary creativity seem to occur when he breaks through the bounds of an intellectual construct into a new, uncharted area. *Nausea* is an account of such a breakthrough. On stage, his heroes enact the surge of energy that comes with Sartre's discovery of some new realm to be drawn into the orbit of his understanding. In *The Flies*, Orestes leaps beyond Sartre, ensconced in his Paris café, working out his ontology; he projects Sartre's determination to free his fellow citizens from the mythical constraints of the past rather than immediately from the Nazis. In *Les Mains sales* (*Red Gloves*), Hoederer, the Communist leader, anticipates Sartre's "liberation" from bourgeois "idealism"; while Goetz, in *The Devil and the Good Lord*, enacts Sartre's decision to do away with intellectual quibblings and throw the full weight of his authority on the side of Russia and political revolution in France: to work wholeheartedly in that context for the social good. The drama on stage mirrors the various movements of Sartre's mind as it progresses toward a synthesis and a decision, a "totalization" and its "dépassement" in a mental resolve: the action is symbolic. Sartre's plays are real Sartrean psychodramas projected in imaginary situations enacted by imaginary characters who "realize" them and play out to their resolution the conflicts and peripateia of the Sartrean dialectic: thence their verbosity.

This, in effect, is the way Sartre lives the "real". Each concrete configuration, each political situation becomes a psychodrama, until Sartre "resolves" it by absorbing it into the complex interplay of psychological conflicts that, within his system, constitute men's history in the making. Sartre's "concrete world," for him, is the world he reconstructs and the "real" human being he describes is the "concrete man" of his own invention. Interpretation and reality have changed places to the point that, when Sartre confronts the everyday world of debate and diversity, wherever it fails to fit into his patterns, it becomes in his eyes the locus of men's bad-nonSartrean-fictions; and he sees it as his task to "demystify," which often, in his polemics, means denouncing them. That Sartre is aware of the ambiguity his own description of his re-creation of Flaubert makes clear. He calls it a fiction and—to adopt his somewhat ponderous neologism—a "presentification": that is, a means not of presenting Flaubert to the reader, but of making Flaubert intelligible to us in terms acceptable to the modern mind.

One facet of Sartre's activity has been widely publicized: his willingness to take positions on the issues of the day, whether national or international, large or small. In postwar France, to sign petitions, partake in demonstrations, support victims of political injustice, does not require exceptional courage. But it does call for the expenditure of time and energy. These Sartre has given generously, thereby bringing to each, with his name, the benefit of publicity.

But Sartre's concern for injustice, genuine and generous, has not been impartial, precisely to the degree that the theoretical frame he has adopted has sometimes served to shield him from the real implications of his verbal commitments; there is little point, for instance, in branding the bewildered, uprooted, Algerian-European worker as a "colonialist," or in weighing on the scales of his own justice lynching in America as against the hundreds of thousands of denizens in Stalin's camps. The arguments may be dialectically consistent—or not—but the whole process mocks human pain. Human beings caught in the mechanisms of war, oppression and disorder cannot be expected to look at their situation from the point of view of the future. Sartre has merely designed a hell and a heaven which assuage his conscience and af-

ford him the illusion of intellectually dominating a dis-
ordered world. Sartre equates his positions with the social
good as defined by his vision—theoretical—of that good.
This need for certification from within a system he himself postulated and modified is responsible for some of
Sartre's more questionable pronouncements, and for his
progressive relinquishment of the claims he had made for
literature in the thirties. In literature he had seen the
single most obvious evidence of man's freedom; at the
time of *The Words*, he saw it rather as the expression of
man's conditioning. His *Flaubert* now seems to announce
a re-evaluation and a qualified return to the earliest of
his positions.

It sometimes seems today that Sartre, weary of the immense intricacy of his present undertaking—to synthesize
our chaotic views of ourselves and not least among them
the conflicting Marxian-Freudian-Structuralist approaches
—has come at times to equate freedom with freedom
from the excruciating mental labor he has undertaken. His
enthusiastic response in 1968 to the students' call to "wreck
the system," no matter to what end, and to live uncon-
strainedly in the present, is rather indicative, and so are
the somewhat rueful statements he made on that occasion,
on the creative power of the spontaneous as against the
consciously calculated act.

In Camus, there is no trace of Sartre's dialectical strat-
egies: he was unable, he somewhat ironically recognized,
"to argue beyond the limits of concrete experience." What
horrified him most about the war was that it had been
made with the flesh and blood of millions of people—a
concrete fact lost in the abstract calculations and auto-
matic projections of men's minds.[7] It was consistent with
his whole outlook that he should weigh his experience
from that angle. A stimulus to Sartre's thought, the war

weighed heavily on Camus's sensibility. His concern
was not how to make the human scene intelligible but
how to reason out and communicate his deep moral revulsion. This led to his confrontation with Sartre.

In the immediate postwar years, it was Camus's conception of his role as journalist that had brought about
the first dissensions between the two men. For Camus, the
task of a journalist was to make all facts available to the
public: among these the unpalatable facts concerning
the Russian camps. Sartre eventually took the same position but carefully weighted it, as we have seen, in terms
of its situation in the historical process. Camus's concern
was with the present, with the practical needs of the
moment. He was not trying either to detect or to regu-
late the current of history. As it turned out, the moment
having past, the historical facts could not be eluded, nor
ultimately their significance in terms of the victims, the
dialectic notwithstanding.

The "conflicts" that were built into Sartre's schemata of
the world, inherent in the reciprocal antagonism attendant, in his view, upon "the look" (each individual first
appearing to another as a threat to his freedom), were,
for Camus, abstractions. World War II after World War I,
spelled actual wreckage, murder on a stupendous scale,
consequences so shocking that they called for a radical
appraisal of the human attitudes that had perpetrated
and tolerated them. *The Rebel* was one such appraisal:
not exhaustive, not demonstrative, in intent a personal
assessment. It brought the final confrontation of Sartre
with Camus. "At the root of all literary works," Camus
wrote, "one usually finds a single deep emotion, long
mulled over, which, without justifying the writing, is
enough to explain it. I should not myself have written
The Rebel if, in the forties, I had not confronted men

whose system [of thought] I could not explain and whose acts I could not understand . . ." (*Essais*, p. 1702). But what he had understood was that "ideas were not merely pathetic or harmonious games, that on certain occasions, to accept certain ideas was equivalent to accepting unlimited murder." He was more distrustful than was Sartre toward the myth of social progress as embodied in revolutionary violence (*Essais*, p. 1704).

It is not my purpose here to discuss *The Rebel* and its arguments, but to define the nature of Camus's commitment. Life, he had long known, sets limits; and he had opted to hold life precious, to enhance and enlarge it by putting the powers he felt he had to work on some chosen aspects of it—yet ever holding in mind the presence of the rest. Both *The Stranger* and *Caligula* invite us to remember the actual stuff of which people's days are made. The most telling part of *The Rebel* is without doubt the particular use Camus makes of the legend of Prometheus: Prometheus, Camus's Prometheus, arises in rebellion against the pain and suffering of the world, fires men's imagination, and leads them ever further into the desert, exacting from them an ever greater toll of labor and suffering, while slowly he turns into Caesar; until a new Prometheus arises to challenge him, as the community of men continues to eke out its life and its small chances of happiness upon the earth it inhabits. Whatever the flaws in Camus's tracing of the impact of the Promethean posture on Western civilization, it furnishes an answer to his dissension with Sartre. Reliance on a "praxis," based on the unverifiable assumption that rational coherence, dialectic or otherwise, was a sufficient guide in political decision seemed to him downright folly. In conjunction with any utopian view of the end of history it subverted man's moral sense catastrophically. Camus's Prometheus-

Caesar is clearly an intellectual; it was the doctrinal quarrels of the hour Camus was attacking, with a plea to lay aside unresolved contradictions and serve the practical needs of the moment. The patterns of order, created by men's minds, he saw as partial constructs that do not give men complete "meanings." A man's responsibility then must go beyond them to needs that lie deeper than the mind's ordering which attempts to dominate.

The confrontation of Camus with *Les Temps modernes* was merely an epiphenomenon. It reveals the familiar human flaws in many intellectuals: the taunting tone and smug assumption of intellectual superiority on the part of Jeanson; his deliberate *reductio ad absurdum* of Camus's argument; the mocking parody of imagery and style. The need to refute was obviously overriding. Camus was incensed: Sartre, Camus felt, and to a certain extent, was right to feel, had betrayed the tacit code of friendship by delegating the hatchet job to an accomplice; and it is true that, involved in his own crisis, about to "commit" himself in the opposite way, Sartre made short shrift of Camus's point of view—discussing it in terms of his own postulations. But something humanly precious was lost in the debate, which was just what Camus had wanted to prove. In a small way, the incident verified his contention: a totalitarian view of the world is antihuman.

Camus's strength in practical action had its source in his genuine passion for truth, clarity, in his belief in certain values, and his intense respect for human lives. It did not lie in the realm of abstraction, which he suspected, as *The Rebel* shows, of having distorted the intellectuals' grasp of reality. Life around him was extraordinarily real for Camus. His own, in the temporal perspective he had so early perceived, seemed absurdly unreal, and yet he knew it was not to be recklessly spent—as was sometimes his impulse. There was no theory or system he wanted to communicate to others. It was of the one-sidedness of doctrinaire ideologies that he was critical: thence the role played by *The Rebel* in the demythicizing of Marxist eschatology. Whereas Sartre was engaged in the project of revolutionizing his and our knowledge of our minds, Camus was engaged in weighing and appraising those things that enhance human lives. During the war years, happiness was a word that was outlawed. And it was outlawed, too, in the endless ideological discussions in Paris. Hatred, violence, and death had confronted him and he had partaken of them. In the fifties, he felt the need to break away from their obsessive grip; the theme of the opening and final stories in *Exile and the Kingdom* is the welling up of the "water" of wordless understanding in two human beings who are thus carried into a realm of their own being where the narrow horizons of their lives open upon wider realities. Literature, for Camus, had not ceased to be the privileged realm he had discovered in his young manhood, where barriers fall and intimacy is established. But he would never again be able to separate his own intimations of the pain and joy of living from those common to all men. Where Sartre sought unity, Camus spoke of harmony. Art in a time of discord he saw as conciliator, healer, however slow in its working.

What had drawn Sartre and Camus together for a short while was a brutal and stark crisis. In the mid-forties they were extremely close to each other in the immediate range and nature of their preoccupations and in their genuine revulsion against the explosion of barbarism in the West. This took its toll of them. It launched Sartre on his relentless and humorless pursuit of total understanding, as though he and he alone were charged with righting the evils of the world and because of his brilliant mind could lord over it in omnipotence; and it put upon the young Camus's imagination the stamp of austerity and a kind of moral reticence, constraining the writer and exhausting the man. And yet—tedious though the laborious wrestling of their minds with a reality that revolted them may now seem—it was that rebellion which proved for both a salutary thing, and made them the spokesmen of the mid-century years. And indeed, both weighed the perils of an age that requires minds to break away from current modes of thought. But no two men could in fact have felt the times more differently. Sartre's volubility and racing thoughts, the flow of words issuing incessantly from his lips or pen, the grand tirades and monumental works, contrast with Camus's self-imposed restraint, his caustic humor, his need to withdraw and meditate in tranquillity. As one of the workers on the *Combat* team remembered, "he couldn't create anything worthwhile without long hours of solitary meditation."[8] Sartre's mobility and often abrasive aggressiveness contrasted with Camus's quiet attentiveness to others and firm adherence to a position, once he had elected to take it. Volatile, constantly solicited by new ideas, by the flow of words and notions that seems endlessly to pass through his mind, Sartre is a man who fixes his attention on those ideas that most deeply stir him at certain moments of uncertainty because they seem to provide a rational frame of reference that can contain and order the chaotic whole. His own mind is the stage on which issues are weighed and this absorption has cut him off, much to his distress, from the common man. Part of Camus's personal charm and authority, in contrast, was due to his easy relations with ordinary human beings. Of this there is no better testimony than the homage of the "men of the stone"—typographers and proofreaders—who had worked with him on the newspaper, *Combat*. All stress his warmth, his gaiety, his understanding, "his handsome face and warm smile." "He was better at listening than at talking about himself. That's how we became friends. He liked to hang around the stone with the typographers, who liked him. He was friendly and slightly ironic at the same time, always a charming comrade. After you had chatted with him for fifteen minutes, life seemed a little more bearable!"[9]; and, again, "I was a workers' representative. We had to deal with Camus concerning specific problems. . . . Right away he understood the most complicated matters, the various problems of the workers which I had outlined, and they were pretty tricky. Camus understood; he really was one of the boys in the composing room. . . . He was a friend and you could be completely open with him, he never changed."[10] What these men liked about him was the directness of his approach. "We found him simple, real, without false modesty, not a demagogue. . . . Indeed that's how he was then at that meeting, in the dimly lit hall with dirty windowpanes and the smell of two or three hundred men. . . . It began with Camus's refusal to read a prepared speech, to refer even to notes, or to begin a discourse. There wasn't the slightest sign of affectation nor of that pride which may be hidden but which resides, at least to some extent, in every man's soul. He was waiting for our questions, and they came. . . ."[11] It was in this meeting that he bluntly stated twice his position concerning the "social question." In response to a question concerning the "social question," Camus agreed this was a serious matter, which the writer should approach with care. He had to avoid "taking responsibility for the workers' lot" and turning out hackneyed works in the style of Ilya Ehrenburg, or becoming a "boy-scout of social activism";[12] and when asked in what ways he thought a writer could serve as a guide to the proletariat, he answered that "he had never been a guide, that he couldn't dream of being one, and that he felt too much real humility to put himself in the place of the multitude."[13]

Camus's sensuousness, his disengagement from and impatience with the petty maneuvers and "accountings" of daily intrigue are shown by his preference for concrete accomplishments: a paper to bring out; a play to realize on stage. He did not share Sartre's compulsion to elucidate verbally every small incident and relationship in his life. For Camus, emotion was the path to thought, and aesthetic emotion ranked high among the productive, creative emotions in human lives. The things that counted for him were few and deep. He was rooted in humanity.

Impulsive, Sartre mistrusted emotions as being the source of illusion and mystification. Yet, in the long run, one senses that—the dialectic notwithstanding—it is emotion that underlies the generous record of his political activities and his belatedly relinquished—not quite relinquished—preoccupation with men's "salvation." Of these emotions, not the least is the sense of guilt at his own privileges, and at the frustration he has long felt at the intellectuals', meaning his, "marginal" existence. Thence his struggle to destroy the bourgeois image of himself, and to pour new content into his writing. Of all the literary forms, drama was certainly the best suited both to his psychological view of "human reality" and to his view of the socio-historical process. It is, besides, the most immediately effective form of social literature, the one most immediately involving other human beings. He could attack, persuade, conquer "the others," dominate and instruct them, at will. It was essentially suited to Sartre's vision of commitment as crisis—as a moment when a man is wrenched free of self-delusion and accepts his "role," from which there is no escape; accepts the play and role Sartre has meted out to him. There the stage world and the world of Sartrean reality coincide. Sartre is a born dramatist, although an uneven one, too easily satisfied with a dramaturgy of the past whose elements are the tirade, demonstrative rhetoric, literary eloquence, and moral conclusions. It is notable that his two most powerful plays—one of the first—*No Exit*—and the last to date— *The Prisoners of Altona*—are plays that create obsessive, baroque metaphors of sequestration and impotence. From Sartre the political polemicist to Sartre the artist in spite of himself, the connecting line is stretched almost, one feels, to the breaking point. But the tension which led— regrettably in my eyes—to Sartre's sacrifice of the writer to the philosopher-polemicist, is thoroughly recognizable to us all, one of the horizons of our experience. It is inherent to forms of intellectual romanticism quite prevalent among us.

In a thoughtful essay on the recurrence, in modern literature, of the myth of Orpheus, Walter Strauss points to the two predominant and antithetical myths that characterize modern literature: the myth of Prometheus and the myth of Dionysius-Orpheus. Camus recalled them both—the myth of Dionysius via the adventure of his first character, Mersault; the myth of Prometheus in *The Rebel* as a paradigm of an outworn political myth, transformed by him to fit the modern situation. The Sartre-Camus confrontation to a certain extent recalls the Orpheus-Prometheus conflict. Prometheus defies the established powers in the interests of men, in order to liberate them and make them the equal of the gods. He is the rebel— Faust, Satan, or Sartre, as Sartre sees himself, and he is punished. Sartre seems still to be awaiting a punishment which is not forthcoming. Camus in the Orphic tradition seeks transformation from within.

Prometheanism, Strauss tells us, seeks to change the outer conditions of men's lives, Orphism seeks to "alter society only indirectly, through the changes man can effect in himself." It was a change of consciousness that Sartre first wanted to bring about in others, progressively becoming the social rebel and ideological revolutionary under the pressure of events. Camus's quest in contrast followed ever more intensely the Orphic pattern of descent into the self, of confrontation and self-renewal. Action was always accompanied in his case by a movement inward; what he sought was the Orphic inner and outer reconciliation. The order he attempted to create was an esthetic order and his was the self-awareness of a man in search of his own elusive truth. This was Camus's essential commitment. He had no sense that he occupied a special place in the world; he was aware that he shared the fate of many others, that historical moments and perspectives were relative and soon passed. *The Plague* was his parting salute to the mid-century crisis and to his involvement in its political and ideological patterns. He had never assumed that either art or political activism had redemptive powers. But life, he felt, in its reality had its own rich compensations. He had spelled out his commitment to the fullness of experience early. "I do not want to choose between the right and wrong sides of the world, and I do not like a choice to be made . . . The great courage is still to gaze as squarely at the light as at death . . ." And he stated it again much later in a lyrical essay entitled *The Sea Close By* which discloses the full range of his involvement with and love for the world: "At midnight, alone on the shore. A moment more and I shall set sail. The sky itself has weighed anchor with all its stars, like the ships covered with lights which at this very hour throughout the world illuminate dark harbors. Space and silence weigh equally upon the heart. A sudden love, a great work, a decisive act, a thought that transfigures, all these at certain moments bring the same unbearable anxiety, quickened with an irresistible charm. Living like this, in the delicious anguish of being, in exquisite proximity to a danger whose name we do not know, is this the same as rushing to our doom? Once again without respite, let us race to our destruction.

"I have always felt I lived on the high seas, threatened, at the heart of a royal happiness." The sense of the urgency of political action had receded but not his concern for others, the tensions he hoped to resolve, the art to which he looked for support.

All now were again polarized around Camus's central concern: human happiness. From the very start it had been against the forces that militate against that happiness, or deny men's need of or their access to it that he had struggled—whether the destructive forces in himself or those apparent in society. His art then was the single, necessary expression of an experience that could not logically be proved.

No reconciliation is possible between the two men on the intellectual plane. Camus's creations are often "mythical" embodiments of different drives he sensed in himself. The postwar soliloquist of *The Fall* and prophet of man's impotence, Jean-Baptiste Clamence, is one of the best-known of these—a figure to be recognized and measured in terms of each reader's knowledge of life. But others rise beside him: the silent figure of a schoolteacher, on the high plateaus of Algeria, who stands alone, ineluctably condemned, yet firm in his own integrity; the men who fight the plague, obstinately refusing to give in to the

sense of their impotence; and in one of Camus's last stories, "The Growing Stone," the engineer whose inner life
is restored by the warmth and friendship of simple men.
Reduced to abstract themes, Camus's work seems simplistic, therefore the impatience of critical minds who
deal with his "ideas." What is not simplistic is the subtly
intricate yet sober texture of his writing, rich in its un-
stated connotations. It is from within a world they see
and feel and share that Camus's characters move and
meet and, at certain moments, communicate with each
other, or see each other or themselves in a new light. In
spite of his great love for the theater, it was not in the
conflict and collisions of men and ideas that he was at his
best; his theater, as he quite rightly said, is not a theater
of ideas. For his creatures he needed the presence of a
world, and the sense of a permanence that deflates our
dramatic obsession with crisis. That world is singularly
lacking in Sartre. If, on the surface, Camus's writing
seems traditional, the surface is deceptive; it is power-
fully original though sparse. Because he wanted it so, it is
also, at one level, immediately understood. For Camus it
was a necessary component of his life.

Notes to Conclusion

1. For a brief but clear summary of some of these see J. Stuart
   Hughes, *Consciousness and Society* (1958). One need only
   mention Freud, Einstein, Max Weber, Niels Bohr, Julian
   Huxley, Norbert Wiener among many others to recall the
   new vistas opened up.
2. André Gounelle, in an article on the new orientations in
   theology, "Où va la théologie?" (Where is Theology Head-

ing?) notes that, in contrast twenty years ago in the realm of theology and philosophy the favored prefix was "neo-" (in *Études théologiques et religieuses*, No. 2, 1971; 46th year; pp. 125–38.) That this is a post-Marxian era is also the point of view of George Lichtheim in his account of the evolution of French Marxism, *op. cit.*

3. "Philosophy was to become *real*; its principles—liberty and rationality—was no longer to figure as ideals unrelated to human practice. They were to take on flesh, come down from the speculative heavens and assert themselves as the actual practice of a humanity no longer suspended between blind empiricism and the passive contemplation of transcendental aims not realized in actuality." G. Lichtheim, *op. cit.*, 194.

4. This inevitably brought Sartre, reluctantly, to take Freud into account. Both share a preoccupation with the formal coherence of a theory that establishes a connection between theory and behavior and so can predict future patterns. But Sartre had to save from Freudian determinism his assumption that man is a free agent. Naturally, too, it brought him to Marx who played a decisive role in the increasingly complicated development of his schemata.

5. Sartre extended his original pattern to collective entities acting as "mediators" between individuals and the greater community of men, which he now conceptualized as evolving toward the Marxian classless society, each man changing himself as he changed his relations with the collective entities, and changing them—so affecting all the heterogeneous structures involved.

6. One has a feeling, perhaps erroneous, that the violence of some of Sartre's political sallies, judicious or not as the case may be, is a momentary escape from the unremitting pressure of his drive to order the world.

7. Camus's reaction is comparable in a sense to the reactions of Daniel Ellsberg when confronted with the real results of actions theoretically designed in the hermetic seclusion of think tanks.

8. *Albert Camus and the Men of the Stone*, edited by Robert Proix, translated by Gregory H. Davis (San Francisco, California: Jack Werner Stauffacher/The Greenwood Press, 1971), p. 49. Camus here quite clearly stated his position in regard to syndicalism versus Party dictatorship. The whole account of the discussion is all the more interesting because it took place in 1957.

9. *Ibid.*, p. 22.

10. *Ibid.*, pp. 25–26.

11. *Ibid.*, p. 56.

12. *Ibid.*, pp. 50–51, 59.

Index